Self Hatred i

Detoxifying the Persecutory Object

The persecutory object is the element of the personality which attacks your confidence, productivity, and acceptance of reality to the point of no return. Persecuted patients torture themselves, hurt their loved ones, and torment their therapists.

In this book, the authors integrate object relations and Kleinian theories in their way of working with tenacious persecutory objects and persecutory states of mind. This is vividly illustrated in a variety of situations, including:

- individual, couple, and group therapy
- serious paediatric illness
- working with persecutory aspects of family business.

It is argued that the persecutory object can be contained, modified, and in many cases detoxified by the process of skilful intensive psychotherapy and psychoanalysis.

Self Hatred in Psychoanalysis: Detoxifying the Persecutory Object will be invaluable to a variety of practitioners including psychoanalysts, psychotherapists, social workers, psychiatrists, and mental health counsellors.

Jill Savege Scharff is Co-Director of the International Institute of Object Relations Therapy, Chevy Chase, Maryland, Clinical Professor of Psychiatry at Georgetown University, and Teaching Analyst at the Washington Psychoanalytic Institute. She is in private practice in Chevy Chase, Maryland.

Stanley A. Tsigounis is Executive Director of the Florida Institute for Object Relations Therapy and is on the core faculty of the International Institute of Object Relations Therapy in Chevy Chase, Maryland. He is a Clinical Psychologist in private practice in both Sarasota and Tampa, Florida.

Self Hatred in Psychoanalysis

Detoxifying the Persecutory Object

Edited by Jill Savege Scharff
and Stanley A. Tsigounis

Brunner-Routledge
Taylor & Francis Group

HOVE AND NEW YORK

First published 2003 by Brunner-Routledge
27 Church Road, Hove, East Sussex, BN3 2FA

Simultaneously published in the USA and Canada
by Taylor & Francis Inc
29 West 35th Street, New York, NY 10001

Brunner-Routledge is an imprint of the Taylor & Francis Group

Cover design by Terry Foley, Anú Design
Typeset in Times by Mayhew Typesetting, Rhayader, Powys
Printed and bound in Great Britain by TJ International Ltd,
Padstow, Cornwall

British Library Cataloguing in Publication Data
A catalogue record for this book is available from the British Library

Library of Congress Cataloging-in-Publication Data
Self hatred in psychoanalysis : detoxifying the persecutory object / edited
by Jill Savege Scharff and Stanley A. Tsigounis.
    p. cm.
   Includes bibliographical references and index.
   ISBN 1-58391-926-0 (hbk) – ISBN 1-58391-925-2 (pbk.)
    1. Self-acceptance. 2. Psychoanalysis. 3. Self-hate (Psychology)
I. Scharff, Jill Savege. II. Tsigounis, Stanley A., 1950–

   RC489.S43 S44 2002
   616.89'17–dc21

                         2002066741

ISBN 1-58391-926-0 (hbk)
ISBN 1-58391-925-2 (pbk)

Contents

Contributors

Marianela Altamirano, M.Ed is a psychologist with a degree in educational psychology and is in the private practice of individual, child, and couple psychotherapy in Panamá City, Republic of Panamá where she is on the faculty of IIORT Panamá, the satellite programme of the International Institute of Object Relations Therapy (IIORT Washington).

Charles Ashbach, PhD is a faculty member of the Institute for Psychoanalytic Psychotherapies in Philadelphia, Pennsylvania and is a clinical psychologist in private practice in Philadelphia and Wyndmoor. He co-authored *Object Relations, the Self, and the Group*, and contributed a chapter to *Tuning the Therapeutic Instrument: Affective Learning of Psychotherapy* (2000). He is Chair of IIORT Philadelphia and Editor of the IIORT bulletin.

Carl Bagnini, CSW, BCD is on the faculties of St John's University Post-doctoral Program in Couple and Family Therapy and the Suffolk Institute of Psychoanalysis and Psychotherapy and is in private practice in Port Washington, New York. He contributed to *Tuning the Therapeutic Instrument: Affective Learning of Psychotherapy* (2000). He is Chair of the Couple, Child and Family Therapy Program at IIORT Washington and Chair of IIORT Long Island.

Hilary Hall, MA, LMHC is a licensed mental health counsellor in private practice, Sarasota, Florida. She is a Fellow of IIORT Washington.

Leslie A. Johnson, PhD, LPC is in private practice as a licensed mental health counsellor in Charlottesville, Virginia. She is a Fellow of IIORT Washington.

Michael Kaufman, MA, LPC is in private practice in Charlottesville, Virginia. He contributed a chapter to *Tuning the Therapeutic Instrument: Affective Learning of Psychotherapy* (2000).
He is coordinator of the Charlottesville Program in object
relations theory and technique, IIORT Charlottesville, and is on
the faculty of IIORT Washington.

Kent Ravenscroft, MD is Associate Clinical Professor of Psychiatry
at Georgetown and George Washington Universities where he
was formerly Training Director in Child and Adolescent Psychiatry and was also Director of Medical and Surgical Consultation services at Children's Hospital in Washington DC. He
is in the private practice of adult and child psychoanalysis and
psychotherapy and testifies as a forensic expert on custody,
visitation, adoption, trauma, and Munchausen by Proxy syndrome. He has published on psychiatric consultation, trauma,
Munchausen by Proxy syndrome, eating disorders, family
therapy, multiple personality, and voodoo. He is on the faculty
of IIORT Washington.

David E. Scharff, MD is Clinical Professor of Psychiatry at the
Uniformed Services University of the Health Sciences and at
Georgetown University, Teaching Analyst at the Washington
Psychoanalytic Institute, and past Director of the Washington
School of Psychiatry (1987–1994). He is in private practice in
psychoanalysis and psychotherapy in Chevy Chase, MD. His
books include *Fairbairn and Relational Theory Today* (ed. with
F. Perreira 2001), *The Psychoanalytic Century: Freud's Legacy
for the Future* (ed. 2000), *Fairbairn Then and Now* (ed. with N.
Skolnick 1998), *From Instinct to Self* (ed. with E. Birtles 1994),
Object Relations Theory and Practice (ed. 1994), *Refinding the
Object and Reclaiming the Self* (1992), *The Sexual Relationship*
(1982). He is senior co-author with Jill Savege Scharff of *Object
Relations Couple Therapy* (1991), and *Object Relations Family
Therapy* (1987). He is Co-Director of IIORT.

Michael Stadter, PhD is a clinical psychologist in private practice in
Bethesda, Maryland and is on the faculty of the Washington
School of Psychiatry. He is the author of *Object Relations Brief
Therapy: The Relationship in Short-Term Work* and a contri-
butor to *Tuning the Therapeutic Instrument: Affective Learning*

of Psychotherapy (2000). He is on the faculty of IIORT Chevy Chase and is the Chair of Weekend Conferences at IIORT Washington.

Yolanda de Varela, MA is a clinical psychologist with a Masters degree in educational psychology. She is in the private practice of individual, child, and couple psychotherapy in Panamá City, Republic of Panamá. She is a Past President of the Panamanian Psychological Association and a contributor to *Tuning the Therapeutic Instrument: Affective Learning of Psychotherapy* (2000) and *Comparative Treatments for Relationship Dysfunction* (2000). She is Chair of IIORT Panamá, a faculty member of IIORT Washington, and Chair of the Summer Institutes at IIORT Washington.

Editors

Jill Savege Scharff, MD is Clinical Professor of Psychiatry at Georgetown University, Teaching Analyst and Associate Supervising Child Analyst at the Washington Psychoanalytic Institute. She is in private practice in psychoanalysis and psychotherapy with adults and children in Chevy Chase, MD. She is the author of *Projective and Introjective Identification and the Use of the Therapist's Self* (1992), and senior author with David E. Scharff on *Tuning the Therapeutic Instrument: Affective Learning of Psychotherapy* (2000), *Object Relations Individual Therapy* (1998), *Object Relations Therapy of Physical and Sexual Trauma* (1996), and *A Primer of Object Relations Therapy* (1992). She edited *The Autonomous Self: The Work of John D. Sutherland* (1994) and *Foundations of Object Relations Family Therapy* (1992). Formerly Chair, Object Relations Theory and Therapy Program Washington School of Psychiatry (1993–1994), she is Co-Director of IIORT.

Stanley A. Tsigounis, PhD is on the faculty of the Tampa Institute for Psychoanalytic Studies and is a clinical psychologist in private practice in Sarasota and Tampa, Florida. He contributed a chapter to *Tuning the Therapeutic Instrument: Affective Learning of Psychotherapy* (2000). He is Director of the Family and Group Institute for Integrative Psychotherapy, Chair of IIORT Tampa, and Dean of IIORT Washington.

Acknowledgements

We are grateful to our colleagues and students for their enthusiasm as we put this book together, and especially to those who agreed to join us as authors. We particularly want to thank Nancy Bakalar, MD, Betty de Benaim, MA, Chris Norman, PhD, Samuel Pinzón, PhD, and MaryJo Pisano, PhD for being sympathetic to our project goals. Special thanks go to our spouses who not only contributed chapters but also cheerfully supported us while we were preoccupied with writing and editing tasks. We appreciate the generosity of patients and clients who have shared with us their inner worlds. Writing about our work with them has increased our understanding. We hope that their experiences and our efforts on their behalf contribute equally to the understanding of other patients and other therapists. Lastly, we are grateful to the editorial staff at Brunner-Routledge, especially Kate Hawes, who saw the potential in our manuscript, Kathryn Russel, who shepherded it to conclusion, and Kirsty Wood, who arranged its promotion.

Early versions of some of the papers in this book were presented at the weekend conference 'Advances in Object Relations', organized by Stanley Tsigounis for the International Institute of Object Relations Therapy, Chevy Chase, Maryland, 7–9 April 2000.

Jill Savege Scharff, MD, Chevy Chase, Maryland
Stanley A. Tsigounis, PhD, Sarasota, Florida
January 2002

Preface

The persecutory object is our term for an intrapsychic structure that causes self hatred by persistently attacking the confidence, productivity, likeability, and value of the self. Persecutory objects may inhibit or defeat individuals, hurt their loved ones, and torment their therapists. Our goal as clinicians is to create conditions in which each person who consults us can experience and modify the persecutory object and its toxic effects on self and others.

Our aim as authors is to provide plenty of direct clinical material so that readers may decide for themselves whether the theory fits the clinical situation and how it informs technique. Identifying details have been altered to protect the privacy of the analysands, psychotherapy patients, clients, or students from whose work we have drawn vignettes, but the dynamics remain true to our recollection. Our goal as editors is to bring together theoretical and clinical contributions from various authors to reveal the viciousness, hatefulness, and tenacity of the persecutory object, the breadth of its influence, and the object relations approaches we bring to understanding and detoxifying it.

We begin Part 1 with an introduction to the nature and development of the persecutory object, using vignettes from patients who illustrate its action inside the self and in interaction with others, especially with their babies. The authors examine the concept of the persecutory object from Freudian, Kleinian, and Fairbairnian perspectives, with an emphasis on the death instinct, the tie to the bad object, and the affects of shame and guilt. We give an example from marital and sex therapy to show how the persecutory object is projected into sadomasochistic sexual fantasy, enters the interpersonal field, and fills the couple relationship with contempt and despair. In an individual case study, we report on the noise of the persecutory object and trace its effect at different stages in a woman's life. We describe cases of Munchausen by Proxy to show how the persecutory object is projected into the body by disturbed women whose love for their children is totally contaminated by self hatred.

In Part 2, we examine how to work with the persecutory object in individual therapy with a terrified, grieving adult and a fragmenting adolescent, in conjoint therapy with divorcing couples, and in group therapy where the therapist has to cope with a debilitating countertransference. We present and review theories and illustrate techniques that have been developed and applied in the clinical situation to assist patients in resolving their psychic pain. From experience with medical consultation and liaison, we illustrate working with persecutory aspects of physical deformity and surgical intervention. We describe family transferences that become persecutory in the context of the for-profit situation of a family business and show how consultants work to understand the family tensions and restore good management. The chapters are rich in description of the therapeutic struggle with the persecutory object and the ultimate rewards for individuals and organizations. We conclude with our recognition of the frustrations and failures of this type of work when detoxification remains incomplete.

Part 1

The theory of persecutory states of mind

Chapter 1

Introduction to the persecutory object

Stanley A. Tsigounis, PhD and
Jill Savege Scharff, MD

WHAT IS A PERSECUTORY OBJECT?

The persecutory object is a part of the self that is imbued with a sense of harassment, suppression, subjugation, tyranny, torture, vengeance, and self hatred. The term *persecutory object* refers both to the mothering person as actually being, or being perceived to be, threatening (the external object) and to the trace of early relationships inside the infant self (the internal object). The persecutory internal object is structured in reaction to the nature of the external object: to the parents' physical and psychological holding and handling, their temperaments, and their capacities to contain anxiety and give meaning to experience in interaction with the infant's constitutional energy, esprit, and capacity for relating. A persecutory internal object, then, is a harsh, retaliatory part of the self that controls and torments self and other (Klein 1935).

We will raise questions about the persecutory object in formation as the infant deals with the mother in the first year of life. We will illustrate the ways the persecutory object exerts its hateful effect on the self and others, and conclude with examples of the adult refinding the persecutory object in the baby.

HOW DOES THE PERSECUTORY OBJECT FORM?

As human beings we have the gift of self-consciousness and reflection. We recognize our vulnerable state of being, both physically and psychically, and realize that the world contains real threats to our existence. We are conscious of feeling anxiety and capable of anticipation. Whether threat is real or imagined, survival becomes a dominant concern and motivates our behaviour towards preserving life. The wish to survive creates anxiety that acts as a warning system, alerts us to real danger, and triggers an adaptive response. If anxiety becomes too intense, we deal with it using a number of defence mechanisms designed to protect us from being overwhelmed, projective and introjective identification being the most fundamental.

When a person who is the object of our dependency and desire for relationship (the external object) is oppressive towards us, we take in the experience to control it inside our self. There forms an internal object with which the ego is in a dynamic relationship inside the self (the internal object relationship). The external object may be actually oppressive or just felt as being so. Theorists disagree over which is the defining variable. Frosch (1990) argued that many adults who struggle with persecutory anxiety were actually persecuted in some form earlier in their lives. They have been hurt, humiliated, tortured psychologically and often physically, and are compelled to repeat this process symbolically throughout their lives. Abraham (1924) thought that self-criticism and self-reproach stemmed from the introjection of objects or self-objects experienced with ambivalence and hosility due to sadistic libido. Klein (1946) thought that the constitutionally given aggressive force of the death instinct drives unconscious fantasies that, if unchecked by the loving power of the life instinct, interact with external reality to fuel the growth and development of the persecutory object. Once there is the nidus of a persecutory object in formation, its presence leads to expectations of persecution, draws more bad experience to it, and continues to build intrapsychic structure of this kind. It is the complex interplay between actual events and the individual's emerging internal structure that leads to the formation of persecutory internal objects, affecting both the individual's sense of self and perception of significant others.

WHERE DID CONCEPTS OF PERSECUTORY PROJECTIONS ORIGINATE?

Freud suggested that a harsh superego forms in direct proportion to the degree of harshness of the father, through a process of identification and introjection of his qualities. Later he suggested that the severity of the harsh superego is determined by the destructive impulses of the child and the need for modulation of drive energies. According to him, a person is vulnerable to both external and internal forces arising from aggressive and sexual impulses. These sexual and aggressive impulses supply the necessary ingredients for positive growth and development while simultaneously providing a threat to existence. Freud suggested that directing the impulse back towards one's own ego modulates aggressive impulses.

> There it is taken over by a portion of one's ego, which sets itself over against the rest of the ego as superego, and which now, in the form of 'conscience', is ready to put into action against the ego the same harsh aggressiveness that the ego would have liked to have satisfy upon other, extraneous individuals.
>
> (Freud 1930, p.123)

This, Freud postulated, becomes the foundation for guilt and subsequent punishment. However it appears that this superego can mutate and become overly punitive. Klein later called this the harsh superego and Bion described it as the ego-destructive superego. The influence of a primitive superego denies the individual the normal use of projection to expel the persecutory feelings and he is left with only the mechanism of turning it back against the self.

Anna Freud gave importance to the defence of identification with the aggressor. She discovered that children identify with an aggressive individual (the external object) so as to modulate inherent anxiety. The identification with the aggressor becomes introjected into the child's character structure (the internal object in object relations terms). The child imitates the aggressor and thus transforms himself from the person threatened into the person who makes the threat (Freud 1936). Having introjected the aggressor, the child projects the aggression outward to be rid of the persecutory anxiety.

Melanie Klein extended Freud's thinking on superego formation in her extensive work with young children and developed a theory of psychic structure formation. In 'Personification in the Play of Children' Klein (1929) described the superego formed by the child's use of multiple identifications and splitting. She suggests that through the mechanisms of identification and introjection, and in order to deal with the infant's destructive aggressive impulses, the superego is split, resulting in the formation of a harsh superego. Contrary to Freud's notion that superego development begins during the anal phase and consolidates after the oedipal phase, Klein thought that the infant superego starts to form during the first few months of life. Through experiences with the environment, the infant modifies its harsher aspects. Until then, the cruel superego fills the infant with persecutory anxiety, the hallmark of the paranoid-schizoid position.

This paranoid-schizoid position develops during the first two months of life (Klein 1946). The infant, besieged with anxiety and aggression emanating from the death instinct, must defend the self from the threat of annihilation. It uses the mental mechanisms of splitting, projection, projective and introjective identification (Scharff 1992). In Kleinian theory, the idea is that the projection of anxiety and aggression is specifically directed towards the mother's breast or other body parts, which then become the repository of the infant's persecutory anxiety. The breast is experienced as either a good breast or a bad breast, with the bad breast containing the anxiety.

The baby then fears retribution from the mother and her breast, which becomes a persecutory object. If the life instinct dominates and the breast is felt to be reliably there for nourishment and nurture when needed, death anxiety is held at bay. The breast is experienced as a satisfying, good breast, and that gives rise to a good internal object. When the death instinct dominates the life instinct, the need for the breast is too great, and it is experienced as a hostile bad breast, ready to devour or poison the infant, which gives rise to a bad internalized object. The object is split into good and bad. The ego and superego are split accordingly, resulting in the formation of a harsh superego which directs its aggression at the bad internalized object for failing to provide satisfaction. If the infant, or later the patient in the paranoid-schizoid position, cannot expel anxiety and aggression arising from the death instinct through projection, the developing person is forced to contain the persecutory anxiety in the form of an internal persecutory object.

Bion (1959) described the abnormal superego as the ego-destructive superego. He saw this ego-destructive superego developing from failures of communication between mother and infant, leading to the destruction of the ego, links with the object, and links between thoughts. It becomes a 'super' ego that destroys links. It becomes easy to imagine why a child would want to rid itself through projection of any process that could be experienced as destructive to the ego.

Example: Superego projection into the baby

Mr Alvez, a 35-year-old Hispanic man, was a New York City bus driver. He was a polite and deferential man who had driven for the Port Authority of New York for the previous fifteen years. He felt honoured to be entrusted with an expensive piece of equipment and the responsibility of its passengers. He took great pride in his ability to navigate a large, cumbersome machine through the crowded and narrow streets of Manhattan in a timely and safe manner. He had never had an accident, quite an accomplishment in New York.

One day, while on his regular route, a mother boarded his bus carrying a screaming, inconsolable infant. As Mr Alvez guided the bus along the route he began to feel anxious, provoked by the crying infant. Perspiration flowed down his face and his respiration quickened. His anxiety grew with each block he travelled. He became so anxious that he worried that he would not be able to drive the bus safely. Simultaneously, he began to grow angry. The baby would not stop screaming. He thought to himself, 'If only the baby would just stop. Why did the mother pick my bus? Why couldn't she quiet the infant? What am I going to do? The incessant crying and screaming is making me crazy.'

His anger and anxiety grew to such proportions that he became certain that he could no longer safely control the bus. He pulled the bus to an abrupt stop at the kerb and, with a shaking voice, ordered the woman and infant off the bus. The woman, shocked and confused, stood and slowly began to gather her belongings. By this time Mr Alvez was in an uncontrollable rage and state of acute anxiety. As the infant and mother passed to disembark, Mr Alvez raised his fist to strike at the infant. At that instant, with arm raised and poised to strike, Mr Alvez's arm became paralyzed in mid air. He looked at his arm in amazement and fear, wondering if God himself had intervened and both protected the baby and punished him in one swift stroke.

The woman and infant quickly left the bus. With his arm frozen above his head, a shaken Mr Alvez called his dispatcher on the radio and requested a supervisor and relief driver. By the time the supervisor had arrived Mr Alvez could lower his arm to waist height but both his arm and hand felt paralyzed. He was seen by the company physician who prescribed tranquillizers, placed him on sick leave, and instructed him to get psychological assistance.

It was five days after the incident when I first met Mr Alvez. His arm and hand had minimal mobility and he felt frightened. Mr Alvez felt ashamed about his behaviour on the bus and humiliated at having to attend psychotherapy. His perfect employment record was ruined. This would stay as a smear on his personnel file forever. He desperately wanted to return to work yet he remained conflicted, fearful that he might see the woman and infant and repeat the whole experience. He felt guilty and ashamed about his reaction to the infant and mother; a true man would never strike or even pretend to strike an infant and mother. He also expressed great concern that his arm would not improve and that he would never be able to return to his bus, his passengers, and his route.

In fifteen years as a bus driver Mr Alvez had certainly encountered crying babies. It wasn't clear whether he was directing the anger and the raised arm towards the infant, the mother, or both. It wasn't clear what this particular mother and infant symbolized for Mr Alvez. What was clear was that Mr Alvez felt attacked and persecuted by the crying, screaming infant, felt that the infant was out of control and inconsolable, and then became himself out of control and inconsolable. His inability to think and thus to verbalize his experience was destroyed. He could only express his internal experience through the gesture of an affective outburst and subsequent paralysis.

If language is the cure for infancy as Phillips (1998) wrote, then the inability to form language represents a regression to infancy. We can hypothesize that the baby and/or mother–infant interaction acted as a symbolic catalyst, stimulating tremendous anxiety and rage in the bus driver. The crying, screaming, inconsolable baby was felt to be an intolerable persecutory object, attacking his internal sense of stability. He began to feel overwhelmed by his own inconsolable affects and, as is often the case, attempted to gain control by switching roles himself from victim to persecutor. Now he would rid himself of these overwhelming affects by attacking and destroying the external symbol of his distress, the baby. In his mind, only an act of God saved the baby, mother and himself from real tragedy. Of course we would say that the three-some was saved by an act of his unconscious mind in the form of a hysterical conversion reaction of the type that so interested Freud throughout his career. We could speculate that the bus driver was himself inconsolable as an infant and the crying infant represented the repressed pain of that primitive experience.

Fairbairn (1943), writing about the formation of internal objects in response to persecutory experience, noted that if a child is given a choice between a bad external object or no object the child will always choose the bad object. The need for relatedness supercedes the avoidance of the pain of relating to a bad object. Over time this bad object becomes internalized. As the child relates to the bad object the child feels bad himself. This appears similar to A. Freud's observations regarding identification with the aggressor. Feeling worse than the bad parental figure, the child will argue vehemently that it is she who is bad, not the parent. This gives the child the illusion that her badness is under her control and con-ditional on her own behaviour. This process serves a defensive function against the realization that it is really the parent who is bad. As long as the child sees herself as bad she retains hope that her parent is bad only in response to her and that the parent is really good after all.

Fairbairn showed how the ego that is whole at birth is split in response to rejecting and need-exciting experiences with the mother. If the mother is experienced as rejecting or exciting, the objects that are internalized are rejecting or exciting objects. The ego splits off parts of itself called the antilibidinal and the libidinal egos to repress the rejecting and exciting objects respectively. This creates rejecting and exciting internal object relationship systems, each consisting of ego, object, and affect. Both systems threaten to return from repression and either of them may be of persecutory dimensions depending on the excessive quality of the original experience, the thoroughness of repression, and the strength and flexibility of the central ego.

Fairbairn was particularly interested in traumatized patients whose difficulties with ego integration interfere with metabolizing and transforming internal persecutory objects and confuse what is real from what is imagined. They may resort to a delusional world in order to sustain the relationship with the persecutory object. They maintain the status quo of their internal world of bad objects as a closed system that resists contact with others and blocks the therapist's attempt to break the closed system.

Guntrip continued the work begun by Fairbairn, and then formulated his own theory of the creation of the persecutory object. He emphasized the role of the environment. He said, 'Fear, persecutory anxiety, arises in the first place as a result of an actually bad, persecutory environment' (1962, p.199). This experience is taken inside and repressed as a rejecting object in relation to the antilibidinal ego, which Guntrip saw as a persecuting ego that directs its energies to hating its own weakness. Thus the persecutory object permeates the sense of self. The degree of this unconscious self hatred determines the level of the individual's psychic stress.

WHY DO PARENTS FEEL PERSECUTED AND HATEFUL?

Winnicott brought into focus the actual relationship between mother and child, unlike Klein who emphasized the phantasies of the child and the mother and the processes of projective identification between mother and child. Winnicott pointed out that good and bad things happen that are quite outside the infant's range of control (Winnicott 1965). In his classic paper 'Hate in the Countertransference' Winnicott (1947) gave 18 reasons why a mother hates her baby, 11 of which clearly reflect the mother's experience of her baby as a persecutory object, listed as follows:

The mother's experience of the baby as a persecutory object

- The baby is a danger to her body in pregnancy and at birth.
- The baby is an interference to her private life, a challenge to preoccupation.
- The baby hurts her nipples even by suckling, which is at first a chewing activity.
- He is ruthless, treats her as scum, an unpaid servant, a slave.
- He tries to hurt her, periodically bites her all in love.

- He shows disillusionment about her.
- His excited love is a cupboard love, so having got what he wanted he throws her away like an orange peel.
- He is suspicious, refuses her good food and makes her doubt herself, but eats well with his aunt.
- After an awful morning with him she goes out, and he smiles at a stranger who says 'Isn't he sweet!'
- If she fails him at the start she knows he will pay her out forever.
- He excites her but frustrates – she mustn't eat him or trade in sex with him.

Of course many of these items are also true for the father's role with the infant. We might extend Winnicott's list for fathers, as follows:

The father's experience of the baby as a persecutory object

- The infant takes the wife's interest away from the husband.
- The infant taunts the father with his relationship with the mother.
- The mother–infant bond is more powerful because the infant grows inside the mother.
- The father loses some of the mother's libidinal interest.
- The infant damages the mother's body, which had been the province of the father.
- The infant restricts the father's interest in the outside world.

Example: The baby perceived as a competitor

A young father expressed feelings that reflect the ways in which both mother and father commonly see the infant as a persecuting object. He said, 'I didn't really realize how much time and energy a baby takes. My wife and I were very active people, hiking, sailing, going to road rallies with the sports car. Now it is not even clear if I'm able to keep the sports car. It's only a two-seater. I didn't have a sense of how demanding a baby can be. I hate to admit it but sometimes I feel like I am competing with the baby for my wife's attention. Even our sex life isn't what it was. I think she enjoys feeding the baby more than me!'

The parents' projections into the baby

Fantasies of the preconception baby

The baby exists long before the mother conceives. The baby exists in the conscious and unconscious mind of the mother, father, siblings, grandparents, and other members of the extended family and parents' peer group. All bring their histories, wishes, hopes, fears, and unresolved conflicts to bear on the construction of this fantasized baby. This complex of fantasies surrounding the baby has been described as the ghosts in the nursery (Fraiberg 1987) and as the beast in the nursery (Phillips 1998). Brazelton and Cramer (1990) describe specific dynamics related to these ghosts or beasts in the nursery: the child as reincarnation; the child as parent; the child as a dead infant; the child as a judge; the child as a competitive sibling. The baby is pregnant with meaning for the family.

Example: The lost baby as a persecutory object

The absence of a baby may be more powerfully persecutory than the presence of a difficult one, as the following example shows.

> Mary Bright, 39 years old, married with one child, Jeff, age seven, presented for couple therapy with her husband Jerry, a robust and droll man. Mary complained of depression, a result of her inability to conceive a second child despite valiant efforts with a fertility physician.
>
> Mary exclaimed, 'We've tried almost everything the past two years with no success! I'm so disappointed and frustrated. I want to continue and try additional methods but Jerry wants us to stop and let nature take its course. I understand it's been emotionally draining for him as well as me but he isn't as motivated as I am to have another child.'
>
> Jerry cut in, 'Motivated isn't the word for you. Obsessed is more like it. We've spent countless hours and over $30,000 of money we don't really have, not to mention the emotional investment. Now you want to go even further, it just doesn't

seem reasonable to me. I know this is important to you but it's starting to feel that this has become even more important than our marriage. Your obsession with this unconceived child makes me feel that I am not adequate and I don't count. I am worried that as our son gets older he will begin to feel the same way, that he is not enough, that all that matters is this phantom child.'

Mary cried, 'You just don't understand how important it is for me to have two children.'

Identifying with Jerry, I (S.T.) began to feel that in the session I didn't count. 'How curious,' I thought. 'He and his son don't count, and now he and I don't count. Only this missing baby counts. No. She didn't say "missing". That's my word not hers. Why do I feel as if there is a baby missing?' Using these feelings as my guide I said, 'This is clearly very upsetting for you. Can you help us understand the importance of this second pregnancy?'

Mary's cries turned to sobs. She sounded like the missing baby, crying out for its mother.

Through her tears, Mary answered, 'I don't know. I just feel so sad every time I think about it.'

I said, 'This feels very powerful. Like there is a baby already missing.'

Mary sobbed and cried out, 'There were two!'

Surprised I said, 'Two?'

'Yes,' she answered. 'Two. But I feel like only one is missing now. When I was in my early twenties I became pregnant. I was unmarried and in the middle of college. I didn't know the boy very well so I decided to have an abortion. It was terrible. I never wanted to go through that again. I swore to myself I would never let that happen again. Then, two years later, oh, I'm so ashamed. I did it again. I can't believe I did it again. It was great sex, just a one night stand. What was I thinking? No I wasn't thinking. So . . . I had a second abortion. Now I think God is punishing me for those two abortions by making it so difficult to get pregnant.'

'If you become pregnant you'll have replaced both children and perhaps feel that God has forgiven you?' I suggested.

Sobbing harder Mary replied, 'Yes, yes if only he would let me have another child then I wouldn't feel guilty any more. I'd have the two children.'

Here we see how the trauma of the previous pregnancies and abortions was encapsulated, resulting in a current crisis for Mary personally, and in her marriage with Jerry. The birth of her current child and the desire to have a second child represented reparation for her past losses and sins. The image of the aborted baby became a persecutory image. The wish for a pregnancy and live birth of a second child represented a fantasy of a detoxification of the earlier trauma. Only through the exploration of the earlier trauma and painful feelings could Mary and her husband puncture the encapsulation, work through the painful feelings, and resolve their current difficulties.

HOW DOES THE PERSECUTORY OBJECT EXERT ITS EFFECT?

We will now look at how the persecutory object exerts its effect in various ways along the continuum from self to other. It may define the primary sense of self, may lead to a conflicted sense of self, or may be projected outside the self. It both arises from and then further colours the perception of significant others and how they are to be dealt with. We will look at the parents' relation to the baby as an object and the baby's identification with the parents to understand how persecutory objects are mutually co-created.

The persecutory object as the central part of the self

When the persecutory object is the essence of our experience of our self, we are continually in a state of self-persecution, terrorizing ourselves with a harsh, aggressive inner voice and ever-present anxiety and aggression. In this case we are not aware of internal conflict as we would be when one side is representing the persecutory object and the other side is representing the part being persecuted, the victim of persecution. Rather we identify only with the part that does the persecution, unable to react in any other way, like the man in the following example.

Leo Russell is a tall, attractive, well spoken and distinguished professional man in his early sixties. He has been separated from his wife for the previous four years and is having trouble finalizing the divorce, fearful of being alone despite his obvious strengths. In a recent therapy session he described his feelings about himself.

'I have so much anxiety about being alone. What decent woman would want me? I am ugly in so many different ways. Without my money I have absolutely nothing to offer a woman and if I get divorced I'll have even less money. I hate myself. I have always hated myself. Even when I was a quote "big man on campus" I felt that I was a fraud. One of my coaches knew it. He would tell me that I was only filled with hot air and had no real substance as a ball player, but I knew he also meant as a person. Every time I had to be around him his very presence reminded me of what a wretched individual I really was. I would score points on the court with cheap baskets and make sure that if the game was close I would keep away from the ball by passing it to my teammates as quickly as possible. That way I wouldn't have to take the last shot and lose the game by missing. Of course I would miss. My father was right. He once told me that he was sorry he wasted his sperm on me. I haven't lived up to anyone's expectations. I had no real expectations of myself because I knew how limited I really was. What an asshole I am. You're wasting your time with me Doc. You would do better putting your energy into someone who has potential.'

Here Mr Russell experiences his primary sense of self as deserving his attack. He does not feel victimized by his self-attack because he feels it is all true, completely ego-syntonic. He has identified with the persecutory figure of his childhood, his disappointed father, and has internalized that experience as a persecutory object.

The persecutory object in conflict with the self

When identification with the persecutory object is not total, the self is split, one part identifying with the persecutory figure and the other with the victimized self. The individual is caught in a helpless conflict, identifying first with the persecutor and then the victim. These part-objects are caught in an oscillation between hate and aggression on one side and anxiety and terror on the other side.

Al Baxter, a forty-five-year-old man with different dynamics than Mr Russell, sees himself as being caught in a terrible conflict between warring sides; a harsh, attacking, punitive part-object and a victimized, helpless part-object.

'I can't seem to stop this self-attack. It's brutal. One side of me realizes that I am being far too harsh with myself for my mistakes but that side doesn't seem to be able to ward off the attack from the other side of me. I attack myself and then feel hopeless and depressed. I am constantly shifting from a state of attack on my self to a state of feeling victimized by myself. I then attempt to mediate the entire experience without much success.'

Mr Baxter experiences himself as caught in the crossfire of the persecutory part-object, the victim part-object, and a weak rescuer part-object. This dynamic creates a conflicted sense of self which itself becomes persecutory.

The persecutory object projected outside the self

The self may identify completely with the victim position by projecting aggression outside the self. A particular individual seems to be persecutory or the entire world may seem to be in a conspiracy. Clinically this can take the form of a paranoid projection.

Brian Berger experienced his therapist as hostile, cold, and rejecting. He experienced his interpretations as criticisms. 'I don't know why I continue to come here to suffer this abuse,' he said. 'You don't really have an ounce of understanding about me. All you can do is criticize and belittle me. I feel humiliated by you. You treat me just like all the other authority figures I've met, arrogant and stupid.'

Mr Berger experiences himself as a victim to a cold and punitive therapist. He unconsciously holds feelings of arrogance and stupidity that he attempts to eliminate through projection, projective identification, and introjection. Now it is the therapist who holds these feelings towards him. He believes that if he gets rid of the therapist he won't have to experience the feelings of arrogance and stupidity himself.

The persecutory object projected into the imagined baby

Just as the baby projectively identifies the mother and her breast as a part-object that is either all-good or all-bad from moment to moment, so parents may split their perceptions of their baby along good and bad lines too. They may split their image of the baby in response to the strength of the baby's projective identifications, or the cycle of projection may begin with them.

Ask people at random to conjure up their image of a baby and ideally good and bad images emerge:

- Baby: a bundle of joy, a coo, a smile, a laugh! A symbol of life, renewal, change, growth, purity, innocence, idealized love, and hope for the future. A pure seduction. A peaceful cherub.
- Baby: a frown; a cry; a scream! A symbol of frustration, dread, overwhelmed feelings, inadequacy, hopelessness, envy, and hate. A terrifying banshee. A persecutor.

We see the best of ourselves and the worst of ourselves in the baby. The infant provokes a range of reactions (Bick 1964). Even before the baby is biologically conceived we construct, both consciously and unconsciously, images of 'our baby' or 'my son' or 'my daughter'. The imagined baby is a powerful object, stimulating us to project our hopes, dreams, and wishes as well as our fears, nightmares, and unmet needs. The baby in actuality may or may not be a suitable object to accept the projections.

Example: A loving mother whose aggressive baby does not match her fantasy baby

Samantha Smith, thirty-four-year-old mother of three reported, 'I dearly wanted to nurse my baby. But he was so aggressive, biting down on my nipples with a force I couldn't believe. It felt more like an attack at each feeding rather than the warm, intimate experience I had originally imagined. I finally couldn't handle it any more and had to stop breast-feeding. It was my first major disappointment as a mother. I still don't know if I've gotten over it, and it was years ago. It just was not what I expected. Why did he have to be so aggressive? Actually, he's still aggressive.'

Example: An immature father who is afraid of a dependent baby

At the age of sixty, years after the birth of his baby and long after his divorce, Bob Tuckman, a sixty-year-old divorced father vividly remembered the experience of fathering his baby. He recalled, 'My wife told me she was pregnant. I felt a cold sweat of terror run across my body. A baby. I was no more prepared to have a baby than the man in the moon. A baby. An appendage that needs to be constantly taken care of, emotionally and financially supported. I felt overwhelmed for months. All my plans for the future would now have to be forgone. I was going to be a father. I felt that the baby would suck the life out of me. All I could see and feel was a burden of responsibility.'

We look into an infant and see ourselves as an infant reflected back. We search the eyes of the infant for signs that we exist in that pure, innocent state that long ago was lost to the vicissitudes and disappointments of reality. If we had good-enough parenting in our own infancy, we relate to the baby in a warm and positive manner (Winnicott 1965). We seek that pure, innocent part of ourselves that cannot be consciously remembered but only imagined.

If a woman's parenting experiences were not good enough, she looks to her infant to find reassurance that the possibility still exists for good-enough parenting. If the infant behaves in ways that do not give her a sense of herself as a good mother, she may experience the infant as an intruder, provoking her most primitive feelings of envy and hate and awakening dreadful feelings of loss and inadequacy. Her baby becomes a reflection of what is wrong with the world and her. In this disappointing situation, many adults feel diminished. They experience the innocent infant as the source of persecutory anxiety.

Example: Refinding the bad maternal object in the baby

Becky Landau is a 39-year-old new mother. In a therapy session, she said sadly, 'I love my baby yet at times I don't want anything to do with her. She wants my attention. She wants me to hold her and play with her. She's a really good baby, but when I'm tired, I resent her and try to pretend she is not there.

'I hate it when my mother visits. I'm glad we don't see her often. I wish she didn't come over at all. She's always on me for one thing or another. I can never do anything right. She doesn't really get the idea that this is my baby and that any mistakes I make will be my mistakes.'

Becky's baby was born with an outgoing nature and a need to relate that was greater than Becky's. Her healthy, well-regulated, and resilient baby pushed Becky to relate to her, but Becky felt persecuted by her asserting her normal needs. This had its origins in Becky's distant relationship with her mother whom she felt to be both uninvolved and demanding. With her baby, Becky finds a part of herself to be like the withholding mother with whom she is in conflict. She refinds her demanding mother in her baby. If Becky had not come for help, she could have entered into a negative projective cycle that cemented her view of her infant as a persecutor. This could lead to infant behaviours that provoke more withdrawal by Becky. To cope with the pain of this experience, the infant may create a persecutory internal object on the model of her mother's aggressive misperception of her.

LOVE AND HATE

The infant comes into the world predisposed to feel love and hate. When the infant is satisfied, love is more likely to emerge. When the infant is frustrated or denied, hate emerges. In states of frustration, hate is projected on the adult caregiver. The infant becomes a persecutory object and the caregiver feels the impact of the hate and absorbs it or retaliates. The actual experiences between mother and infant and between father and infant are important in determining the nature of the internal objects. Equally important are the aggressive, envious fantasies that the child directs against the parents who are the objects of dependency and desire. The demands of the real world, the infants' constitution, and the family interactions produce everyday successes and inevitable failures. If there are too many failures, the mother and the infant experience one another as a source of bad feeling, the prototype for the persecutory object.

It is the parents' capacity to tolerate and work with the child's fantasies, their own fantasies, and the real events of child-rearing that predict successful development with the detoxification of the persecutory aspects of the object. It is the therapist's capacity for containment that secures metabolization of the previously toxic aspects of the persecutory object, the eventual integration of hate and love, and the ability to relate to whole objects.

REFERENCES

Abraham, K. (1924). A short study of the development of the libido, viewed in the light of mental disorders. In *Selected Papers on Psycho-Analysis*, pp. 418–501. London: Hogarth Press, 1927.

Bick, E. (1964). Notes on infant observation in psychoanalytic training. *International Journal of Psycho-Analysis*, 45: 558–561.

Bion, W. (1959). Attacks on Linking. In *Second Thoughts*, pp. 93–109. New York: Jason Aronson, 1967.

Brazelton, T. B. and Cramer, B. G. (1990). *The Earliest Relationship: Parents, Infants and the Drama of Early Attachment*. New York: Addison-Wesley.

Fairbairn, W. R. D. (1943). The repression and return of bad objects (with special reference to the 'war neuroses'). In *Psychoanalytic Studies of the Personality*, pp. 59–81. London: Tavistock, 1952.

Fraiberg, S. (1987). Ghosts in the nursery: A psychoanalytic approach to the problem of the impaired infant–mother relationship. In *Selected Writings of Selma Fraiberg*, ed. L. Fraiberg. Columbus: Ohio State University Press.

Freud, A. (1936) *The Ego and the Mechanisms of Defense. The Writings of Anna Freud*, Volume 1. New York: International Universities Press, 1966.

Freud, S. (1930). Civilization and its discontents. *Standard Edition*, 21: 64–146.

Frosch, J. (1990) *Psychodynamic Psychiatry*, Vol. 2. New York: International University Press.

Guntrip, H. J. S. (1962). Devitalisation and the manic defense. In *Personal Relations Therapy: The Collected Papers of H.J.S. Guntrip*, ed. J. Hazell, pp. 187–212. Northvale, NJ: Jason Aronson, 1994.

Klein, M. (1929). Personification in the play of children. In *Love, Guilt and Reparation and Other Works 1921–1945*, pp. 199–209. London: Hogarth Press.

—— (1932). *Psychoanalysis of Children*. London: Hogarth.

—— (1935). The psychogenesis of manic-depressive states. In *Love, Guilt and Reparation and Other Works 1921–1945*, pp. 262–289. London: Hogarth.

——— (1946). Notes on some schizoid mechanisms. In *Envy and Gratitude and Other Works 1946–1963*, pp. 1–24. London: Hogarth.

Phillips, A. (1998). *The Beast in the Nursery: On Curiosity and Other Appetites*. New York: Pantheon Books.

Scharff, J. S. (1992). *Projective and Introjective Identification and the Use of the Therapist's Self*. Northvale, NJ: Jason Aronson.

Winnicott, D. W. (1947). Hate in the countertransference. In *Through Paediatrics to Psycho-Analysis*, pp. 194–203. London: Hogarth.

——— (1965). *The Maturational Processes and the Facilitating Environment*. New York: International Universities Press.

Chapter 2

Sources of persecutory anxiety: Death instinct or bad objects?

Jill Savege Scharff, MD

What lies at the root of persecutory aspects of the self? What explains the existence of a part of the self that is haunted by destructive impulses and fears of annihilation? Freud and Klein thought that this part of the self (called the death constellation) arises from a primarily innate death instinct, so powerful that it must be deflected by projective identification, the most effective mechanism of defence to prevent the self's demise. Fairbairn and other object relations theorists thought that the signs Freud attributed to the death instinct are breakdown products seen only in pathology. They believed that destructiveness and fear of death develop in response to identifications following difficult experience in the early years of life.

Is the death drive a powerful, primarily innate death instinct as Freud and Klein thought, or is it a drive that arises in response to experience and identifications as object relations theorists thought? Britton, a Kleinian, showed how the death constellation can result from the denial of oedipal murderousness contained in the rivalrous child's perverse fantasy of the self in relation to the envied parental couple. His work provides a bridge between the classical position on the death instinct and the object relational position on the tie to the bad object as the source of persecutory experience.

In this chapter I review arguments for and against the death instinct as an explanatory concept from Freudian, Kleinian, and Fairbairnian object relations theories. Some argue that such an abstract concept as the death instinct cannot be proved or disproved by clinical material. But the concept of the death instinct was conceived to explain clinical and societal phenomena. So I discuss its relevance to clinical examples and to animal behaviour in general. I offer an object relations view of the clinical material as an alternative for consideration.

FREUD'S CONCEPT OF THE DEATH INSTINCT

After years of dealing with sexual, self-preservative, and life instincts as explanatory concepts, Freud found them inadequate to account for the presence of repeated self-destructive behaviours. He concluded that there must be a death instinct operating in opposition to the life instinct. Freud thought that the death instinct arose from a biological source in the cell and in its molecules, its aim being to return the cell to inorganic matter and to conserve energy (1920).

Why did Freud have to introduce the death instinct? As an analyst, he wanted to explain clinical phenomena that seemed to discount the instinct theory of the pleasure principle – namely primary masochism, the repetition compulsion, the sadistic super-ego, the traumatic war neuroses, repetitive traumatic dreams, and the societal phenomena of anti-Semitism and the devastation of World War I (1920, 1924, 1930). As an old man, Freud was thinking about death – the death of his nephew in the war, the death of his grandson from tuberculosis, the death of his daughter Sophie, and the possibility of his own death from the illness that was emerging as cancer of the jaw. Hamilton (1976) suggested that Freud as a toddler may have been guilty about the death in infancy of Julius, the baby who came closely after him, and arrived at the idea of a death instinct to avoid feeling personally responsible for death wishes against the baby rival.

The biological argument brought up to date

Where did Freud find back-up for his concept of the death instinct? He found it in biology. He thought of his psychoanalytic theory of the balance between the life and death instincts as a dynamic corollary to life and death at the cellular level of the multicellular body of the higher organism. There, once the germ cells have achieved their aim, the rest of the body cells gradually become expendible and may conveniently die. If injury and illness do not intervene, death comes anyway from internal, natural causes that lead the organism back to the inorganic state. Death is the ultimate aim of life. According to Freud, the force that returns the human being to the inanimate state is the death instinct.

In his biological analogy, Freud anticipated modern theories of cell biology that deal with *apoptosis*, a term for programmed cell death in cells with nuclei (Meier et al. 2000). Apoptosis is a genetically determined, carefully orchestrated process in which the normal cell is singled out for death when its usefulness is outlived. One might argue that the single dying cell is indeed imbued with the death instinct, but programmed cell death at the level of the individual cell makes no sense until the whole cell cluster is considered. As Freud knew, cells live in communities. Individual cells die so that other cells in the community of cells may divide and so multiply to build tissue.

A number of triggers go together in a complex sequence to achieve the aim of cell death (Hengartner 2000, Hoffman 2000). A complex assortment of mechanisms collaborate to receive and transmit the signal of cell weakness, the decision for death, the instruction to destruct, the inhibition of cell protective agencies, and the concentration of conditions for successful elimination. Many people find it hard to believe that, in this way, nature can make death a default option (Yarmolinsky, personal communication). Nevertheless, research shows that in a carefully coordinated way the cells normally set in motion and neatly achieve their own death. One might argue that these cells are imbued with the death instinct. But the point of their death is to facilitate differentiation of other cells and so support growth and development.

Freudian arguments for the death instinct

Alexander (1929) agreed with Freud that the death instinct was primary because, he argued, only a death instinct could produce a state of primary masochism without which the sadism of the super-ego is insufficient explanation for suicide and many other self-destructive tendencies. Fayek (1981) argued for the death instinct because he could not explain narcissism without it. Garma (1971) believed that the use of the term death instinct was warranted since the accompanying behaviour patterns are as deeply ingrained as those pertaining to the pleasure-seeking instinct. He suggested that the main reason for anyone rejecting the theory of the death instinct was distaste for admitting something in oneself that is opposed to the pleasure principle (p. 152). Like Freud, he thought that the death instinct arose from and evolved with humanity's past experiences and that the destructive conflicts that it causes, increase or diminish according to the nature of each person's experience (p. 152).

THE KLEINIAN ELABORATION OF THE DEATH INSTINCT

Klein maintained allegiance to the death instinct and in this regard she considered herself Freud's true daughter. Whereas Freud's instincts are physiological, Klein's are said to be psychological (Spillius 1994). The infant Klein describes is haunted by the death instinct, terrified of its potential for self-annihilation and terrified of the resulting aggression against its objects. Driven to protect the self by projection of life-threatening levels of aggression via omnipotent phantasies of spitting, biting, devouring, and excreting, the infant is then terrified by the return of the projected aggression in the form of retaliatory, persecutory objects. Later the infant is worried about the damage that ensues from directing excessive aggression against its primary objects. Some infants have anxiety-provoking amounts of death instinct to cope with, and others have too little life instinct to counteract the death instinct.

According to Klein, deflecting the death instinct that otherwise threatens the self with destruction is the infant's most urgent task. The infant does this through the unconscious mental process of projective identification in which the infant expels the destructive wish and the associated aggressive affects towards the object, namely the mother's breast, and relocates them as if they had arisen from the object (Klein 1946). The infant misidentifies the good breast as absent and the remaining breast as actively hostile to the infant. To deal with the loss of the good breast, the infant takes in the breast as it now is, experiences it as an internal, persecutory object, and identifies with it by *introjective identification*, which leads to having a bad object inside the self (Klein 1946, Segal 1964, J. Scharff 1992). The good breast may be turned bad by the infant's greedy devouring of its supplies or envious attack of its goodness – which leaves the infant feeling deprived. The infant feels threatened with depletion, disturbance or, at worst, annihilation due to the force of the death instinct. Fortunately the situation is ameliorated by the simultaneous projection of loving feelings, emanating from the life instinct. Projection under the force of the life instinct colours the perception of the breast as good. When this is re-introjected and identified with, it leads to the formation of a good object inside the self. It is not that the instincts themselves are in opposition in the way Freud thought. In Kleinian theory, the perceptions of the object and therefore the self as good or bad are in conflict in the immature infant.

Segal (1993) agreed that the death instinct is a biological drive to return to the inorganic and the status quo, a drive towards destructuralization, dissolution, and death. She further defined the death instinct as a drive to annihilate need, the experience of need, and the needed object. As the death instinct is projected to relieve the terror of annihilation, the ego experiences fear, pain, dread of persecution, and guilt. Segal concluded that 'the satisfaction of the death instinct is in pain, rather than in death' (p. 59) and that 'the wish to annihilate is directed both at the perceiving self and at the object perceived, hardly distinguishable from one another' (p. 56). The infant ego avoids pain and envy by not recognizing the separate existence of the need-satisfying object. In addition, Segal made an interesting distinction between earlier and later manifestations of the death instinct: Earlier manifestations are dread of annihilation and accompanying terrors, while later manifestations include death wishes and fear of death.

Like Klein, Bion (1962a) held that the infant experiences an internal threat called nameless dread and deals with it by projective identification, in Bion's terms a type of omnipotent fantasy. In his early papers on psychosis that were not collected until later, Bion (1967) was still thinking in Kleinian terms of conflict between the life and death instincts, but in his subsequent writings he stopped referring to the death instinct. He continued to write about destructiveness to the self and the object, but he did so in terms of fear, hate, envy, and greed as infantile emotions that get in the way of love and gratitude. He emphasized the fear of death rather than the threat of the wish for death, but he made clear that this fear of death is innate. The sense of imminent danger is not created by actual deprivation but is simply a preconception that is confirmed when an actual danger occurs (Bion 1962b, Ogden 1986). Bion was well aware of the fragmenting effects of infantile hatred and destructiveness, but he attributed them to the infant's reaction to the frustration of the absent-but-needed breast, rather than to the death instinct. To the Kleinian concept of projective and introjective identification, Bion added the concept of alpha function (1962a), an empathic function of the mother's reverie that detoxifies and metabolizes overwhelming anxiety (beta elements) and turns it into thinkable, manageable experience (alpha elements). Bion's concept of this maternal capacity for containment of the baby's anxiety takes us beyond the death instinct to an interpersonal dimension to the Kleinian understanding of infantile experience.

ETHOLOGICAL ARGUMENTS AGAINST THE DEATH INSTINCT

Ethological studies of the young of all species do not support the concept of the death instinct. Bowlby (1969), an analyst and ethologist, demonstrated that human beings show the same instincts as animals – following (in human infants this is done with the eyes), clinging, crying, rooting, and sucking – all of them in the service of securing survival through proximity to safety and nutrition. Animals do not seek death but encounter it as a result of unprotected exposure to predators (including jealous parents and siblings), lack of food, congenital deficiency, lack of stimulation from caregivers, intervening illness, and eventually old age. Infants show behaviours that are clearly the expression of a survival instinct, but Bowlby couldn't find a similar set that would support the concept of a death instinct. Surely there is fighting to the death, but it occurs in order to protect status, territory, and loved ones, not to fulfil the desire for the animal's own death. There seems to be no evidence for a primary death instinct among the young across animal species.

Animal behaviour in old age, however, might seem more suggestive of the existence of a death instinct. Ageing caribou know when to lie down in the snow and die. Ageing humans maintain relationships until they must gradually let go of the family and the community because their time has come. Dying may be protested against, accepted gracefully, or actually welcomed. All animals have to accept mortality. Like apoptotic cells in the community of cells, they die to make way for the next generation.

FREUDIANS AND KLEINIANS OPPOSING OR REVISING THE DEATH INSTINCT

Noting that masochists seek pain only towards the end of receiving pleasure, Symons (1927) thought that masochism could be explained by the pleasure principle alone and so there was no need of a death instinct. Jones (1955) believed that aggression turned against the self secondarily, that there was no primary masochism, only masochism following sadism, and that therefore there was no such thing as a death instinct. Simmel (1944) held that the destructive energies are derived from the demands of the gastrointestinal tract and are aroused in reaction to object frustration. So, in his view there was no death instinct. Simmel, Symons, and Jones subscribed to Freudian principles and yet argued against the death instinct on theoretical grounds.

Contemporary Kleinians have modified Klein's original view of the death instinct. Grotstein (1985) preferred to think of the death instinct as a set of inborn defences that alert the self to internal and external sources of danger and secure the self against threat. Britton did not emphasize the death instinct but he was interested in the fusion of sex and death in the hysteric. He wrote that 'unconscious sex and death are combined in a pathological organization (Steiner 1987) in the form of a fantasy in which the patient becomes one of the members of the parental couple engaged in a perverse fantasy of mutual death so as to defend against recognizing the oedipal situation and taking responsibility for murderous wishes against the couple' (Britton 1999, p. 12). This conceptualization of the primal scene draws attention to a source of self-destructiveness. In my experience, the fantasized re-creation of the internal couple is commonly associated with tremendous excitement, envy, and destructiveness.

FAIRBAIRN'S ALTERNATIVE: THE TIE TO THE BAD OBJECT

The major object relations theorist, Fairbairn (1951, 1958) held that Freud's concept of the death instinct was not a universal motivating force. In his theoretical system, the only motivating force is the drive to be in a relationship. He thought that self-destructive manifestations are not evidence of the death instinct but are breakdown products of a poorly integrated ego unable to maintain the state of relatedness. In his view, the pleasure principle and the death instinct are essentially psychopathological phenomena, not normally occurring instincts. He thought that these self-destructive processes enabled his resistant patients 'to maintain their inner worlds as closed systems, and to resist every attempt to convert these systems into open systems and so render them amenable to change through the impact of influences in outer reality.' He concluded that 'Freud's . . . concept of the death instinct is an obstinate tendency on the part of the patient . . . to keep his aggression localized within the confines of the closed system of the inner world' (Fairbairn 1958, p. 90). In the same vein, when discussing the explanation for a fear of annihilation, Sutherland said, 'I don't think we need Klein's death instinct. What we need is a protesting organism' (1994, p. 389). Hamilton (1976) asserted that the death instinct is one of the least tenable of Freud's discoveries.

Even if we redefine death instinct as death wish, we have not solved the problem. Certainly people who suffer mentally or physically may wish to die to end their pain, but surely that wish results from distress rather than the force of an instinct. When human beings speak of the wish to die or enact suicidal behaviour, their motives in seeking death are largely interpersonal. They may wish to kill the pain of unrequited love, avoid conflict, or spare a loved one from pain. They may hope to experience sexual excitement in proximity to death or escape from the fear of being overtaken by death by taking matters into their own hands. They may be trying to escape the stress of relatedness and responsibility, avoid punishment, or take revenge for past hurt. They may intend to hurt a loved one by exposing them to loss. Without regard to their effect on others, thinking only of themselves, they may take suicidal action to destroy an internal object or obey a delusionally experienced internal object.

In the course of arguing *for* the death instinct, Alexander (1929) at the same time maintained that the psyche takes in destructive tendencies by acts of identification, a point that seems to me to argue *against* it. I think that Alexander is talking about the embedding of destructive tendencies in internal object relationships. My reading puts his view in keeping with Freud's view of the individual psyche as being composed of 'subject-matter-memory traces of the experience of earlier generations' (Freud 1939, p. 99) and 'harbored residues of the existence of countless egos' (Freud 1923, p. 38, quoted in Garma 1971). These ideas point me towards thinking of a transgenerational transmission through internal object relationships as the source of the material that constitutes the phenomenon called the death instinct.

A RE-EXAMINATION OF SOME CLINICAL EXAMPLES IN THE LITERATURE

Segal (1993) described vignettes from two analysands, a woman who wishes for her own sudden death rather than experience slow torture, and a man who is filled with deadness and deals with it by projecting it into the analyst, who feels killed off. My summary does not do justice to the case she makes that these phenomena illustrate the action of the death instinct, but my point is to suggest a different conclusion.

Dr Segal mentioned that the woman's wish to die and die quickly intensified as the patient faced a break in the analysis, and that the man's feelings arose as he faced the end of his analysis. That information suggests to me that the feared loss of the object is at least as good an explanation for their symptoms as the death instinct. I think that sudden death and the obliteration of the self and of all feeling seemed more bearable to the woman than the slow torture of gradually feeling the loss of her analyst. In the case of the man, I think that the self's relation to an important object was a crucial precipitant in the experience of deadness in the self and its transmission into the analyst by projective identification.

Both patients were fighting off the idea of separateness as a total catastrophe. Both patients were defending against their longing by evoking the death of the self that is in a state of longing or the annihilation of the object for which they yearn. In keeping with Fairbairn's observation that the unconscious antilibidinal object relationship further represses the libidinal internal object relationship, I suggest that Segal's patients' longings for connection to her and fear of losing her were expressed indirectly as material about death.

At another place in the same paper, Segal showed that the environment does play a part in shaping the manifestations of the death instinct. She wrote, 'The fusion and modulations of the life and death drives are part of developing relationships to early objects, and, therefore, the real nature of the environment will deeply affect the process' (1993, p. 60). In this respect Segal tends towards an object relational point of view.

Feldman (2000) described the clinical destructiveness of a male patient who attacked links between thoughts, obfuscated meaning and differences, spoiled the analyst's therapeutic efforts, and undermined the competence of both the analyst and himself. Feldman emphasized that the man's destructive drive did not aim at total annihilation of self or other but at creating a state of constant near-death in which the life was sucked out of his self and his object projected into the analyst, and therefore diminished the analyst's power to evoke admiration, dependent longings, grief, or envy. Like Segal's patient, Feldman's patient was facing a break in the analysis over the weekend and this brought out his pleasure in deadly negativity. The break was short and routine, but the man associated it with the traumatic loss of a previous analyst and his repeated experiences of being left by his father in childhood, and so it tapped into a reservoir of grief and rage.

The man's destructiveness took the form of spoiling his capacity for thinking and working, and invading his analyst's capacity for thinking and working, instead imprisoning both of them in a tormented union. Between them they created a cruel and useless couple that is reminiscent of the couple that I cited from Britton (1999) earlier. The couple the man created in the transference with Feldman revealed the man's identification with parents who were not sexually vital, but who were ill and weak, drawn to death and forcing abandonment on him. (As Alexander noted, the tendencies to destructiveness and deathliness are internalized by identification with important external objects.)

Feldman argued against Freud's idea that the gratification of destructiveness is produced by fusion of the death instinct and the life instinct. Although he agreed that the drive to spoil and attack is anti-life, Feldman argued that it could not accurately be called a death instinct because its aim is not annihilation but the maintenance of a tie to a tormenting, paralyzing, or terrifying object. In this respect, Feldman departs from the Kleinian position towards an object relational point of view.

CURRENT CLINICAL EXAMPLES FOR DISCUSSION OF CONCEPTS

Example 1: The persecutory object projected into the genitals

This example, from my own practice, explores the connection between sex and death and shows how the persecutory object gets projected into the genitals of the partner.

> Mr B loved and admired his wife but she avoided having sex with him because sexual arousal made her angry at him. He attributed his sexual frustration to his wife's sexual reluctance, criticism of his ineptitude, and frighteningly aggressive reactions if ever she were aroused. Remembering the first time he had sex helped him to see that when he was aroused he, himself, had a heightened sense of feeling other than desire.
>
> Mr B said, 'I was 17 and I was home with my parents in Panama for the summer. I'd met this older girl at a cocktail party my parents gave at their country house in the interior. We arranged to meet later and I had to sneak out of the house behind my parents' back. I'd taken a sleeping bag with me, and we put it down over some soft pine needles near the edge of the lake. We started making out and I suddenly realized that she was very aroused, much more experienced than I was, and that she was expecting to have intercourse. "Oh, my God," I remember thinking, "This is what I've thought about for years. This is the moment I've been waiting for!" And I couldn't get an erection! I couldn't do it. I felt so excited, I wanted to, and I just couldn't do it. There I was in the dark, and no one knew we were there. This was in Panama, and there were real alligators in that lake. Having sex, I could have been eaten alive! It was terrifying. And to think of my parents finding what was left of me there like that. My only thought was to get home as quick as I could.'
>
> 'Because the vagina and the biting mouths around you in the dark were so scary,' I said.
>
> 'Oh definitely,' he agreed. 'I felt like a complete loser.'

Fusion of sex and death instincts or tie to exciting and rejecting objects?

Mr B's first sexual experience felt dangerous and traumatic. Sexual desire became linked with death. But I do not think that happened because of a death instinct. His sexual curiosity and desire contaminated with anxiety and fear of discovery by his parents led him to invest the alligators with retaliatory castrating powers that inhibited his potency. The same cycle of projection was evoking the aggressive response in his wife. Mr B felt close to his mother who was capable of great intimacy, and so he felt abandoned by her when she dealt with her frequent rages by leaving the house impulsively. He felt lonely and rejected in his marriage to a woman to whom he felt close and loving and in whom he refound the rejecting and exciting aspects of the maternal object.

Example 2: Self-destructiveness; death instinct or tie to the bad object?

The next example, also from my own practice, presents a young man who hates his homosexual orientation. He shows a repetition compulsion to destroy himself, a history of suicidal feelings, guilt, and a sadistic superego – some of the clinical features that led Freud to think in terms of a death instinct. I will present a single session from the early mid-phase, and will then apply first the death instinct and then object relations concepts to the task of understanding his experience.

> Mr A is a twenty-seven-year-old banker who is suffering from homosexual conflict about which he is ashamed and guilty. He is deeply distressed because he loves children and would like to be a father and create a family but can't imagine himself happy in either a heterosexual or a homosexual marriage. His homosexual desire takes the form of watching gay pornography, wanting to suck on a penis and get the semen into his mouth, and experiencing arousal in masturbation to homosexual images. His heterosexual desire takes the form of experiencing a more intense orgasm in masturbation in response to heterosexual images and longing to be in a family with a wife and children. He values heterosexuality above homosexuality, but in fantasy he prefers homosexuality.

Anxiety and depression were manifest in his obsessing over whether or not he will be openly gay or live as a heterosexual, and in overeating, oversleeping, drinking, and abusing drugs, habits that he guiltily hides from his parents whom he loves and respects, and from his colleagues at the bank. He hates his body, thinks that he is hugely overweight, and regards himself as vile. He is not actively suicidal, but his dreams are filled with fatal plane crashes. He has been in analysis for over a year and has not discovered the discrete trauma that he hoped to find to explain away his homosexual wishes.

He has, however, progressed in his understanding of his early experience and its impact on his identity. He has discovered that his current fascination with sucking on a large penis to get fluid out of it connects to his daily exposure as a child to an adult penis as his father sat with him in the shower. As a child, he felt revulsion at seeing his grandmother's sagging breasts, and a frustrated desire to see his beautiful young mother's hidden breasts. Both these reactions to the breast and the penis are connected to his continuing bottle-feeding until he was three. One day on a car journey with his mother and father, he threw away his beloved bottle in disgust, because he said it had a nipple with too big a hole. He wishes he could find an explanation for his homosexuality that would allow him to throw it away as easily.

The material that I will report is from the second session following my absence when I unexpectedly had to cancel two sessions to attend a family funeral out of town. The session began with a dream within a dream.

Mr A said, 'I had a dream the other night. I was in a hotel-like building that had been reduced to fire or something. It was like a place that I used to see on my way home as a child driving with my mother. I saw myself in there. Then I woke up in the dream and thought (still in the dream), "Gee, I remember this building from my childhood; so maybe my brain is giving me a message to pursue this avenue in analysis." So then I thought of you. I realized that there was a connection. The dream continued, the narrative proceeded to a thriller-like conclusion and everything fell into place. "Gee!" I thought, "That hotel and that rubble contain the answer to all this."

'I woke up from the dream and realized that I had been in a twilight zone between sleeping and waking, thinking back on the dream. Finally, when I was truly awake, I realized that nothing fell into pieces and there were no connections.'

I said to Mr A, 'I was quite struck by your expression that in reality "nothing fell into pieces" whereas in the dream "everything fell into place".'

He said, 'Nothing falling into pieces, hmmm – that's even worse than nothing. Yes. And I saw myself as a tiny person in the dream. In the dream, I thought to myself that someone had harassed me at this hotel and that that explained my homosexual conflict, but it didn't seem the right answer when I was awake. It was really disappointing. I had been so excited to come and tell you about it.

'Well that was the dream. Now I would like to speak in detail about this fantasy of mine that we have been talking about, this fantasy in which I am driven to inflict pain on myself and hurt myself. It hit me yesterday that it's not just with drug abuse and cigarette smoking, but it's also with overeating and lack of exercise that I am signing my own death warrant. It's not that I *wish* to hurt myself. I wish I were healthier so I could live longer. I don't want to die that young.'

He fell silent for a few minutes.

'My mind totally wandered off,' he explained. 'Here's what train of thought popped up. I recently requested a Delta mileage award for a round trip upgrade from Washington to home, and that's why I imagined myself flying business class. Suddenly you appeared there in the business class section. I was wondering if you were going to a seminar near my home and wondering how I would react, or how you would react, if we met on the plane. I was wondering whether, if I needed an emergency session, you would conduct it on the plane. And other absurd thoughts like that.'

I said, 'This fantasy has you and me meeting on a plane. Not only does the fantasy have this plane able to land, unlike your dreams in which the plane crashes, but it has me there in the future with you in your home town.'

He replied, 'Now I remember, the fantasy actually did start with the thought of the plane crashing. I really did have death wishes at times, particularly when I was in love with this girl at school. I thought these death wishes were really childish. I once wished that my plane would crash so that I wouldn't go to hell for feeling suicidal over her! No matter how deep trouble you're in, it must be really difficult to commit suicide.'

I was thinking that this sounded like evidence of the death instinct – an irrational force dominating his thoughts. Then I thought about his attachment to me. In this fantasy he had me accompany him on the plane where he could continue his analysis and so avoid separation, a reversal of what had actually happened. At first, he had suppressed the fact that he had initially imagined that the plane would crash. In that case we might die, and in reality analysis would be ended, but in his fantasy, we are together forever doing analysis, connected by death. The crash would obliterate any evidence of his wish to be with me and would erase any guilt about possessing me when I was with others in my family and doing my own mourning. I didn't speak.

'Well, this is turning out to be one of our more boring sessions,' he said in disgust. 'But I am feeling very tired.'

I said, 'This session has become like the dream. The wonderful clues in the dream have led you to a sense of nothing.'

Apparently switching topics, he continued to describe bisexual sexual desire, making an association between boredom, nothing, death, and the relative lack of heterosexual desire. 'At school, within the female group, there was one, or maximum two girls I might want to sleep with. Within the male group, the number was five or even six. This is how many men I could visualize myself having sex with.'

I noticed the distinction he made between the sexes, the women being girls and the men being men.

He continued, 'Obviously, the male side is overwhelmingly favoured. Of the six men, two or three are actually handsome, whereas most of the girls are not. Even so, I said to myself, "God, I can't believe how desperate you are."'

I asked, 'Desperate?'

He replied, 'Desperate for male flesh, although admittedly most of the girls are below average but even if not they might go unnoticed.'

I began to feel extremely sleepy. As a woman, I felt extraneous.

Mr A continued, 'If I had the same amount of lust and had been a girl (and a footnote here is that I have no desire to be a girl) I would have been one of those girls who are sexually active, sleep with every other guy. You know?'

I said, 'You think that I know something about girls like that?'

'Everybody does,' he answered. 'I don't mean personally.'

I continued, 'I was thinking perhaps you did mean personally. I thought you might be thinking of me as having behaviours like one of those girls who doesn't really care about any one man, seeing a series of patients for intimate meetings as I do, and going off unexpectedly.'

'No, I wasn't,' he said. 'I'm desperate for male flesh because I haven't had it for ages.'

'In conclusion,' he said, 'I'm a bigger homosexual than a heterosexual. I acknowledge my heterosexuality, but I don't embrace it. Overall, I'm not critical of my life, but the one thing I hate about myself and my life is I'm forced to watch gay porn and masturbate to it all alone, like I'm a prisoner, or a slave, or in a concentration camp.'

Mr A has a history of suicidal feelings and addictive behaviours. He has a sadistic superego. His repeated attempts to destroy himself can be thought of as a repetition compulsion. He has a drive to be sexual with a man without being in a relationship. These qualify as some of the clinical features that led Freud to the concept of the death instinct. But the history of his life and of his transference led me to doubt that Mr A's self hatred, depression, and self-destructiveness were due to the death instinct.

A survey of Mr A's symptoms shows that he has a tremendous desire to take in. By the mouth he has taken in milk, food, semen, alcohol, and drugs, and by the eyes he has taken in the shape of breasts and sexual interaction between body parts in homosexual and heterosexual interaction. He attacks the nurturing female body that he finds in his own fatness and in unattractive girls and he idealizes men with large penises, especially when I am not available. He has conflict over his objects, his own body, and his sexual desires. He longs for relatedness and procreativity. He longs for the breast, but he can't have it. He threw away his bottle, and now he throws away his self as a useless object. It seems to me that this attitude occurs because of guilt at his level of desire for the sexual organs of both parents, rage at being denied access to pleasures that his parents as a couple enjoyed, and shame that he does not have a sexual partner.

In the session, Mr A refutes my interpretation that his homosexual desperation was due to a frustrated need for relatedness, or due to a wish to incorporate the man he might have imagined I had left him for. His next associations point to the association of unrelated sexual excitement with slow torture and death. Mr A's devouring homosexual urges seem to fit the theoretical explanation that they derive from a frustrated instinct, as he prefers not to think of himself as searching for relatedness to a man either as a primary love object or as a substitute for a frustrating woman.

In the transference, Mr A wants to be with me on the plane and yet he thinks of killing me off. I think that this is a response to my leaving him to do my own mourning. He connects to me by the shared threat of death and then disconnects from me by imagining unattractive women at school. It is the handsome, exciting men who are there – not the abandoning, ugly women – who arouse his excitement. Mr A lives in a closed system of internal object relationships in which his attachment to rejecting and rejected female objects leads to hostile attacks both on his heterosexual longing and on his homosexual longing for idealized and exciting paternal objects.

SUMMARY: THE DEATH CONSTELLATION TIED TO THE BAD OBJECT

Alexander, Fayek, and Garma joined Freud in thinking that the death instinct was the necessary explanation for narcissism, primary masochism, the sadism of the superego, the repetition compulsion, mass aggression, and self-destructiveness. Freud introduced the death instinct as the normal opposing force to the life instinct, rather than the aggressive instinct as a drive in support of life and the living space (marking out territory different from Adler's term 'aggressive instinct'). Klein and Segal accepted the validity of the concept of the death instinct. They elaborated its manifestations in normal infants, children, and adult patients. Like Alexander they noticed the impact of identification in the development of an internal nidus of destructiveness in the individual, but they thought that destructiveness emanates from the death instinct leading to the projection of aggression onto the breast, not that it arises in interaction with aggression in the personality of the mother. Bion did not actively refute the death instinct but it fell out of his lexicon.

One difficulty in accepting the concept of the death instinct comes from research into living systems that shows that they do not tend towards a resting state. Freud thought that the aim of the death instinct was the conservation of energy, the maintenance of the status quo, and the return to the inorganic state. We now know that living systems do not show entropy, as Freud thought. On the contrary, living systems are constantly growing, developing, and changing (Bertlannfy 1950, Prigogine 1976). They receive feedback from the environment and oscillate between chaos and order as they adapt to changing circumstances. They are particularly sensitive to conditions at the beginning and at transitional moments between one phase of growth and the next. Their patterns of behaviour are pulled into chaos and into order in association with the dynamic forces of neighbouring systems. Contemporary study of living systems does not support the idea of a death instinct. Still, it has to be admitted that the system does eventually organize into a pattern that ends in death.

Further difficulties in accepting the death instinct follow from the use of the word 'instinct', infelicitously translated from the German original '*Trieb*' and chosen to describe a deeply ingrained repetitive behaviour (Bettleheim 1982). The word 'instinct' refers to innate behaviours of the animal species. Nowhere in studies of the young in the animal kingdom do ethologists find a death instinct. There is a self-preservative instinct manifest in attachment behaviours. There is a sexual instinct that ensures mating, nest-building, and reproduction. There is an instinct to kill predators or competitors, and sometimes the father will destroy an imperfect baby animal, but there is no normal drive of the young to die.

The claim that the ultimate aim of life is death argues for the existence of a death instinct near the end of life. Certainly the end of life is always death, but the aim is reproduction of the species prior to death. The soma cells of the multicellular organism such as the human being exist to support the germ cells that reproduce and differentiate, and then, admittedly, the soma cells gradually die. Beyond the cellular level, the argument can be made for survival and sexual life instincts, but not for a death instinct – at least, not until death becomes inevitable.

Research findings on programmed cell death seem to confirm Freud's theory of the biological basis of the death instinct, and Hoffman (2000) presented them in detail in the spirit of reviving the concept of the death instinct. But can cellular mechanisms really argue in favour of a death instinct at the level of the whole organism? Clearly, there is genetically programmed, carefully controlled cell death. That fits the description of a death drive, but only at the cellular level. The purpose of this death drive, however, is adaptation, differentiation, balance, renewal, and the perpetuation of life until the moment of death from senescence, not the return to the status quo. Programmed cell death occurs only in the multicellular organism. The unicellular organism clings to life for ever (Stoica, personal communication). Even more relevant is the fact that a human being is much more than a collection of cells, however carefully orchestrated they may be.

Like the single cell in the community of cells, each human being lives in a community with other human beings in a state of interdependence throughout the life cycle. Life and death are events of the individual's internal physical milieu, but they are also functions of the family and the social environment. Babies without mothers die not because of their death drives, but because of lack of care, nourishment, appropriate stimulation, holding, handling, and a good rhythm of frustration and satisfaction. Babies fail to develop because of a failed entrainment of the infant brain in association to the more mature, affectively attuned brain of their mothers. Prematurely terminally ill people may carry genetic vulnerability to contract the disease that kills them but that is not the same as an instinct to get ill and die. The species dies because it is unable to adapt to the external demands of a changing environment. Death is socially constructed.

Symons, Jones, Reich, and Simmel thought that there was no need of a death instinct – because the pleasure principle was sufficient, there was no primary masochism, and destructive energy arose from the instinct for self-preservation. Fairbairn agreed that there were antilibidinal trends in each personality, but he reframed the death instinct as an obstinate tendency to cling to a bad object – bad because it is inherently frustrating or because the infant's needs are too great to be met. For him, manifestations attributed to the pleasure principle and the death instinct are not evidence of normal fundamental forces but are breakdown products of failed relationships and poor ego strength.

Reviewing the clinical examples that Segal gave to illustrate the death instinct and applying object relations theory for understanding them, I find that identification with the abandoning object is central. Feldman's clinical example shows how the tie to the tormenting object is the crucial aspect driving the behaviours that might otherwise be attributed to the death instinct. The examples from my own practice are given to show how fantasies of death and sex are fused in response to early object relationships. My conclusion is that impulsive sexual activity, self-destructive behaviour, and aggressive fantasy derive from the internalization of the parents as individuals and as a couple, based on the child's feelings and perceptions appropriate to various developmental phases and to the parents' actual behaviour.

My review of Freudian, Kleinian, and object relations theory and clinical practice leads me to the conclusion that the constellation of death threat and destructiveness is not simply instinctual. Instead of thinking of the death instinct as an innate threat to the infant, we can think of the infant becoming aggressive when frustrated by the needed breast, whether due to the mother's non-attunement or the child's inability to tolerate delay. Then if it does not secure the needed object or is not defused by the mother's holding and handling, the child's aggression may become destructive to the self, the object, or the relationship. Instead of thinking of the death instinct as the motive force of death and destruction, we can see aggression as defending territory, driving curiosity, ensuring learning, adaptation, and the mastery of new situations, and only in states of extreme frustration leading to violence and war. Aggression aims at supporting the human need to be in a relationship and yet enjoy increasing autonomy. Instead of seeing the death instinct as an innate potential for annihilation of self and other, we can see the deathly constellation as the trace of aggression that has failed to possess the loved object and now engenders feelings of protest or hopelessness and doom, locked in a closed system of internal object relationship (D. Scharff 1992, Scharff and Scharff 1998).

The death constellation is seen when the aggression and the desire of the helpless, anxious infant is frustrated by the mature, nurturing, and limit-setting responses of the mother and father who feel both love and aggression towards their child, who both loves and hates them individually and as a couple. It is seen in adulthood, when individuals alone or in partnership cannot create a sustaining sexual relationship, as Mr A and Mr B found themselves unable to do, or when the pain of illness is too much to bear. The impact of loss, separation, and death normally affecting family members and friends through the life cycle is conveyed to the child. Along with these ordinary experiences, the family transmits to the growing child its experiences of annihilation, sudden death, torture, and aggression towards self and other in its culture. From this substrate, the child creates psychic structure that may then include a preoccupation with death or repetitive self-destructive behaviours.

In my view, the death constellation is not due to a death instinct. It is interpersonally constructed and it consists of persecutory internal objects.

REFERENCES

Alexander, F. (1929). The need for punishment and the death instinct. *International Journal of Psycho-Analysis* 10: 256–269.

Bertlannfy, von L. (1950). The theory of open systems in physics and biology. *Science* 111: 23–29.

Bettleheim, B. (1982). Reflections: Freud and the soul. *The New Yorker* March 1, pp. 51–93.

Bion, W. (1962a). *Learning from Experience*. New York: Basic Books.

—— (1962b). A theory of thinking. In *Second Thoughts*, pp. 110–119. New York: Jason Aronson.

—— (1967). *Second Thoughts*. New York: Jason Aronson.

Bowlby, J. (1969). *Attachment and Loss* Vol. 1. New York: Basic Books.

Britton, R. (1999). Getting in on the act: The hysterical solution. *International Journal of Psycho-Analysis* 80: 1–13.

Fairbairn, W. R. D. (1951). A synopsis of the development of the author's views regarding the structure of the personality. In *Psychoanalytic Studies of the Personality*, pp. 162–179. London: Routledge.

—— (1958). On the nature and aims of psycho-analytical treatment. In *From Instinct to Self* Vol. 1, ed. D. Scharff and E. F. Birtles, pp. 74–92. Northvale, NJ: Jason Aronson.

Fayek, A. (1981). Narcissism and the death instinct. *International Journal of Psycho-Analysis* 62: 309–322.

Feldman, M. (2000). Some views on the manifestation of the death instinct in clinical work. *International Journal of Psycho-Analysis* 81(1): 53–65.

Freud, S. (1920). Beyond the pleasure principle. *Standard Edition* 18: 7–64.

—— (1923). The ego and the id. *Standard Edition* 19: 3–66.

Freud, S. (1924). The economic problem of masochism. *Standard Edition* 19: 157–170.

—— (1930). Civilization and its discontents. *Standard Edition* 21: 59–145.

—— (1939). Moses and monotheism: Three essays. *Standard Edition* 23: 7–207.

Garma, A. (1971). Within the realm of the death instinct. *International Journal of Psycho-Analysis* 56: 145–154.

Grosskurth, P. (1991). *The Secret Ring*. Reading, MA: Addison-Wesley.

Grotstein, J. (1985). A proposed revision for the psychoanalytic concept of the death instinct. *Yearbook of Psychoanalysis and Psychotherapy, Vol. 1*, pp. 229–326. Hillsdale, NJ: New Concept Press.

Hamilton, J. (1976). Some comments about Freud's conceptualization of the death instinct. *International Journal of Psycho-Analysis* 3: 151–164.

Hengartner, M. O. (2000). The biochemistry of apoptosis. *Nature* 407: 770–776.

Hoffman, T. (2000). *Revival of the death instinct: a view from contemporary biology*. Manuscript in preparation.

Jones, E. (1955). *The Life and Work of Sigmund Freud 1919–1939: The Years of Maturity*. New York: Basic Books.

Klein, M. (1946). Notes on some schizoid mechanisms. In *Envy and Gratitude and Other Works 1946–1963*, pp. 1–24. New York: Delacorte Press, 1975.

Meier, P., Finch, A., and Evan, G. (2000). Apoptosis in development. *Nature* 407: 796–801.

Ogden, T. (1986). *Matrix of the Mind*. Northvale, NJ: Jason Aronson.

Prigogine, I. (1976). Order through fluctuation: Self-organization and social system. In *Evolution and Consciousness: Human Systems in Transition*, ed. C. H. Waddington and E. Jantsch, pp. 93–126, 130–133. Reading, MA: Addison-Wesley.

Scharff, D. (1992). *Refinding the Object and Reclaiming the Self*. Northvale, NJ: Jason Aronson.

Scharff, J. S. (1992). *Projective and Introspective Identification and the Use of the Therapist's Self*. Northvale, NJ: Jason Aronson.

Scharff, J. S. and Scharff, D. E. (1998). *Object Relations Individual Therapy*. Northvale, NJ: Jason Aronson.

Segal, H. (1964). *An Introduction to the Work of Melanie Klein*. London: Heinemann.

—— (1993). On the clinical usefulness of the death instinct. *International Journal of Psycho-Analysis* 74: 55–61.

Simmel, E. (1944). Self-preservation and the death instinct. *Psychoanalytic Quarterly* XIII(2): 160–185. [Abstract (by M. Grotjahn) in *International Journal of Psycho-Analysis* 26: 180–181.]

Spillius, E. (1994). Developments in Kleinian thought: Overview and personal view. *Psychoanalytic Inquiry* 14(3): 324–364.

Steiner, J. (1987). The interplay between pathological organizations and the paranoid-schizoid and depressive positions. *International Journal of Psycho-Analysis* 68: 69–80.

Sutherland, J. D. (1994). On becoming and being a person. In *The Autonomous Self: The Work of John D. Sutherland*, ed. J. S. Scharff, pp. 372–389. Northvale, NJ: Jason Aronson.

Symons, N. J. (1927). Does masochism necessarily imply the existence of a death-instinct? *International Journal of Psycho-Analysis* 8: 38–46.

Chapter 3

The interpersonal sexual tie to the traumatic object

David E. Scharff, MD

SEXUALITY, TRAUMA, AND THE TIE TO THE PERSECUTING OBJECT

It is the function of all primary relationships to transform major trauma into healing and growth and to provide buffering against everyday trauma, and regeneration following major setbacks. This transformative function begins with the mother and father's protection of the infant. It extends to adult spouses or partners who offer security, soothing, and stimulation of growth potentials for each other, and then for their children. A particular role in this process is played by the adult's sexual life. A major function of adult sexuality is to provide an experience that makes up for life's wear and tear, and all the more so when there has been actual trauma (Scharff 1982, Scharff and Scharff 1994). Partners who have experienced physical and emotional abuse often transfer aspects of their traumatized object relationships into their sexual life, a psychosomatic conversion in which they attempt to use sexuality to represent internal object relations and to effect repair to their selves and their relationships (Fairbairn 1954).

When the transformative process becomes blocked, we often see the repeated expression of part–object relationships as partners try, over and over, to make good their relationship, each time experiencing defeat as they fail to transform trauma into genera (Bollas 1989). This is one manifestation of what Freud described as the repetition compulsion, which he thought was driven by the destructiveness of the death instinct. To understand this pattern in object relations terms, we turn to Fairbairn's concept of the tie to the bad object. The continued attempt to relate in the same self-defeating way is understood as the repeated attempt to recover lost and damaged parts of the self (Fairbairn 1952, Dicks 1967, Scharff and Scharff 1994). Viewed this way, the repetition compulsion is a sign of undying hope. In the sexual arena, the repetition compulsion takes the form of repeated failures to transform pain into pleasure. This leads to sexual dysfunction and perversion – a part–object way of relating in which the genitalia, through shared projective identification, embody the painful part–object relationships that can never quite be overcome, but that continue to seek transformation into a healing, life-giving sexual relationship.

When a couple's attempts fail to repair painful internal object relations that have been externalized onto the sexual stage, the persecution by painful internal object relations is magnified powerfully by a renewal of persecuting and frustrating relationship to external objects. Previously each partner's primary childhood objects had carried aspects of traumatic object relations. Now the couple's relationship itself acquires a traumatic dimension that increases the power of the persecutory inner objects, as the individual failures are compounded by the daily retraumatizing effects that accrue from the couple's ongoing external failure in the intimacy of their shared sexual relationship.

I will now describe couple therapy with a husband and wife whose intimate life was dominated by trauma-induced persecutory internal objects that were eventually graphically revealed in their sexual relationship. This therapeutic approach leans heavily on object relations theory and on behavioural techniques that I have modified from Masters and Johnson and Helen Singer Kaplan (Masters and Johnson 1970, Kaplan 1974, Scharff 1982, Scharff and Scharff 1991).

PERSECUTORY DYNAMICS IN A COUPLE

The history of the marriage

Ricardo and Maria were in their mid-40s when they sought help for their marriage which was filled with chronic resentment and frustration. Many years ago, they had been sweethearts, both from a small village in South America. Ricardo came from a poor family but was always the smartest in his village school and the most outstanding soccer player. Maria had adored him. She sacrificed herself for her boyfriend, the superstar who went off to the capital city and eventually to university – an achievement previously unheard of in his village. He was both a fine athlete and a driven intellect, the one whom everyone expected to leave others in the dust. If he had a hint of arrogance she did not notice, such were the stars in her eyes.

At 19, Ricardo was dealt a crushing blow. He developed a benign but recurrent tumour of the lumbar spine. Because of his poverty, he did not get medical attention for the early symptoms. One day he was a star student and athlete at the national university, and three months later he was in a wheelchair for life. A wealthy professor at the university befriended him by paying for his medical care and rehabilitation. Several operations by an excellent surgeon prevented further damage from the tumour. Ricardo's capacity for erections and his sexual functioning were unimpaired, but his legs were permanently paralyzed.

Maria had expected throughout her adolescence to marry Ricardo, and thought herself lucky to be attached to him. At the time of the onset of the paralysis, she stood by him without question. She wanted to stay with him because she still loved him, and because, in an unspoken way, she was afraid to be alone or to look for someone else. She thought secretly that she would never catch another husband and so she stayed with him through university, hostage to her own insecurity. No one thought he could manage the ambitious workload he had carved out for himself after his illness, but he did. Ricardo persisted, and graduated at the top of his class. He drove himself relentlessly. He thought – and it was probably true – that everything was harder for him than for others, that his paralysis meant that he had to work many times harder than his peers to convince teachers to take him seriously, but he carried on.

In retrospect, we could see that the illness crystallized Ricardo's pre-existing conviction that he would never escape the scourge of poverty and ignorance. In the wake of this conviction, he became single-minded in his studies. Maria visited him periodically, supported him from home, and waited. Where Ricardo had been funny and loved jokes, there was now a deadly seriousness about him. While she had been light-hearted and counted herself lucky in many ways, she developed a dour sense of herself, connected now to damaged goods, even though quite special damaged goods. The fun seemed to have gone out of their life, although from the outside they still looked like a special couple.

During their long pre-marital relationship, they observed strict Catholic social and religious sanctions on sexuality and did not have intercourse. When Ricardo graduated, they got married. He had good intentions and strove to succeed in ways his teachers said were impossible. He worked night and day while Maria supported him in many ways. She worked as a secretary, she went out to buy the books to help him keep up his studies, she accompanied him on trips beyond the known perimeters of his academic world, and she went with him on a year's fellowship in Madrid. They went to parties, had friends, and seemed to be a magical couple. They were popular, funny, and successful. But with each other they were miserable. Sex was not good although there continued to be no physical impairment of Ricardo's erectile potential. Although the marriage seemed to be in ashes from the beginning, Maria thought she should be self-sacrificing and guiltily carried on.

In time they had a son and a daughter, and Ricardo went to work on the science faculty of the university. He did well, supported by mentors, assistants, and students at the university, and by Maria who stood by him at every important occasion, every new situation, and stayed home to raise their two children and take care of him. The marriage revolved around Ricardo's injured pride and his fierce determination to show the world he was as fit in the scientific and academic worlds now as when he had been the adolescent soccer star – no matter how much sacrifice it took on Maria's part, no matter how much he ignored her wishes and needs. And she agreed to support him, silently at first, and then with growing resentment which showed in her constant badgering and whining, her cutting remarks at his every effort.

And so their marriage went for more than 20 years in a silent state of compromise. They fought at home. Their children knew it, but no one else seemed to. When they came to me for help with their marriage, theirs had been a long and painful private life. Each of them had now been in individual psychotherapy in South America. Ricardo had had a long analysis with a dedicated analyst in which he had learned about his ruthless self-centred way of steam-rolling over the people most important to him. The experience had been enormously important to him but he still despaired much of the time. He felt he had wasted his academic career. After a spectacular start and a rapid promotion to professor, he had hit the doldrums. For years now, he felt he had not had a single original idea and was simply putting in his time. Experiencing himself as the object of the university's pity, he felt humiliated. By the time he saw me, he was a visiting scientist in Washington, but he was really a scientific ambassador from whom no actual science was expected. He felt belittled by the part he was playing in the international agency, and he dreaded returning to the university, to the same old teaching, to a backwater career with no way out because he had nothing new to offer.

For the last few years he had been deeply depressed at times. Despite the gains in the analysis, despite treating Maria better than he ever had, he would collapse, feeling all was futile. On some recent occasions he had been seriously suicidal. He had again consulted an analyst who had agreed to offer additional treatment, but who also thought that he had an endogenous depression requiring medication. He had taken a variety of anti-depressants that helped, but he remained periodically severely depressed.

Maria had returned to therapy a few months before the couple saw me. When Ricardo began to make it up to her for the years of neglect, she became depressed because he no longer fuelled the anger that had protected her until now. She felt better when she went back to work in the embassy where she was valued and thought of as talented. Working meant that she could no longer back Ricardo up in the way she had spent her life doing, but it was worth it to feel independent and productive.

Although they were similar in coming from the same village, there was a difference in their backgrounds. Maria had an ordinary, secure working-class upbringing, leaving her champing at the bit for something more. Her father had status as a policeman. Her parents were happily married, supportive of Maria and her brother, and had always planned to provide her with a business training so she could take care of herself.

In contrast, Ricardo was from a desperately poor family. His mother took in laundry while the children begged and did odd jobs. His father tried to provide for her and Ricardo's several younger brothers and sisters, doing whatever work he could get. Ricardo's mother bossed her husband around and denigrated him while idealizing Ricardo, her eldest son. Ricardo kept a distance from his father, and scorned him in imitation of his mother. Only after he left home did he realize how much his father had done for the family, struggling with two or three jobs, sleeping little, loving his wife despite her scorn, and, especially, supporting Ricardo's schooling even when the family was in dire straits.

Ricardo's father was killed when Ricardo was an adolescent. The story of his father's heroism came to light only after his death. Even though poor and uneducated, his father had nevertheless been instrumental in political organizing for land reform around the peasant village where they lived. During a period of civil unrest, government soldiers singled him out as a guerilla collaborator and shot him in the town square. This traumatic death came three years before Ricardo's paralysis. Unconsciously guilty at never having a chance to show his father the gratitude he deserved, Ricardo had felt numb in response to the loss until he recovered his grief in analysis. As the couple therapy proceeded, we were also gradually able to link this loss to the physical trauma that had later befallen him. Traumatic in itself, his father's sudden execution had primed him to expect catastrophe around every corner.

At the beginning of therapy

When I met them, Maria and Ricardo were in despair. Ricardo conveyed this to me in the first session. He said, 'We've been a miserable failure in just about everything. My career amounts to nothing really. Our marriage is a sham. Our children aren't doing well in college. The only thing I feel good about is that Maria has gotten free from me for the first time and has a working life of her own, which she loves. And I love it that she has it. But when we go back to our country in two years, I doubt there'll be anything like that for her, and the university now gives me so little support that it's hard to get along without her there to get me places.'

'I wouldn't mind doing that,' Maria said, 'if I felt I got something for it. Ricardo's much more appreciative than he used to be, but now he's so depressed that it's no fun to be doing things for him.'

'She's right. It's no life for a human being,' he said. 'But I feel I can't get along without her, and it's a rotten thing to do to her. And I've done it for more than 20 years. I think she should leave me, but I'm desperate when I think that. I realized about five years ago that I loved her deeply – that I always had. She's the only woman I've ever had in my life, and I abused her for years. Not only did I take her for granted, I ground her down, made her my appendage, just a part of me who couldn't have a separate life.'

'That wasn't really the worst of it,' Maria said, nodding. 'I didn't mind helping him, and I did feel needed. But it was no fun. He was so driven, like the world was going by and he would be left on the refuse heap. And no matter how well he did – and he did extraordinarily well by any standards – he was driven like failure was around the corner. We fell in love when he was 16 and I was 15 – he was fun, on top of the world. When he lost the use of his legs, he lost that *joie de vivre*, at least with me. Others see that side of Ricardo, and we both have it in public. You should see us socially, really. We're the life of the party – so many people are always gathered around his wheelchair to talk. They hang on every word he says, a charmed circle around him. It's partly why he's done so well academically. They don't care if he hasn't discovered anything scientifically in ten years. He entertains the students and smoothes over departmental squabbles. He's a favourite of the university president and of the national scientific society.

'But at home, forget it! He drives himself and he drives me. I don't know if I can take much more, but I don't know where I would go without him. I don't believe anyone else would have me. I don't want to be alone.'

These were two desperate, lonely middle-aged people who had cared for each other, but who were hostage to their own dependence on each other and to the trauma they had shared for 20 years without mourning its impact.

Despite all the support Ricardo needed, he had not done the obvious things: he had not made his house fully accessible to himself by wheelchair and, until the work with his current analyst, he had refused the training to become adept with crutches for the occasions when wheelchair access was difficult. Ricardo had operated for many years with the belief, as he put it, that he was a nimble athlete. Now that he was learning to walk with braces and crutches, he could finally discuss the way he had previously maintained an unconscious belief that he could walk, despite a paralysis that meant that he could not negotiate strange environments. He had acted as though he could have all the accomplishments of a full-bodied person, and he had done well by all outward measures. But the trauma had continued to haunt him in the absence of mourning the loss.

The early response to treatment

Initially, the treatment went spectacularly well. It seemed that they did love each other just as Ricardo insisted. For him, the tragedy was that he had only discovered this during his analysis, after Maria felt that love had been battered out of her. She did not know if she could dare to hope or to love, even though she could see that Ricardo did really want to do things differently now. He had learned to listen to Maria, to himself, to his analyst, and therefore to me. He could be demanding, but he could back off. He could take in Maria's point of view as he had not been able to for many years. But when he did, she pulled back.

> It was not long before Maria was able to say, 'He is different. Whenever I see that, I feel pulled to him. That's when I get really frightened. I just don't know if I can open up to him, to all this again. And I do have something to lose now. Not just the job. I can keep that even if I open up to Ricardo. He supports that. He's very good about it. But something about myself, that's what I'd lose.'
>
> I was thinking that the return of hope for the relationship threatened Maria the most because it would expose her once more to threat of the persecutory object.
>
> I said, 'You're afraid to hope again, to give over part of yourself to Ricardo again when you've been so hurt and felt you surrendered so much of yourself to him when he abused it.'
>
> 'Yes. I felt I had to. He was crippled and needed me, but then I had nowhere to go either. Now that I have protected myself by pulling away from him, I'm afraid to try again.'

It was not difficult to see what had happened in their relationship. I understood it in terms of Fairbairn's (1952) concept of a person's internal dynamics operating so that the painful unconscious anti-libidinal part–object relationship further represses the libidinal one. The chronic bickering between Ricardo and Maria (a sign of the anti-libidinal ego constellation) had covered over their longing (the libidinal ego constellation) so they could not be in a loving, sexually satisfying relationship (the central ego system in communication with the unconscious) and not be enriched by it. Maria was now saying it was too painful to let her longing come to the surface, that she now preferred to live with Ricardo as an embodiment of the persecutory object. And something else had happened that they both felt had corrupted them. Ricardo had become a villain, to himself and to her. He had been a narcissistic youth, contemptuous, arrogant, scornful, king-of-the-hill. Both of them had valued that. But when trauma narrowed their world, it brought the two of them into a secret closed circle. The contempt had nowhere to go. He turned it on Maria. Through projective and introjective identification, it fitted with her self-contempt. Before I learned the details of how the despair of poverty and his father's death had contributed to his arrogance, or why she had become so submissive, I could see the contempt that was part of his narcissistic compensation hurting Maria.

In the early therapy, they had only one fight in my office. While Maria had taken her emotional whacks back at Ricardo, they were nothing compared to the character assassination he carried out in the session I will describe now.

> Ricardo called Maria every name in the book. In his paralyzed fury, he stared daggers at her, waved his arms as though about to pursue and throttle her. I said that the problem was the way Maria accepted Ricardo's outrageous contempt. She looked puzzled, but he was deeply affected. At first he objected, feeling I had called him an unspeakable name, but he then turned and asked her if it were true.
>
> 'I don't even see it any more,' Maria sighed. 'This is just the way it is with Ricardo. It just washes off my back.'
>
> I said, 'In fact you're saying it's so strong you can't stand to acknowledge the individual incidents. You take it, but it's gotten inside you where it has done more than erode your confidence. You feel you're just Ricardo's support. You think you're no better than his legs, just a degraded function. It relates to the way his mother treated his father like a scorned organ of support.'
>
> 'That's true,' she said, and began to cry. 'I wouldn't mind being his legs but the way he walks all over me and the rest of the world is so cruel, and only I know that. People at the university know he can be brutal sometimes, but I've also become the legs and feet he uses to trample others. In a way, it has made me feel powerful and identified with his cruelty. But mainly I feel mean, little, degraded, stepped on.' She was sobbing.

With this work, Ricardo and Maria began to change. Ricardo was a man who threw himself ruthlessly into everything he did. And when he threw himself into trying to be a loving husband, he worked as few patients will. It could not fail to impress, especially when it even included his capacity to relent about the drive to improve. Maria dared to try, to become open to his capacity for caring. She told him that she appreciated the vigour with which he was trying but that, even though she admired it and relied on it, his single-mindedness still scared her. And he seemed to get it. He 'worked on' not working so hard with her. He relaxed, listened to her for longer periods. When this happened, they began to sit near each other on the couch. There was little fury, and they began to look like a much younger and certainly more loving couple.

So much work had been done individually by each of them that the marital difficulty yielded almost as if by magic. A few interpretations went a long way because they worked with them readily and diligently, held almost nothing against each other, and rarely repeated an impasse once we had examined its dynamics. It felt like a therapeutic honeymoon.

The emergence of problems with intimacy and sexuality

After about two months, Ricardo and Maria asked for help with their sexual life. It had been terrible, perhaps one of the causes of their discord all these years. They told me that they had intercourse, but without joy, just a release for Ricardo and a trial for Maria. Their sexual pattern of his need and her withdrawal reflected the heart of their problems.

Beginning sex therapy

We switched formats to object relations sex therapy (Scharff 1982, Scharff and Scharff 1991). I had been meeting with Maria and Ricardo for a double session twice a week even before the sex therapy, and we continued that arrangement, so there was plenty of time for discussion of marital and family issues. Their paired sexual dysfunction captured all the elements of their shared difficulty, the abandoned and buried hope, the awkwardness of their frozen youth, the futility of their young love. Their history and present dynamics related to sex like the spokes of a wheel.

For quite a while, sex therapy went exceedingly well. They began with non-genital massaging, through which they quickly learned to enjoy giving as well as getting. They loved doing the exercises, gave feedback generously, rarely cheated on the limits I gave them, and galloped ahead, scarcely believing and barely trusting the gains in their discovery of each other, unencumbered by Ricardo's limp legs. They felt they had a new marriage, and in the main, they did. Only in the newness of their adolescent relationship more than 20 years earlier had they experienced the pleasure and mutual pride in each other that they now found.

Sitting cuddled in Ricardo's arm, Maria patted his knee and said, smiling but with an ominous note, 'But I don't trust it. It's wonderful, but it's so fast. Will this last?'

Indeed, the work had gone incredibly fast and easily, the way it can only if the neurotic elements are largely resolved before work on sexual difficulty begins. Or so I thought. The sailing was not going to be so easy, for we had not yet dealt with the traumatic aspect of their marriage.

Containment in sex therapy

As they began the penetration exercises, Maria grew frightened again. She could tolerate the penis resting quietly in her vagina, and he was able to remain there without premature ejaculation. They continued to enjoy and employ the whole body pleasuring, the sensual massages which had brought them close. But Maria felt she would not be able to enjoy orgasm. In the past, she reminded me, she had only had orgasms when Ricardo had manually stimulated her clitoris, and she had felt humiliated that she needed that. She felt alone in her need, knowing that he had resented having to do it for so long. With more work on her capacity for understanding her own body, and on their shared capacity for physical intimacy, sexual pleasure continued, but this area remained a point of doubt.

They had had months of steady loving with hardly a lapse – why was she still afraid? Was there an aspect of trauma so encapsulated that I had no hint of it with them?

They moved on slowly. She began to experience occasional orgasms in the shared setting, but she was holding out nevertheless. In the exercises where she had previously been immersed, eager and initiating, even asking to try oral sex for the first time, she now found herself distancing and trembling. Then came a session that opened a new door.

CONTEMPT, SELF HATRED, AND SADOMASOCHISM

Revelation of a shared perversion

In the beginning of this mid-phase session, Ricardo sat in his wheelchair at a remove from Maria. He usually lifted himself from the chair or now walked in to the office using crutches at which he had recently become adept, and came to sit next to her on the couch, even holding hands recently. Today they sat miles apart. After a few minutes, Maria said she felt lonely and asked if he could join her on the couch. When he did, she leaned into him in an uncharacteristically clinging way.

Ricardo said Maria had been finding erotica, especially women's erotica, helpful in becoming stimulated before the exercise phase of containment, that is of insertion of the penis into the vagina and holding it there quite still.

Suddenly they were talking about their disgust with the S-and-M literature they had passed in the bookstore. They seemed to be protesting too much. I felt a momentary worry about being aggressive if I were to connect this to their sexual blocks, but Maria and Ricardo had worked so well with my comments through the months that I took the risk.

'Do you think your fighting might be like the S-and-M literature you both hate?' I asked.

Maria looked like I had hit her. Her head dropped toward her chest.

'Oh, shit!' said Ricardo. 'That hadn't occurred to me. Why do you say that?'

'Because you've told me you had a marriage full of cruelty and suffering emotionally, that is emotional sadomasochism, in which you Ricardo have done things you say have tortured Maria, and you Maria have absorbed them feeling you had no choice,' I said.

'But do you think that has something to do with our sex?' Maria asked.

'What do you mean?' I asked, not knowing where we were going.

'I was having trouble having an orgasm yesterday. So I asked Ricardo to tell me punishing things he might do to me. He did, and I got aroused and had an orgasm pretty quickly. It felt good, but I got nauseated after that and didn't like it.'

'Is this something you've done before?' I asked.

'Maria hung her head and looked upset. 'I don't know if I can talk about it,' she said.

'This isn't the first time you've felt that you couldn't talk about something,' I said. I was dimly aware that my pressing her had the makings of a sadomasochistic encounter in the session. She was dangling this tantalizing but painful material, and then coyly refusing to discuss it. As I look back, I see that this was a re-enactment of the problem in the transference and countertransference, including the way Ricardo put Maria out front to absorb the humiliation while literally sitting behind her, holding her as a shield.

'No, it's not,' she agreed.

'Maria used to like me to tell her what I would do to her,' Ricardo volunteered. 'At some time in our sexual life, she began to ask me to tell her punishing things I would do sexually while I stimulated her. It was like she wanted me to walk all over her!'

'It was the only thing I could regularly get to arouse me,' she admitted. 'I hate telling you this. I don't want to discuss it, really. But it would arouse me. I haven't done it all this time we've been seeing you, and we were having so little sex for the couple of years before that it hadn't happened recently, but it was what I had used over the years to get aroused.'

'This is the sexual version of the part of your marriage you felt hopeless about for years,' I said. 'It represents an attempt to transform pain into ecstasy, and in some ways it's worked. It's also an attempt to transform your emotionally sado-masochistic marriage – the way Maria felt punished by Ricardo and by the circumstances of your shared trauma – into something palatable, even exciting and loving. But it founders on the rocks of your shame and humiliation.'

She nodded. 'Yes, that's true. I've felt punished, and at least this way it gave me something close, something we could share. He helped me with this.'

'What did it do for me?' Ricardo asked.

'We don't know so much about it yet,' I said. 'But it might have given you the feeling you could transform the damage you've caused to Maria and people you care about into something they want, something positive, even orgiastic. You've been concerned about damaging those you care about. This undoes that problem in an odd, almost magical way.'

From this session, I began to see how the shared perversion worked in a paradoxical way for both of them, allowing the transformation of hate into love, of a persecuting object relationship into a loving and exciting one. It relieved guilt and loneliness, vented the confusion of love, hate, neediness, and isolation that each of them tried to bury. It re-established their original shared myth that he was powerful and she needy, that he was the one who could transform their lives and she the grateful recipient of his princely bounty. Sexually, she was the cripple and he was the helper, undoing the trauma by reversing their roles and returning them to the constellation of their adolescence when he was going to take them both out of poverty and into the stars.

Their perverse sexuality attempted to replace guilt with shame. They both began by feeling guilty for damage and disloyalty perpetrated on each other, and then tried to transform their guilt into a sexual triumph over pain and damage by inflicting and suffering more pain. But this perverse script was accompanied by unrelenting shame that came to exist alongside the inadequately handled guilt.

Shame and hurt

The couple began the next session in an emotionally upset manner, saying they wanted to review the issues that had surfaced in the previous session.

Ricardo said, 'Doctor, it's not as though we didn't know it, but when you put a label on our relationship like "sado-masochistic", we couldn't avoid it any more.'

Maria grimaced. 'I know it is not your label. It is ours. But it's too much to talk about. We have been drained ever since.'

I felt their devastation. It seemed as if I had caused them irreparable damage by labelling their behaviour, especially by describing their marriage as sadomasochistic. For the most part, they weren't blaming me. They had known it all before. They fully realized how they hurt each other. They had told me often that they had ruined their children, too, by exposing them to their warring relationship. For the first time they talked about their preferring to keep the perverse elements of their relationship out of awareness, buried, and disconnected from themselves. I felt again the pain that gave the lie to the previous months of progress.

I realized that I had taken in Ricardo and Maria's fear of damaging each other so that in my countertransference I feared that I had hurt them beyond repair. My linking the perverse elements of their sexuality to their relationship had broken through the encapsulation that had threatened to explode from the beginning. They had each felt unbearable guilt that they had tried to handle by blaming each other in order to preserve a remnant of a sense of goodness about themselves. In the process, they struggled to make each other the unrelenting bad object. With the tangible label of sadomasochism now attached to their sexual behaviour, the sense of crushing futility came upon them full force, and with it a renewal of Maria's anger at Ricardo for the hopelessness she again felt. Persecuting object relations had come into our therapeutic space, and sat between us like unapproachable ghosts that embodied not just a single trauma, but the many they had experienced before and since.

Retreat from sexuality and reworking of underlying trauma

For much of this session and in the ones that followed, Ricardo and Maria retreated from sex. Maria said she could not talk directly about it, and I did not press her. Instead I invited them to talk again about the principal trauma in their lives, Ricardo's paralysis.

I had heard it before, but I might now hear it in a fundamentally different way because I was now involved with the sense of trauma. We shared in experiencing the reverberations of trauma within the treatment. They were together in experiencing my traumatization of them instead of being against each other. How could they trust me? They experienced me as another well-meaning doctor who was recommending a procedure that might not be enough and that was coming too late. My intervention might further injure the vulnerable and disintegrating marriage that had been Ricardo's sole source of support even in its damaged condition. The couple worked through their feelings about me as a re-edition of the doctor who failed Ricardo. Work on their trauma in the transference and countertransference is what enabled them to return to the topic of the perverse elements in their sexual relationship.

Returning to sexual issues

I asked, 'Can we continue reviewing what happened to sex as your marriage went on? What kept it from functioning in the ordinary way? Can you elaborate on the short version of your sexual story you've given me so far?'

Maria hung her head. 'I don't know if I can. I'm so ashamed to have you know about it. To be my age and to have to be doing this! It didn't start this way. For several years, when we had sex, it was ordinary. Not much fun – I didn't get anything out of it, but there was nothing to be ashamed of. Then something switched.'

There was a silence, and Ricardo spoke. 'You want to know what happens? OK, I'll tell you. I tell Maria about painful things I am going to do to her while I stimulate her, like squeezing her nipples or using clips on them, tying her up, or hurting her elsewhere. That's all.'

'Do you hurt her physically as well?' I asked.

'Yes, by pinching her nipples while I stimulate her clitoris to orgasm. Most of the time, she can't have an orgasm without that. It lets her have an orgasm, which makes me feel better. I don't do anything else to hurt her. I don't whip her or beat her. I wouldn't want you to think I did that!'

Feeling their shared humiliation, I asked as gently as I could, 'Can you say anything else, Maria?'

'I'm ashamed that I need to do this, but it helps if he tells me his fantasies of hurting people, too.'

'Yes, there are my fantasies,' he agreed. 'And there's some exhibitionism in all this, too.'

'And we did do some of those things,' Maria added, more easily able to talk about what he had her do. 'You tied me up with your pyjama tie and robe belt once.'

'I forgot about that,' he said. 'It was just tying her loosely, just for the thrill of the idea.'

'And he gets excited asking me to tell him stories.'

'What sort?' I asked.

'About all the dirty things I would do with other people and all the affairs I could fantasize,' she said.

At first it had seemed that only Maria needed sadism and suffering, but then it emerged that what Ricardo was putting into her excited him, too. I felt sadness at the humiliation and hopelessness of the couple, at the pattern they had fashioned to get some relief from their aching distance from each other, at what it took to relieve the logjam of feeling in this intensely proud woman. I thought that part of the logjam came from the lack of acknowledgement of how much of his own pain Ricardo put into her. He relieved himself of the suffering imposed by his persecutory objects by becoming her persecutor, but in a perverse solution through which he gave her a pleasure that seemed to triumph over the persecution.

By now, the outline of meaning embodied in their shared perversion had declared itself, but there was much still to learn about its relationship to Ricardo's childhood pride and fears for his safety, his identification with his mother's scorn, the childhood losses, the daily degradation. The emotional standing of his father who was so demeaned by Ricardo's mother left Ricardo joined with her in suffering poverty and daily degradation while she coped as best she could. Then when his father was killed, he realized that he had been unfair in his judgement and treatment of his father, but it was too late. His disadvantaged social background and the personal trauma of the murder exposed him to a climate of cumulative trauma (Khan 1963) which set the stage for the focal trauma provided by his paralysis. That trauma threw Ricardo fully into identification with his own vulnerable and anxious mother, and at the same time into a lifelong attempt to compensate for the guilt over his treatment of his father. It heightened the desperation of his drive to survive.

But we had also to understand the meaning that Ricardo's trauma had acquired for the couple, why Maria became in essence nothing but Ricardo's legs. She had been willing to submit to him and live through him to fulfil herself because she felt only a part-person herself, fit only for supporting someone else. She had thrown herself into the relationship with Ricardo hoping to use it to heal an image of herself as ineffective and worthless, an image which made her prone to the self-sacrifice she compulsively lived out, resulting in resentment that grew with every year. This resentment kept her from seeing how much she also hated herself for the humiliating servitude from which she could not extricate herself because of its reverberation with her own childhood trauma.

Maria had experienced her mother as loving and caring much of the time, but also brutally caustic, disapproving and sniping. In an angry mood, her mother would predict that Maria would amount to nothing and once, wrongly suspecting sexual activity, she slapped Maria for staying out late with Ricardo. This response had given Maria a pervasive sense of sex as a trigger for her mother's disapproval, a sign of her own badness, and a model for joining sexual promise with pain and guilt. Maria had idealized her mother and buried her feelings about the painful interactions, but her mother's disapproval and ready sarcasm had undermined Maria. When Ricardo did similar things she was unable to integrate a view of him and hold him responsible. This inability to hold him accountable became frozen in time when she stood by Ricardo after his paralysis.

The perversion that Maria and Ricardo described was mild. Indeed, we might not necessarily even call it a perversion if adding pain to their physical sexual life was a small element in a more flexible and regenerating overall relationship. It was perverse because a frozen, self-destructive pattern of behaviour, the tip of the iceberg of the hateful, persecutory object relationship, came to be the centre of the relationship itself. It captured excitement and a sense of transcendence that had eluded them when boredom and failure permeated their shared sense of themselves. Their sexual pattern gave them a way of elevating pain and degradation to a climactic excitement, a periodic moment of triumph over the pain of their life together. Together, they had unconsciously invented the perversion and floated it like a buoy marking the explosive mine of their agony buried beneath the troubled waves. It was this depth charge we had triggered in our work. Once it had exploded, it littered the waters of their lives with the previously hidden wreckage they could no longer avoid. Ricardo and Maria's sexual pattern qualifies as a perversion because it embodies the fear of destruction as part and parcel of sex. Its hope is the use of sexuality to transmute punishment to ecstasy. Its result is an obligatory conjunction of orgasm and distance.

Working through this constellation involved facing the issues that the couple's combined psychic forces had marshalled to keep out of their awareness for years. They had used encapsulation of trauma as a defence against the fear of annihilation (Hopper 1991). Their life together was invaded every day by the leakage of these issues from the encased pain, by the constant sense that things were always about to explode. That leakage also fuelled their unconscious sense of shame and guilt, which only fully surfaced in therapy. They had come for therapy because they felt they could no longer carry on. They felt they had no choice but to face these issues even though their sexual activity remained the hardest part of their life to discuss.

The work on the couple's perversion gradually became subsumed into the general work of couple therapy – on the sadomasochistic patterns that permeated their relationship, the mutual abuse and despair, and the depression that passed back and forth between them. Late in therapy, the punishing potential of their everyday life became the everyday talk of the therapy, one that was more general than specifically sexual, and the relationship slowly became more integrated. They could more fully consider the pain evident in daily misunderstandings and mistreatment, in withdrawal and anger, and in the transference when I challenged them to face things that recalled the trauma. Slowly, despair became more connected to hope, and they began the process of inching through the difficulties of years of accumulated trauma which had taken root and grown on the scars of the original trauma.

SHAME AND GUILT IN PSYCHIC ORGANIZATION OF INDIVIDUALS AND COUPLES

In this couple, Ricardo had come to hold most of the guilt for his narcissistic use of Maria in the wake of his trauma. Maria expressed most of the shame for the couple, a derivative of repeated interactions with her shaming mother as magnified by her own harsh self-judgement. With modification of the pattern between them, shame and guilt, persecution and healing could be redistributed and reintegrated in each of the partners.

Psychotherapy following trauma is always uneven, marked by setbacks when encapsulated trauma erupts, only gradually to be integrated into the fabric of the couple's life. Vulnerabilities remained for this couple, but there was progress in the detoxification of the persecutory object relations, in the transformation of perversion to ordinary pain, in lessening the splits that had captured traumatic precursors in a perverse enclave and had impeded the healing of pain and trauma, and in the working through of unconscious shame and guilt. We will leave the couple here, well into their difficult therapy.

Object relations couple therapy can deal with deeply ingrained, largely unconscious perverse constellations thought in the past to be affected only by psychoanalysis or intensive individual analytic psychotherapy. Conjoint couple therapy has the power to do this because each partner has become closely associated with the other's painful internal objects, and because persecutory qualities of internal object constellations are magnified through the lens of persecutory external relationships. To illustrate the way that individual issues of depth psychology are illustrated during couple therapy, I will briefly discuss aspects of shame and guilt as illustrated in the vignettes above.

Sexuality has the potential to add bodily emphasis to either healing or wounding aspects of inner experience. When it echoes with the persecutory elements, it draws on aspects of shame and guilt that derive from developmental object relationships. When efforts unconsciously intended to repair the early persecutory quality of internal objects fail, they are increasingly accompanied by the unconscious affects of shame and guilt associated with the persistent unconscious domination by persecuting object relations that have not been healed. Couples vary in the degree to which it is shame or guilt that predominates in the shared unconscious, but in any case, the shame and guilt are closely related to each other. In Chapter 4 on the dynamic role of components of the superego in shame and guilt, Charles Ashbach distinguishes between the guiding role of the ego ideal and the judgemental role of internal persecutory objects in the expression of shame and guilt. We can extend his argument by drawing on Fairbairn's formulation of the superego in terms specific to his object relations theory of personality (1954, 1963).

Fairbairn thought that the internal structures that participate in superego function include three discrete parts: the 'rejecting object' that is internalized from split-off rejecting and persecuting experiences; the 'anti-libidinal ego' or 'internal saboteur' – his terms for the part of the self that is split from the central ego and repressed in connection to the internal rejecting object; and the 'ideal object' – the object of the central ego, a structure that he derived from Freud's concept of the ego ideal. Conceptualizing these components of the superego separately allows us to see dynamic interaction among them, and thereby to describe superego action in the case of shame and guilt more accurately because the three structures combine in varying ways that give differing weight to aspects of superego function. For instance, if the voice of the rejecting object is dominant, the superego will be harsh and judgemental, and the self will feel criticized and bad. On the other hand, when the voice of the anti-libidinal ego or internal saboteur dominates, the person feels and expresses self-punishing ideas or actions. Finally, if the ideal object is dominant, the superego will be more gently or creatively guiding and softer in its internal judgements. Fairbairn's formulation of object relations suggests that guilt stems mostly from the self-pole of ego organization, from the self's concern for harmful treatment of the other – that is from the action of the anti-libidinal ego, often augmented by the judgement of the ideal object. In contrast, shame stems from the self's identification with the other's contemptuous attitude towards the self, a set of judgements rendered by persecutory inner objects – that is from the action of the persecuting object.

While guilt and shame are related closely to each other, in its pure form guilt is an affect of the self's attitude towards the object, while shame is an affect of the self's feeling of persecution at the hands of the object.

THE DETOXIFYING POWER OF COUPLE THERAPY

Couple therapy provides insights into the role and treatment of persecuting objects beyond the purview of the spouses' previous individual therapy and analysis, as illustrated by the unfolding of the shared constellation of shame and guilt in Ricardo and Maria's relationship. Couple therapy can detoxify persecuting object relations because the partners know each other so well that they often have the potential to help each other through insight and through the provision of improved psychological holding in their relationship. Because the partners have been tied to each other through the persecutory relationship that masks (and even protects) their hope and longing, small increments of progress in the task of detoxi-fication can result in disproportionately large gains in libidinal attachment that bring pleasure and secure attachment. These improvements in the overall relationship reverse perverse cycles, create further opportunities for insight and growth, and support the capacity for detoxifying future assaults from persecutory objects.

REFERENCES

Bollas, C. (1989). *Forces of Destiny*. London: Free Association Books.

Dicks, H. V. (1967). *Marital Tensions: Clinical Studies Towards a Psycho-analytic Theory of Interaction*. London: Routledge and Kegan Paul.

Fairbairn, W. R. D. (1952). *Psychoanalytic Studies of the Personality*. London: Routledge.

—— (1954). The nature of hysterical states. In *From Instinct to Self: Selected Papers of W. R. D. Fairbairn, Volume I*, ed. D. E. Scharff and E. F. Birtles, pp. 13–40. Northvale, NJ: Jason Aronson, 1994.

—— (1963). An object relations theory of the personality. In *From Instinct to Self: Selected Papers of W. R. D. Fairbairn, Volume I*, ed. D. E. Scharff and E. F. Birtles, pp. 155-156. Northvale, NJ: Jason Aronson, 1994.

Hopper, E. (1991). Encapsulation as a defense against the fear of anni-hilation. *International Journal of Psycho-Analysis* 72(4): 607–624.

Kaplan, H. S. (1974). *The New Sex Therapy*. New York: New York Times/Quadrangle and Brunner/Mazel.

Khan, M. M. R. (1963). The concept of cumulative trauma. In *The Privacy of the Self*, pp. 42–58. London: The Hogarth Press and The Institute of Psycho-Analysis, 1974.

Masters, W. H. and Johnson, V. E. (1970). *Human Sexual Inadequacy*. Boston: Little, Brown.

Scharff, D. E. (1982). *The Sexual Relationship: An Object Relations View of Sex and the Family*. Northvale, NJ: Jason Aronson.

Scharff, D. E. and Scharff, J. S. (1991). *Object Relations Couple Therapy*. Northvale, NJ: Jason Aronson.

Scharff, J. S. and Scharff, D. E. (1994). *Object Relations Therapy of Physical and Sexual Trauma*. Northvale, NJ: Jason Aronson.

Chapter 4

Persecutory objects, guilt, and shame

Charles Ashbach, PhD

Guilt and shame are powerful affects that signal the action of persecutory objects affecting human experience, identity, and behaviour in both individual and social dimensions. They herald the pain and danger of disapproval, persecution, and rejection by those objects, and thereby help individuals align themselves with their ideals and regulate their behaviours with significant others. I think of them as the emotional latitude and longitude of human interaction and relationship, locating individuals in relationship to both themselves and their social context. In this chapter I discuss the formation and effects of persecutory objects and the regulatory agencies that give rise to shame and guilt; for they play a central role in generating suffering in the self's experience of persecutory objects and in promoting or blocking recovery.

THE AGENCIES OF REGULATION

The superego and ego-ideal are the main regulatory agencies enabling the self to control and order its internal equilibrium. They are made up of selective identifications with the limit-setting and inspiring aspects of the parents and with the lost aspects of the narcissism of childhood (Freud 1914, 1923; A. Freud 1936; Grunberger 1971). Both of them are internal objects with conscious and unconscious elements that generate emotional energy in the form of anxiety – guilt from the superego and shame from the ego-ideal. Guilt and shame are the affective instruments through which the agencies perform their regulatory functions, compelling the self's adherence to the rules of the superego and the aspirations of the ego-ideal. Guilt determines whether we *feel* good or bad for having done wrong, whereas shame pertains to whether we *are* good or bad. The superego and ego-ideal are like observation posts that look out onto the inner cosmos to protect and preserve the life of the inner objects.

Persecutory primal objects, superego, and ego-ideal

According to Klein (1957) the inner objects are associated with the reality of the parents, their functions, prerogatives, bodies, and relationship. It is within this narrow circle of meaning that Klein locates the basic human agenda: enter the mother's body; figure out the contents therein; control those contents, and find some way to survive the struggle without killing the self or damaging the mother who is the receptacle for the father's penis (leading to generativity), other babies, and excrement (leading to damage of objects). The outcome of the struggle is the creation of good and bad objects inside the self. Meltzer (1973) thought that these areas of good and bad become experiential centres around which the self organizes its sense of well-being on the one hand or tortured inadequacy on the other.

When envy is not too strong and the good object has been able to be established as a vital, internal presence, the child is capable of allowing such primal objects to co-exist in a pleasurable productive union in which they support pleasure, procreation, and knowing of self and other. These objects, taken together, are good. When trauma stops the internalization of the good object and brings about a profound narcissistic injury and the explosion of envy, then the child cannot allow for the combination of these objects within the mind and psyche. Learning stops and the generativity associated with parental intercourse is stopped, frozen, or perverted. This is the breeding ground for persecutory experience, guilt, terror, and inhibition.

Envy, flowing out of the traumatic experience of separateness from the ideal other and from the parental pair, brings with it a hellish reaction of injury, torment, revenge, and spite. The unceasing experience of malevolence due to a deep sense of being wronged brings with it an enduring desire to revenge the self upon the object, made manifest in therapy as the negative therapeutic reaction in which the self and the therapist are defeated (Rosenfeld

1987). Such a persecutory internal environment leads to a kind of psychic anorexia where the patient refuses to take in anything from the therapist in order to deprive the internal object of the pleasure associated with the feeding experience, as well as to protect the self from the poison of the mother's love. Encounters with anything felt to be alien or evil evoke substantial persecutory anxieties and arouse powerful defences against them.

In therapy: The superego

From a therapeutic perspective we are interested in understanding and modifying the objects, rules, and emotions that endow the superego with its unique configuration. The violence that is characteristic of the superego derives from three sources: (1) from the trauma and injuries associated with the actual, external events and individuals; (2) from the projectively identified aggression identified by Freud as the outcome of repression of instinctual forces, constellations, and yearnings; and (3) from the intense aggression associated with the loss of the ideal. This last loss is perhaps the most compelling because it is experienced as a narcissistic trauma and one that leads to threats against the very core of the self. When they are not neutralized and modulated by later relationship experience, these elements lead to the common experience of the superego as a violent and relentless inner judge. Obviously, with such a reservoir of aggression and narcissistic injury contained within it, the superego is a breeding ground for the accumulation and intensification of bad-persecutory objects.

Clinically, we seek to help the patient establish a mature relationship to the superego, which will lead to a deeper understanding and appreciation of the forces and wishes that are under its repressive power. Understanding the superego's punishing, castrating, or moral force is central in treating a broad spectrum of disorders that involve acting-out, including alcohol and drug-abuse. Recovering lost aspects of the self in therapy leads to greater self-integration and personality cohesion. The modulation of unconscious guilt decreases masochistic acting out and depression. The metabolizing of primitive superego elements acts as a catalyst for the release of libidinal attachments, creativity, and reparative interactions with objects. Releasing the guiding functions of the superego from its attack mode frees the self to function autonomously.

In therapy: The ego-ideal

The impact of psychotherapeutic relationships and interventions is to ameliorate toxic, and at times perverse, ideal objects and the unconscious scenarios that emerge out of them. The message 'Fly ever higher above the squalor and suffering of life' is frequently at the unconscious core of the narcissist's yearning (and in psychological treatment leads to negative therapeutic reaction). Here the ego-ideal and its objects exist in a plane of experience that is beyond time where they are not subject to persecutory and depressive anxieties. Why would narcissistic people want to be helped to descend into the travail of life when their essential striving has been to be lifted up, out of life? How are we to help them recover their direction?

The experience of being the persecutory object has to be gathered in the transference if there is to be any chance of detoxification. These transference–countertransference configurations are among the most complex and demanding that therapists have to work through because of the danger of engaging the therapist's damaged inner objects. With successful containment by the therapist, recovery of split-off, feared aspects of the self leads to personality cohesion and a diminution of unconscious guilt and therefore of masochistic self-destructiveness and depression.

PERSECUTORY OBJECTS: A CLINICAL VIGNETTE

Miss Goss is a 53-year-old woman who has been in twice-weekly therapy for about 9 years. Her father died recently and her relationship with her mother has been a continuing struggle. She has been complaining about a difficult situation at work. The session that I will report began with three dreams.

> In the first dream, Miss Goss's father is in hospital and she realizes that no one has been to visit him in some time. She feels guilty and wonders how he feels. She attempts to get her mother to visit him but he objects.
> In the second dream Miss Goss is walking down the street with me and another woman. At some point I leave and she is in an awkward silence with this other woman.

In the third dream a colleague is making a presentation in a hall, and Miss Goss is there to witness it. She sees her parents sitting together and takes up a position, behind a big pillar, so that she cannot be seen by them.

Miss Goss went on to say that after the last session in which she complained about her work situation, she felt much better. The next day she was able to confront her abusive boss and begin a process of job change that she had been helpless to deal with for many months. The three dreams followed that session and the successful confrontation with her boss. Her next associations pointed to her guilt about not thinking about her dead father.

I interpreted the dreams as revealing a continual attack against the coupling of the mother and father. In the first dream she puts into her father the wish to split from her mother. In the second dream she separates her therapist from the woman he is with and sends him out of the dream. In the third dream she is paired with a colleague whom she is there to support and admire. Instead she focuses on hiding from her parents as a pair. This time she allows them to remain a couple, but only by putting a large pillar between them and her. In her dreams and associations, her father is alone in hospital, her therapist sent away, her boss about to be left, and her parents cancelled out through hiding. The couple containing the generative penis is banished (the phallus preserved only as a tall pillar of stone).

I said that Miss Goss was unable to tolerate a couple finding each other, for such a pairing excludes her and fills her with the wish to destroy the couple in order to control the maternal object.

Following her attacks, Miss Goss's mental state is one of guilt and persecutory anxiety, which she deals with by freezing. A deep sense of sterility and deadness follows. In therapy with me, an exhaustive process of non-thinking protects her from discovering her agenda against her primal, inner objects. To immobilize the breast-mother and penis-father is to prevent the catastrophe of her separation from the mother who cannot live without her and without whom she cannot survive. The deadness of her life and lack of ongoing relationships with men at any time in her adult life is paradoxically the only way to maintain sanity and keep herself alive. She lives by not living. She survives by stopping intercourse, fun, and spontaneity.

Miss Goss was able to hear my interpretation regarding her attack on the couple. She responded by acknowledging another attack, this time on the couple's love object, their son. She had driven her brother mad on the phone by subjecting him to a torturous recitation of her problems at work. When he started yelling at her, she knew, after some reflection, that she must have been attacking him, for why else would he be so agitated and unsettled? Such a discovery of her unconscious aggression marked a significant gain, one that would be reversed in the short term, but that laid the foundation for a more secure realization of the depressive position. For that moment she was able to transform her experience into a recognizable communication about her central dynamics.

Therapeutic working through should provide Miss Goss with a somewhat detoxified superego that might enable her to acknowledge and moderate her destructive attacks against couples and against external reality. With this recognition in the transference, she may hope to understand and then master this primitive, destructive component of her self. Working through should also help her to realize the cost to her of maintaining such a perfect, unsullied ego-ideal, and appreciate the value of modifying it.

In therapy I have observed that Miss Goss has sometimes seemed more interested in consuming the menu than in eating the meal. She has responded that the picture of the food sometimes tastes better than the actual food. Detoxification and working through may free her enough to find her place at the banquet of life.

The persecutory object

Persecutory objects predominate in the paranoid-schizoid position where their existence is the by-product of defensive splitting processes. The good has been separated from the bad. The bad part of the self acts as a kind of tormenting ghost seeking to gain re-admittance to the now defended good component of the self. The movement into the depressive position is a sign of a more integrated ego and object system. Persecutory anxieties can arise within the depressive position but they are contained within a more neutralizing and metabolizing context which works to strip away the pressing, contagious aspects of the fears of annihilation and castration. The anxieties of the paranoid-schizoid position are more intense and unmodified and the ego in that position is more split and polarized. As content is modified, ego structure improves and the interactional effect between container and contained produces a more modified and manageable set of internal experiences and leads to a more mature and communicable inner experience.

In Klein's (1946) view, persecutory objects derive from the infant's attack on the goodness of the breast and then they continue the attack against the external object and against the self. The empty, hungry infant devours the breast greedily and envies its capacity to replenish its supplies apparently by itself. Merely because the breast exists outside the omnipotence of the infantile self, it must be attacked and brought under the control of the self. We struggle to hold onto the sense of personal goodness in the face of recognizing the shocking effects of our fantasized or perceived desires, emotions, and fantasies against the parents that nurtured and sustained us. Discovery of this aspect of the self breeds a deep sense of persecutory assault from inside the self.

That assault on the self also comes via projective identification from the parents' internal objects, which cause toxic parent–child transactions that are then internalized by the child as bad and persecutory objects. Then bad has to be split from good to maintain sanity. If the resulting separation is precarious, then the good has to be even more split off and elevated into the realm of the perfect. Such an ideal object is the brittle antidote to powerful feelings and fantasies of hate and destructiveness against the unsatisfactory objects.

Whereas Freud thought that persecutory experiences arose from punishment by castration for sexual desire, Klein thought that persecution occurs by annihilation of the self and destruction of the envied object.

GUILT AND SHAME

In an excellent but little known contribution, Piers offers a succinct delineation of the structural, affective, and dynamic origins of guilt and shame and how they relate to each other (Piers and Singer 1953). Piers holds that there is significant clinical benefit to be derived from considering the different aims, goals, and techniques of the ego-ideal and superego in the exercise of their regulatory functions within the personality. In the clinical setting, the process of keeping these two agencies separate helps us to clarify the impulses, needs, and yearnings of the patients and the anxieties they are suffering.

Shame and narcissistic injury seem to be the essential affects of failure of the ego-ideal; guilt, castration, and loss of love the prime issues associated with the superego.

Guilt and the superego

According to Piers, guilt is 'the painful internal tension generated whenever the emotionally highly charged barrier erected by the super-ego is being touched or transgressed' (Piers and Singer 1953, p. 16). The transgressions occur when sexual or aggressive impulses expressed as drives, phantasies, or actions collide with the boundaries that the superego has constructed to preserve the homeostasis or structure of the personality, and by extension, the social group. Originally guilt was seen as flowing from the taboo against unconscious desires of sex and aggression during the oedipal stage and continuing into later years because of the persistence of the Oedipus complex (Freud 1905). Impulses to destroy the rival and win the desired parent are the central forces that activate the superego into deploying the guilt experience. In its unconscious aspect, guilt is associated with the feeling that the barrier against the incest taboo and patricide has been breached and therefore punishment must be the inevitable result.

Emanating from the superego, the punishment to fit the crime is governed by the principle of retaliation according to the Law of Talion, literally the 'law of the claw' epitomized by the modern saying 'an eye for an eye, and a tooth for a tooth'. This Law of Talion demands either mutilation or annihilation of the offending organ, the erect penis that intends to penetrate and possess. This leads to castration anxiety. The conscious feeling of guilt, or guilt anxiety as it is sometimes called, is the evidence that the unconscious transgression has already occurred. The experience of guilt may be simply an affect or it may produce idiosyncratic behaviours such as wincing, shaking the head, talking to the self, and disagreeing with an imaginary other.

Guilt occurs only if there is awareness of the ability to harm another directly or do damage through violation of a valued standard. Guilt is a manifestation of the *self's sense of responsibility* for its actions: '*I* have done this, and it is wrong.' Further, it is a sign of object relatedness: 'I am aware of the world around me and I register the fact that *I* have brought pain and suffering into it'. Empathy is clearly a basic element of the guilt experience, closely followed by concern for the suffering of others, but these aspects are generally under-appreciated in most writing on the subject. Following the theory of Klein, we can appreciate the infant's movement away from narcissism and denial prevalent in the paranoid-schizoid position into the depressive position where concern for the object breeds guilt and the pain of taking responsibility. Awareness of the separateness of the object, recognition of aggression towards it, and love of it blend together to act as the primary motive force for translating concern into a reparative impulse that is thereby activated.

Shame and the ego-ideal

Until recently, guilt was considered, from a psychoanalytic viewpoint, as the pre-eminent regulatory emotion, with shame positioned as a sub-aspect of guilt. Kohut's (1971, 1977) work on narcissism and other contemporary initiatives into the understanding of the self have brought shame into focus for analytic investigation. Piers uses the structural perspective to view and define shame by means of its relationship to the ego ideal (Piers and Singer 1953). Whereas guilt is generated with the touching or transgression of a boundary established by the superego, shame is generated when a goal that is presented by or embodied within the ego-ideal is not reached. Shame therefore indicates a real shortcoming and generates a feeling of failure, inadequacy, or flaw. In shame the unconscious threat is that of abandonment rather than mutilation. The Law of Talion does not prevail in shame. When we feel shame, we do not expect a punishment as much as a cancellation of our being and the elimination of any sense of personal goodness. Personal identity, self-respect, and self-regard are threatened by the affect-state of shame.

The basic threat with guilt comes from the superego and involves a moral recrimination. With shame the attack comes from the ego-ideal and threatens our very being.

We maintain our identities through a constant relationship with the ego-ideal that is the repository for both the split-off primary narcissism of the self as well as the projection of wishes and fantasies associated with parental identifications. The idea that the ego-ideal is made up of mere wishes for perfection seems inadequate to explain the enormous psychic power of encounters with the ideal. Following Grunberger's (1971) argument, I agree that it is probably more accurate to say that experiences of pre-natal elation and transcendence are encoded within the self as psychosomatic sensations and memory constellations. These memories and emotional-subsystems release what is called narcissism when libidinal energy passes through them. As the repository of narcissism, the ego-ideal holds within its core those feelings and phantasies, and perhaps memories of a total union with the needed ideal object along with a sense of omnipotence, elation, and grandiosity, those by-products of merger with the ideal. Filled with the lost perfection of primary narcissism, the ego-ideal becomes a core component of the self's integrity and acts as a type of gyroscope that provides the self with a guidance system to direct the self's searching to achieve re-union with the source of being.

Through cycles of projection and introjection, we are constantly using our experience of the ideal to shape external objects in the light of what we consider to be absolutely necessary for our being. Correspondingly, we introject the essential and relevant group, social, and cultural ideals and values back into the ego-ideal as a way of keeping a close correlation between internal and external measures of perfection, inclusion, and aspiration. For instance, the 'American Dream' is a societal fantasy that becomes internalized into the unconscious experience of the individual ego-ideal and thereby attains the power to motivate and regulate our behaviours, hopes, and dreams.

Freud (1920) used the ego-ideal to explain the essence of group formation. The leader becomes invested with the power and importance previously attached to each individual's ego-ideal. Once transformed into such an ideal object, the leader can then be related to by the membership as a common and organizing focal element through which to regain the lost narcissism of the individual, as well as to control the forces of competition and envy. The leader as ego-ideal and therefore ideal object subdues the destructive internecine rivalries and battles and therefore provides the group with a modulating presence and reason to control the more aggressive and envious aspects of the self. Freud's discovery of this function of the ideal object enabled him to explain group and social behaviour when it could not be accounted for by instinct-libido theory.

How can these structural considerations help us to understand the affect of shame? Miller (1996) identifies a state called 'shame proper' (p. 33). In this state some disjunctive event causes the self to experience a gap between the perfect ideal object and the self. Within this gap, or space, the negative judgement of the self's badness, worthlessness, and unloveability emerges (Wurmser 1981). This internal experience generates the feeling of being ashamed of oneself. A cluster of physiological responses clearly signal shame: blushing, hunching of the shoulders, shrinking of the body, hiding the eyes, covering the face, gaze avoidance and so forth. I believe that such embodied states are what Fenichel is referring to when he speaks of the 'primitive physiological reflex pattern' that is at the core of shame (1945, p. 139). The projection of this experience out into interpersonal relations or group and social contexts where it becomes public leads to associated states that include humiliation, shyness, bashfulness, embarrassment, self-consciousness, disarray, and disgrace. But shame proper seems to focus on the excruciating encounter with the ideal where, having revealed ourselves, we discover traumatically a response that does not affirm our goodness experienced through union with the object. Instead the response announces our disconnection from the good object and betrays our essentially flawed essence. The private encounter breeds a dread of scorn and abandonment: 'You are a pathetic and disgusting child!' The social encounter with shame breeds a fear of social expulsion and ostracism: 'We don't want you.' With emotionally significant individuals and with members of the social group, we create actual relationships in the here-and-now that reflect, join with, and augment painful internal object relationships.

Behind the fear of shame lies the fear of contempt, rather than the fear of hatred and punishment as is central in guilt.

These primitive roots of shame seem to be anchored in the self's need to locate the maternal object, attach to it successfully, and assure a pleasurable and continuous relationship with it. The anxious, separated infant self scans its environment for the smiling face of the mother. Finding that face but discovering there disapproval or joylessness leads to a *reactive sense* of shame. This reactive experience of shame is not mediated by an internalized ideal object but appears as a primitive, physiological reaction to the still-faced adult, the scowling mother, or the disgusted other. These disjunctive interactions, as they are called in the attachment research literature, lead to a diminishment of the sense of self.

Repeated experiences of such disconfirmation, rejection, or traumatic separateness give rise to a self that is judged as being bad,
flawed, or inadequate.

Applying Bion's (1962) ideas on thinking, I imagine the emer-
gence of reactive shame in the following way. The inherent preconception of the infant in the successful infant–mother pair seeks
an external affirmation in, say, the smiling and encouraging face
of the mother. When that is not found, a negative realization is
created. Within the space of that negative realization emerges the
physiological and psychological distress, danger, and dread we call
reactive shame. With regard to the feeding situation Bion (1970)
says that the negative realization of the good absent breast produces the realization of the bad present breast. As regards shame,
the absence of the affirming good-mother must produce the experience of the bad, present witch-mother. The myth of the Medusa
with the head full of snakes represents such a mother who turns to
stone whoever looks upon her. Here the stone is the cold, dead de-
animated self, frozen with shame. This concept recalls the dream
image of Miss Goss frozen behind the pillar of stone.

Finally, we can think about the relationship between shame and
psychosomatic and hypochondriacal states. The generally diffuse
states of bodily distress including blushing, hunching over, squirm-
ing, and gaze avoidance show how shame experiences utilize the
deepest bodily pathways to express and encode trauma. These
bodily states indicate psychosomatic transformations as well as
hypochondriacal anxieties, concerns, and delusions. The shame
affect moving about the body feels like illness, a 'sickness in the
skin' as the French describe it. Shame affects the skin and organs
by bringing about physiological responses that mimic disease
entities. The ego's inability to record this primitive experience in
the realm of thought leads to the formation of bodily states which
are woefully inadequate containers for shame-based relational
traumas. Attacked by physical discomfort, the ego continues its
relationship with unconscious persecutory objects while acting out
core emotional scenarios with significant others.

The interaction between guilt and shame

Given the interweaving of related experiences in the development
of the superego and ego-ideal, guilt and shame continually interact
in a complex dynamic. Fairbairn (1952, 1954, 1963) described this

interaction of ego and superego as a system of parts: the internal saboteur (the anti-libidinal part of the ego), the rejecting object, and the ideal object, all in dynamic relation. In Chapter 3, David Scharff applies Fairbairn's formulation of superego functions to the close relationship between guilt and shame. He holds that guilt stems mostly from the self's concerned reaction to its harmful treatment of the other, while shame derives from the self's reaction to the other's harsh or contemptuous attitude towards the self. He thinks of guilt as the affect of the self's attitude to the object and shame as the affect of the self's feeling of being persecuted by the object. These views are consistent with the perspective I am presenting.

In his discussion of shame and guilt, Piers describes a situation in which sexual or aggressive impulses can lead to the ego's inhibition of its instinctual longings under the impact of superego injunctions that then undermine the subject's sense of competence and identity (Piers and Singer 1953). Such an undermining leads to the experience of shame that then triggers rage as an antidote for the sense of shame-based ineffectiveness. One then witnesses the re-engagement of the superego to produce guilt as the means to inhibit the aggression just released. The clinical picture can become quite complicated when one affect state is being used to mask another affect lurking in the unconscious. This situation frequently leads to a misdiagnosis of the patient's central conflicts and therefore to an unempathic clinical stance. It is often difficult to discern if 'analytically uncovered shame feelings . . . spring from a deep sense of inadequacy or whether they represent frozen attitudes of atonement for an unconscious guilt' (Piers and Singer 1953, p. 35). Piers concluded that guilt over masturbation masks shame over a sense of sexual inadequacy or passive homosexuality. It is important to keep in mind that guilt is an affect that can be shared, while shame cannot.

Guilt and shame comprise internal objects that use condemnation or abandonment as the regulatory mechanism to reinforce specific behaviours or thoughts. I think of guilt and shame as polarities on the internal-self regulatory continuum.

ENVY, MASOCHISM, AND AGGRESSION

With shame we encounter the problem of envy. With envy we see an attack against the object due to the pain and distress that overwhelm the subject when encountering the gap between itself and the ideal object. The subject has the feeling of being denied a sense of sharing and fusion with the bounty and opulence of the object. The fullness and grandeur which should reside inside the self is experienced as painfully outside, beyond one's own essence and control. One is so small and the other so big. One is so hungry and the other so full. This experience of the gap between the perceived limitations and inadequacy of the self and the imagined fullness and plenitude of the object explains the intensity of the envy experience. In envy, the shame of being separated from the omnipotent other breeds a deep and violent hostility against the object within the self. The pain associated with such a chasm between the self and object is an important source of persecutory experience. The torture of having to be a starving witness to the banquet enjoyed by the idealized object and its partner in the primal scene produces intense suffering of the most destructive form. This was illustrated in Miss Goss's dream images of her exclusion from couples, her attack on the fruit of their union, and her difficulty in taking in interpretations. Related to the concept of envy is the masochistic defence.

In guilt, masochism operates as a means of disguising the hostility against the object by debasing the self. It is the ego's way of submitting to the object in hopes of being forgiven for the crimes and offences that have evoked the object's punishment. In this way masochism is hiding the aggression that caused the attack against the superego's boundaries as well as engaging in an attempt to propitiate the angry superego.

In shame, the function of masochism shifts. It restores narcissistic power to one's self as the author of one's own shaming behaviour (Green 1972). The self withdraws from object relations into a pure atmosphere of moral transcendence wherein good battles evil without the constraints of empathy, relatedness, and human compassion.

Rather than providing punishment of the self for its imagined sins and crimes as it does in guilt, in shame masochism becomes a way to elevate the self and to restore narcissistic wholeness through renunciation, self-debasement, suffering, and defilement.

Aggression in guilt and shame

Our discussion of guilt and shame might give the impression that the ego's response to these experiences is primarily acquiescent or submissive. But therapists know this is not so. We frequently encounter powerful aggressive defence forces deployed against us by the patient who needs to protect the frail self from having to experience the full brunt of registering the existence and implication of substantial reservoirs of unconscious guilt and shame.

Most common is the process of blaming the therapist: 'You should have told me about this', 'Why didn't you help me to see the implications?', 'Why were you so withholding from me?', and the most ubiquitous of all accusations, 'Why didn't we get to this before?!' The effort to transpose the guilt from the patient into the therapist is a central defensive dynamic. Through concordant identification (Racker 1968) the therapist becomes the bad, offending self who has to withstand the onslaught of the harsh superego now lodged within the patient who has identified with the perpetrating object.

As the experience of shame involves a feeling of threat against the existence of the self, aggressive responses associated with threats to the ideal are among the most furious and powerful within the human personality. Any action perceived to be trying to separate the self from its union with the ideal is seen as a deadly menace. The self's attempt to annihilate anything or anyone that stands between it and union/merger with the ideal may be conceptualized as a manifestation of aggressiveness connected to the death instinct. However, such destructiveness does not manifest as a wish to die but rather the preparedness to use every force available in order to maintain linkage and fusion with the perceived source of all that is good. In the same vein, Segal (1981) wrote that the death instinct is perhaps better understood as a drive to annihilate the awareness of need, because it is need more than anything else that informs the self that it has lost its fantasized fusion with the ideal.

Separateness and difference are therefore fought with grave intensity, including the otherness of the therapist. I believe that is why Kohut's (1971) technique of mirroring is so vital: the therapist can begin to form a relationship with the patient as a mirror, without introducing the trauma of otherness. Obviously, negotiating that trauma at some point in the therapy process will mark the success or failure of the therapeutic enterprise. Winnicott (1971) speaks to just such a process whereby the catastrophe of otherness can be the catalyst for psychic growth and development. In his formulation, the trauma and the persecutory feeling suffered when the otherness of the object is registered can, with appropriate holding and containment, lead to an appreciation of otherness as a source of nourishment and reality outside the hallucinatory boundaries of the self. The survival of the object points the way beyond narcissistic solipsism to the expansion of the self. This leads to the birth of true intersubjectivity. That is, to a world of objects actually separate but connected by a bond of empathy and similarity.

One dramatic form that shame-related aggression can assume is seen with the perverse personality. The violence and aggression seen in perversions or in perverse attitudes is manifest in attacks against differences, especially those between the generations and the sexes. Chasseguet-Smirgel (1984) focuses on the narcissistic element as the core of all perversions or perverse attitudes. People with perversions are trying to overcome powerful psychic traumas that are associated with the fact that they are not the centre of their psychic universes. Violence is used to overcome the actual order of the world so as not to be dependent, secondary, and vulnerable. Under such circumstances, the ego-ideal no longer serves as a repository for the ideal elements and aspirations of the self, but rather has become an object with which the person is attempting to fuse in a crude fashion without any sublimation. No longer to have the ideal object, but to be the ideal object, is the impossible demand placed before the perverse ego. Here, persecutory experience stems from the recognition of the true nature of reality. The separateness and generativity of the parents inflict great suffering on the perverted basis of the patient's narcissistic world.

THE CONTAINMENT OF SHAME IN THE COUNTERTRANSFERENCE

Within the countertransference, the experience of working with a shame-based individual frequently involves surviving the patient's attempts to shame the therapist into submission, or in more extreme cases, shame the therapist out of existence. The process of containment with the traumatized individual can demand an inordinate amount of patience, empathy, attunement, and thera-peutic nimbleness. Because the patient feels so threatened with annihilation, projective identification is the preferred mode for inducing the therapist to experience the shameful and inadequate self-experiences that the patient suffers. The battle is frequently waged between the therapist's desire to help the patient become a good enough human being and the patient's split desires: on the one hand to use the therapy relationship to finally realize the life-long dream of the attainment of perfection through fusion with the ego-ideal, and on the other hand to have the therapist contain and detoxify what has previously felt too dangerous or destructive to share with any other person.

McDougall (1980) says that the mother's job is seducing her baby into the human realm. The therapeutic task with shame-based individuals frequently has a similar overall mission. What we need for the task is a therapeutic stance in which we attempt to point out primitive yearnings based on narcissistic identifications that have left the patient in a state of confused identity – part idealized object, part grandiose yet depleted self – both parts suffering from the hybrid nature of the self's experience. The need to continually inflate the self, through addictive behaviours, grandiose under-takings, or violent envious attacks, undermines any sense of comfort and self-acceptance. Guilt is a constant, though generally unconscious element, which is the consequence of relentless attacks launched against reality. Such emotional and ego experience leads inevitably to a sense of diminished selfhood and chronic, guilt-based inferiority.

The therapeutic task of identifying these cycles of shame, attack, guilt, denial, and renewed attack frequently strains the therapeutic container. Holding the patient in an atmosphere of acceptance provides a context for the beginning phases of detoxification. The containment of the injuries to the self, the survival of the attacks launched by the patient against the therapeutic object, and the reverie required to re-order and neutralize the more pernicious elements of the human unconscious, challenge the therapeutic repertoire.

Internal objects are the carriers of life's central force and meaning. Their elaboration leads to a sense of aliveness, creativity, and joining with the great river of life. The attack on them and their fantasized defeat lead to a sense of death-in-life and an endless spiral of defensive denial, paranoid threat, and persecutory unhappiness associated with battling elusive, transcendent demons. These objects carry the 'stuff' of what Bion called 'O . . . the ultimate reality . . . the infinite, the thing-in-itself' (1970, p. 26).

Acknowledging them, recognizing their effects on love and work relationships, gaining contact with them in the transference, and modifying them in the transference experience, allows for psychic reality, symbolism, the establishment of meaning, and the transformation of the persecutory object.

REFERENCES

Bion, W. R. (1962). A theory of thinking. In *Second Thoughts*, pp. 110–119. Northvale, NJ: Jason Aronson.

—— (1970). *Attention and Interpretation*. London: Tavistock.

Chasseguet-Smirgel, J. (1984). *Creativity and Perversion*. London: Free Association Books.

Fairbairn, W. R. D. (1952). *Psychoanalytic Studies of the Personality*. London: Routledge & Kegan Paul, Ltd.

—— (1954). The nature of hysterical states. In *From Instinct to Self: Selected Papers of W. R. D. Fairbairn, Volume I*, pp. 13–40, ed. D. E. Scharff and E. F. Birtles, 1994. Northvale, NJ: Jason Aronson.

—— (1963). An object relations theory of the personality. In *From Instinct to Self: Selected Papers of W. R. D. Fairbairn, Volume I*, pp. 155–156, ed. D. E. Scharff and E. F. Birtles, 1994. Northvale, NJ: Jason Aronson.

Fenichel, O. (1945). *The Psychoanalytic Theory of Neurosis*. New York: Norton.

Freud, A. (1936). *The Ego and the Mechanisms of Defence. The Writings of Anna Freud Vol 1*. New York: International Universities Press, 1966.

Freud, S. (1905). Three essays on the theory of sexuality. *Standard Edition*, 7: 125–243. London: Hogarth Press, 1957.

—— (1914). On narcissism. *Standard Edition*, 14: 69–102. London: Hogarth Press, 1957.

—— (1920). Group psychology and the analysis of the ego. *Standard Edition*, 18: 67–145. London: Hogarth Press, 1957.

—— (1923). The ego and the id. *Standard Edition*, 19: 3–66. London: Hogarth Press, 1957.

Green, A. (1972). *On Private Madness*. Madison, CT: International Universities Press.

Grunberger, B. (1971). *Narcissism: Psychoanalytic Essays*. Madison, CT: International Universities Press.

Klein, M. (1946). Notes on some schizoid mechanisms. In *Envy and Gratitude and Other Works 1946–1963*, pp. 1–24. New York: Delacorte Press, 1975.

Klein, M. (1957). Envy and gratitude. In *Envy and Gratitude and Other Works 1946–1963*, pp. 176–235. New York: Delacorte Press, 1975.

Kohut, H. (1971). *The Analysis of the Self*. New York: International Universities Press.

—— (1977). *The Restoration of the Self*. New York: International Universities Press.

McDougall, J. (1980). *Plea for a Measure of Abnormality*. New York: International Universities Press.

Meltzer, D. (1973). *Sexual States of Mind*. Perthshire, Scotland: Clunie Books.

Miller, S. (1996). *Shame in Context*. Hillsdale, NJ: The Analytic Press.

Piers, G. and Singer, M. (1953). *Shame and Guilt*. Springfield, IL: Charles C. Thomas.

Racker, H. (1968). *Transference and Countertransference*. New York: International Universities Press.

Rosenfeld, H. (1987). *Impasse and Interpretation*. London: Tavistock Publications.

Segal, H. (1981). *Klein*. Glasgow: Collins.

Winnicott, D. W. (1971). The use of an object and relating through identifications. In *Playing and Reality*, pp. 86–94. London: Penguin.

Wurmser, L. (1981). *The Mask of Shame*. Baltimore: The Johns Hopkins Press.

Chapter 5

The noise of the persecutory object: Like a roof caving In

Yolanda de Varela, MA

THE FEAR OF BREAKDOWN

A woman patient presented with many fears of something bad happening to her, her marriage, and her position in her family. She was afraid of the destructiveness of her envious sister-in-law who had previously been her friend and she was afraid of speaking out about it. She was also afraid of airline turbulence and crashes that could damage her husband and her children and she especially dreaded being paralyzed with fear and personally unable to help them if the imagined disaster struck. In general she had a gloomy outlook on her capabilities and a dim view of her future.

The narrative and vignettes from the woman's individual therapy show how her multiple fears of the breakdown of herself, her family, and the security of the social environment were defences against the repetition of an earlier breakdown in functioning due to trauma in the past, which she represented as a persecutory object currently located in her former friend. The fear of a nervous breakdown is the fear of a breakdown that has already been experienced and forgotten. The early breakdown leads to a defence organization, which is geared to preventing a repetition of the trauma but which actually produces persecutory experience. Winnicott (1963) wrote:

> There are moments when a patient needs to be told that the breakdown, a fear of which destroys his or her life, has already been. . . . Unless the therapist can work successfully on the basis that this detail is already a fact, the patient must go on fearing to find what is being compulsively looked for in the future. . . . The patient needs to remember this but it is not

possible to remember something that has not yet happened, and this thing of the past has not happened yet because the patient was not there for it to happen to. . . . The only way to 'remember' in this case is for the patient to experience this past thing for the first time in the present, that is to say, in the transference. This past and future thing then become a matter of the here and now, and become experienced by the patient for the first time.

(1963, p. 92)

Winnicott's concept of the need to remember the earlier breakdown in order to get over the fear of a new breakdown is a useful way to think about detoxifying the persecutory object that is creating a state of emergency.

In once a week individual therapy, the patient recovered from her fear of being broken by recognizing that it had already happened, and getting over it. From the first interview in which she told me of the problems with her husband's family, the flow of her narrative was interrupted with copious unexpected tears, which led me to suspect a basic failure in her early environment. As the treatment continued to evolve, I heard about the early failure more fully and experienced her sense of breakdown in the counter-transference. This helped to connect her with the task of remembering rather than repeating her traumas and so helped her to stop living life by avoiding feared repetitions of trauma. The following examples are taken from the opening phase and from sessions at the end of a year of treatment with this woman. I will call her Mrs Alvarez.

THE OPENING PHASE: BREAKING DOWN IN TEARS

Mrs Alvarez explained that it was for her son's educational and behavioural difficulties that she had first consulted a psychologist, but the psychologist had noticed her own anxiety and referred her to me. Mrs Alvarez is an attractive, 36-year-old woman, married for 16 years, and mother of two children. She began to tell her history with great difficulty, breaking down without knowing why. She described herself as having been an only daughter for eight years and the centre of her parents' attention, especially her mother's, until the arrival of the new baby but she didn't say anything about its impact on her. Her parents were overprotective of their children and prevented exposure to bad news or any unpleasant experience. Mrs Alvarez remembered a painful incident in elementary school when she was shocked to learn from her friends that her dearly loved grandmother had died three days before. She was devastated by the news and upset with her parents that they had not told her about the loss themselves. She broke down, went home, and complained to her parents that they should have told her. She cried a lot while telling me of this, showing the amount of sadness and rage she still held over this.

Slowly and painfully during the following sessions I learned of a highly problematic relationship Mrs Alvarez had with her sister-in-law, Mirta. Mr Alvarez and his brother are business partners in a successful international law firm. Mrs Alvarez feels that Mirta is provoking a split between her, her husband, and her in-laws. She fears that the damage Mirta might do could eventually cause the termination of the Alvarez's 16-year marriage. Mrs Alvarez had known Mirta since childhood when they were school-mates, but she lost touch with her when she changed schools. Life went on and Mrs Alvarez got married and lived with her husband close to his family in Panamá. Mirta got married and moved to join her husband in Colombia.

The next time Mrs Alvarez saw Mirta was on her return to Panamá after Mirta's bad marriage ended in divorce. Mrs Alvarez remembered her vivid impression of Mirta's physical deterioration. She saw that Mirta was overweight, had a severe acne problem, and looked depressed. Mirta explained that her husband had been physically abusive and that she was also mourning the recent death of her mother. Mrs Alvarez felt sorry for Mirta and tried to cheer her up by offering to arrange for her to meet her brother-in-law, also recently divorced. But she never made the calls to arrange the introduction.

Eventually Mirta met Mrs Alvarez's brother-in-law on her own. Mrs Alvarez thinks that Mirta manipulated the situation so she could be introduced to him. Soon Mirta was attending the same family affairs. Quickly and smoothly, Mirta was manoeuvring herself into a position within the family circle, and Mrs Alvarez felt that she was being actively displaced by her. Finally Mirta married Mrs Alvarez's brother-in-law and appealed to her in-laws by portraying herself as a victim of abuse and as a lonely woman without a family of her own. Mrs Alvarez felt Mirta completely took the total love of her in-laws away from her.

This was not Mirta's only tactic. Slowly Mrs Alvarez's friends and some members of her family of origin told her that Mirta was constantly complaining to her husband's mother. For instance, Mirta would tell her mother-in-law that Mrs Alvarez wouldn't telephone Mirta's daughter or invite her daughter to her house while Mirta was away on a trip, which was very bad from Mirta's point of view, since she, Mirta, didn't have any extended family. Mrs Alvarez was very angry because she did call and she did take her niece out, but it seemed that whatever she did was never enough to satisfy Mirta. To make things worse, Mirta elbowed in on the same charity institution where Mrs Alvarez and her husband had been active and where her contribution was highly appreciated. Mirta was selected a member of the Board of Directors, and worked to block the implementation of any initiative from Mrs Alvarez and her committee. She also capitalized on any opportunity at family get-togethers to take Mr Alvarez aside for talks about Board business.

The situation became critical when Mirta complained to her mother-in-law that her daughter was not invited to Mrs Alvarez's younger brother's wedding. The father-in-law called Mrs Alvarez in to meet with him and stated clearly that he would not have any more fights in his family. Mrs Alvarez was devastated. All this time she hadn't talked to her husband about this problem, and now she feared he wouldn't believe her and would take Mirta's side. She was practically paralyzed. Mirta had become a dangerously persecutory object for Mrs Alvarez.

After the first therapy session, Mrs Alvarez felt courageous enough to talk to her husband about her misfortunes and her feelings. She told him of all that had happened to make her fear that Mirta would succeed in separating them. She explained how afraid and sad she felt about losing his love and the love of his family. Her husband's reaction was one of surprise. Confronted with the intensity of her feelings, he was amazed at how quiet she had been about the whole issue. He didn't know about the family situation and his father's orders, but he did know that it was obvious to everyone how manipulative Mirta was. He didn't want any fights with his brother, and that's why he always tried to be polite to Mirta. He offered his wife his support, talked to his parents, and was more careful at social events in not letting Mirta monopolize him.

Mrs Alvarez remained in treatment to continue work on her own issues. Eventually she decided to leave the position at the charity institution in search of her own space. She then opened a small business, a gift store, making a dream of many years come true. Still every obstacle provoked anxiety and a sense of doom about her future.

After we had been working together for about a year, it was time for my vacation. Two weeks before I would be away I announced that I would be out of the office. Mrs Alvarez didn't say anything about what my absence would mean to her. Although she was unable to express directly any transference reaction to this break in the holding, the situation that followed my announcement of my impending vacation showed me in advance the impact on her of anticipating my absence.

THE FORTY-NINTH SESSION: FEAR OF BREAKING APART

Mrs Alvarez arrived at my consulting room in a state of high anxiety. Her husband, who had invited her to a Mexican resort, leaving their children at home, had changed the travel plans to go to London instead, a trip with a much longer flying time. In a previous session, she had told me with some anxiety about an argument with her husband over her wish to do a leg of the trip by car. She preferred to avoid long periods in the air since she had developed a fear of flying after being on an extremely turbulent flight coming home from abroad with her husband and children. Her fear of aeroplanes had been intensified by the occurrence of two recent plane crashes in which Panamanian friends had died. She thought her fear was aggravated by these accidents as her husband is a frequent traveler.

While she was talking, I had in the back of my mind the horror of the plane crashes in which I too had known some of those who died. I knew that we were near the first anniversary of the second of these crashes. I wondered if this was the reason for her anxiety, but I remained silent.

Mrs Alvarez continued talking about her fears and said that currently everything was going along well for her: her business was booming, she and her husband were getting along fine, she was no longer upset by Mirta's behaviour, and her children were happy and doing well in school. Her daughter was to celebrate her fifteenth birthday, a socially important event in Panamanian society. She feared that if something bad happened to her and her husband during the trip, their children would be left all alone and traumatized. She also had in mind the memory of an aunt who lost her son after his graduation.

I said, 'I notice that your fears of flying have intensified with the idea that something bad could happen since everything seems to be going just fine.'

'You are right,' she said. 'I'm very uneasy and I don't want to travel, although I know this will be good for us as a couple.'

She told me that she had not been afraid of flying as a younger woman, not even as a child when on a flight with her father that was particularly difficult. A war refugee, he was afraid of flying and he drank during the trip to relax. Even though there was turbulence, she was not afraid, and this incident didn't affect her. It was only after the violently turbulent trip back with her husband and children that she became afraid. The most disturbing thing for her was that she couldn't take care of her children when she was so scared. Terrified, she had to ask her husband to look after them because she couldn't cope. She had to run to the rest room as soon as the turbulence stopped. Telling me this, she went into panic.

I asked her to tell me the details of the trip. She told me that they were coming back from a vacation in Disneyland. The children were sitting together on the other side of the aisle, when suddenly, turbulence started to shake the plane violently. The plane dropped suddenly and she thought they were going to crash.

'The plane was shaking,' she said. 'It shook a lot, and there was this noise, this noise. I think the noise was what scared me most.'

I asked, 'What kind of noise?'

'I don't know. I can't describe it. Was it a noise coming from above? It was as if the plane was going to be ripped apart. I don't know. Yes, it was a noise coming from the roof, as if the roof was going to cave in.'

She described this with a movement of her hands. She was in a real panic now, crying painfully, terrified at the memory of this incident.

At this moment I was unable to identify with this kind of terror, the only time I had felt anything like that was when I was dealing with a suicidal patient.

I asked if this kind of noise reminded her of some other situation.

She was silent for a while and said that she could only associate it with some movie about a sinking ship or a plane accident.

I asked her, 'Were you ever involved in an accident?'

'I was in a car accident with Uncle José, my mother's young brother, only 7 years older than me.' She paused.

'Do you remember being scared then, or at any other time?' I inquired.

Mrs Alvarez thought about it for a moment and her eyes filled up with tears. 'José was always doing things to scare me. If I happened to be near the edge of the pool, he'd suddenly jump behind me, grab me from behind, and push me in. He'd sneak behind me and startle me any time.'

I then remembered her telling me in a previous session that José died in a car accident.

I said, 'It seems to me that your relationship with José was full of fright, more than you had realized before. I can imagine the uneasy feeling you must have had when you were with him.'

She said, 'He was always scaring me when I was a little girl. There was an incident during a vacation in Atlanta when he got me to leave my mother and grandmother shopping and go join him outside on the street. We were leaving the store behind, and it didn't feel right to me. I tried to persuade him to turn back, but he only said, "Come on. Let's go on a little further." Then we got lost for ages. I was the youngest and yet I was the one who found the way back for both of us. By that time Mom had involved the police in a search for us and we had to ride back to the hotel in a police car. Another time he took me to a mental hospital to see the people there who he said were crazy, as if that was supposed to be fun. As a treat he would take me for a ride in his car, but then he would speed to frighten me. One day he made the car spin around while I was in it with him.

'But,' she insisted, 'José always took good care of me, as he had done always since I was a little girl. He was like an older brother to me, always took me to parties and other social events.'

So he was very good and very bad for her, I thought. Good and bad were merged in him.

I asked her what she thought of José's emotional stability.

'I knew he was unstable,' she said. 'He had been a problem child. When he was 12 years old he was raped. In adolescence, he became a drug addict. He took an overdose and had to be hospitalized a year prior to his death. Once I grew up, I tried to take care of him. He had just returned from an institution for addiction. He was recuperating, he had bought new clothes, and he had learned that his former girl friend was recently divorced, and was hoping to renew the relationship. I am very angry that he died at a moment when things were going better for him.'

I said, 'I think that what made you so scared was José's suicidal potential. I can imagine how terrifying it must be to know about this level of self-destruction in a person you love and, at the same time, realize there is nothing you can do to help.'

Mrs Alvarez burst into tears. 'I knew something was going to happen that long holiday weekend,' she cried. 'José was just 29. I was 22 and already married. José wanted to use my mom's beach house because it is in one of the small towns where he wanted to spend the holiday and he didn't have a place of his own to spend the night. Mom was out of the country, so José asked me for the keys to the beach house that she owned.

'I always worried about José at the beach. He was so impulsive, and he was always worse at the beach. A few days before, he had shown me a turbo chip that he had bought for his car engine to make it run faster, and he had asked to break-in my new car. I refused to lend him my car and I avoided giving him the keys to the beach house by pretending I didn't have them. I tried really hard to dissuade him from going to the beach, but he said he had already made plans with his friends. He kept saying over and over that he would just have to "sleep in his car". Next thing I knew, José had had a car accident and he was dead.' Mrs Alvarez cried with deep sorrow while she was telling me this. 'I felt terrible that I couldn't prevent that from happening. There was nothing I could have done to prevent it, but I still feel awful about it.'

We were coming to the end of the session, and I made a lengthy summary of the linkages I had noticed. I said, 'I think that the fear you felt on that turbulent plane ride put you in touch with the terror you felt about José as a risk-prone man you couldn't protect. There you were travelling in the air with the children and your husband whose name is also José and suddenly you were unable to protect them because the terror was paralyzing. The noise you heard in the plane provided the link between your fear for your children, yourself as a child exposed to danger in José's car, and your image of José crashing and dying with no one there to help him.'

It seemed to me that up to this time Mrs Alvarez had been unable to accept José's death as a covert suicide. So when she thought of a plane crash as a likely accident in anyone's fate, she transformed a fear associated with not being able to stop something that had already happened, and that for years was on the verge of happening, into a fear of something likely to occur now.

Mrs Alvarez told me, 'It was so hard to accept José's death. If Mom had been in the country, being the oldest sister she might have had more influence with José, or she could have told their mother what he was going to do, and she might have had the authority to dissuade him from going to the beach. José was finally going to find happiness with his old girl friend, and then this tragedy struck. The way it happened was he had been speeding out of a main highway and almost hit a second car and then, trying to avoid it, his vehicle spun out and crashed into a lamp post which then fell on the car top. I can still hear José boasting about that car, telling me it was so powerful, telling me he was going to sleep in his precious car, and then I see the totally destroyed car. He sleeps forever in that car in my mind.'

Mrs Alvarez knew that José was in danger then, and for years before that, but this awareness provoked so much terror in her that she felt paralyzed and stood by, helpless to intervene. A feeling of guilt and a sense of impotence for having failed José has remained with her ever since. What scared her so much on the flight was the fear that she might again fail to save her loved ones. I sensed that this traumatic experience might have been built upon an even earlier experience. A sense of chaos, of not being contained, of feeling paralyzed and incapable of containing her children's anxiety, might be the replay of an even earlier catastrophic internal situation from the first few years of life.

THE FIFTIETH SESSION: BREAKING FROM THE DEAD EXCITING OBJECT

Mrs Alvarez seemed less anxious in the next session. She told me that she had felt great relief at being able to talk about her feelings around José's death. During the weekend she had attended a seminar on hypnosis with a well-known presenter. She had never read his books, nor did she believe in the power of hypnotic suggestions, but still she had an incredible experience.

In one of the segments of the seminar, the presenter induced an hypnotic state in the participants and made them remember things from the past. Mrs Alvarez saw the scene of a car accident. In this vision, there's a child lying on the floor, she doesn't know if he's dead or not, and she sees herself leaning over and helping him. This vision filled her with panic, because she thought it might be a premonition and that something bad was going to happen to one of her children. Anxious, she went to the presenter during the recess and told him about her experience. He said this experience was not about something that was going to happen but symbolized something that had already happened. Mrs Alvarez had interpreted her recovered memory as a fearsome future event just as she interpreted the actual accidents of other people as if they referred to her own future.

Mrs Alvarez told me that she had thought about what the presenter had said. She concluded that the child represented José, and the woman in the dream was herself feeling desperate and impotent about being unable to bring him back to life. She then felt brave enough to go and talk with her grandmother (José's mother). For the first time she confessed to her that she had been the family member who talked to José before his death, and told her how guilty she had felt for his death over the past years. Her grandmother listened to her and comforted her by telling her she was not to blame. She knew that José was looking for his death, and that there had been something wrong with him since he was a child. She said that José's death was a painful blow to her. Her own mother (and José's beloved Granny) had passed away only three months before José's death, and she always thought that Granny had taken him away. Her mother had stolen her child from her, she felt.

Mrs Alvarez told me that she had also talked with her mother (José's oldest sister). Her mother remembered the young Mrs Alvarez giving her the bad news on the phone and yelling at her, 'Why weren't you here?' Mrs Alvarez's mother also felt guilty for José's death, but none of the three women was able to talk about her feelings of loss and guilt, and none of them had spoken about what José's death had meant for each one of them.

José's sister Nora, who also went to parties as a teenager with the young Mrs Alvarez and José, was so affected by her brother's death that she sought professional help. Nora hadn't visited the cemetery before, but a few months after his death, she called Mrs Alvarez and told her they should visit José's grave. So at her insistence they went to the graveyard. Mrs Alvarez remembered being scared when she saw José's grave, and next to his, she read the name of a neighbour who had committed suicide. She then started to read the headstones on the other graves and saw the names of her grandparents and many acquaintances. She started feeling ill. It was as if all these people were suddenly coming back from dead, and she had to run out of the cemetery.

I asked Mrs Alvarez, 'How close was José with Granny?'

'José was Granny's favourite, and he adored her.'

'Was this the first time you heard your grandmother saying that Granny had taken José away?' I asked.

She replied, 'No, I heard that many times, but I can't locate the first time.'

I asked, 'Were you ever afraid that he would take you with him?'

She said, 'Yes, I always thought I would die before I was 29 (José's age when he died), and I felt very relieved when I reached that birthday.'

I asked, 'Might Granny's death have depressed José?'

'Yes, he adored her,' she answered.

'It seems to me,' I said, 'that it is not the dead who take the living away, but some of the living who follow the dead.'

Mrs Alvarez responded, 'I was always afraid José would take me, but I comforted myself by thinking that José loved his grandfather even more than Granny, and he hadn't taken him, so he might not take me either.'

At the end of the session Mrs Alvarez said that she felt relieved at understanding the fear she still carried from her relationship with José. Talking about all this alleviated her fear of the imminent flight to London with her husband, just the two of them. She left the session saying she could now look forward to her trip.

Mrs Alvarez was able to remember José's death, but she forgot the fear and the guilt she had felt then and many times before then when she had feared for his life. Her fear of an impending tragedy was really a way of remembering her reaction to the tragedy that had already happened and that had always been about to happen. I see the process of therapy as the unwinding of a net. Sometimes you can find the principal knot and follow it, but you can't figure out exactly how the whole thing was tied together. As therapy progressed, we unravelled another thread connecting current and early experience.

Mrs Alvarez spoke about a frightening incident. She was home alone with her children when a man shouted, banged on her front door violently, and tried to break into her house. As her house is set apart from others, nobody could hear her. She called a neighbour and the police and fortunately the man ran off. This event brought up the issue of a scary noise again. This time Mrs Alvarez recalled an early experience when she was around 6 years old. She had been out shopping with her grandmother. Upon arriving home they heard her mother in the bathroom, screaming and making loud, banging noises. Grandmother ran upstairs with the 6-year-old Mrs Alvarez and opened the bathroom door. Mrs Alvarez found her mother crying and hitting herself against the wall, all covered in blood. Grandmother quickly removed the little girl from the scene and took her to her house without any additional explanation. Mrs Alvarez didn't know then that her mother was distraught because she had had yet another miscarriage.

ACTIONS AND LOCATIONS OF THE PERSECUTORY OBJECT

In these vignettes from therapy with Mrs Alvarez, we see the different actions and locations of the persecutory bad object. For her, the threatening situation was one of not being able to hold on to the good object. She had created a phobic situation in which the danger was outside her and consisted in the bad object being merged with the good object. She defended against anxiety by staying within known, safe places and experiences. For her, any new situation or event could endanger the peace and safety of the good object. She maintained herself in a state of constant vigilance against the bad object and prepared her moves so she didn't bump into it. But it took many forms, and by the time I met her it was everywhere and she felt she was getting out of control. Very early in her life the message was that she couldn't retain the people she loved. Her paternal grandmother died when she was 5 years old. Her mother's life was threatened with a series of miscarriages at least one of which she witnessed. She had a long relationship with José that had her always at the edge of tragedy. She lost José in a crash. Having lost friends in an aeroplane crash, she worried about losing her husband when he was on frequent business trips. She lost the secure love of her husband and his family to her sister-in-law, fortunately only temporarily, but that was the final version of loss that brought her into therapy.

The extent of damage of a trauma has to do with its intensity and amount of repetition (Scharff and Scharff 1994). At the centre of Mrs Alvarez's trauma is the vision of herself as a mother unable to hold her children safely, linked to her experience of her own mother being unable to care for her when she was haemorrhaging and when she was unable to protect her from risky escapades with Uncle José. Mrs Alvarez's mother's trauma consisted of losing many pregnancies, losing her husband's mother at the same time, and then losing her brother José. Her father's trauma was that of being a war refugee. The internal chaos of each parent was crashing inside her creating, not an integrated protective internal couple, but a scared and scary couple that metaphorically made the noise of a roof caving in.

The importance of containing, of being able to sustain not knowing, of maintaining a safe holding environment during the process of therapy is vital to the unfolding of this kind of trauma and to its eventual detoxification. On many occasions, while in session with Mrs Alvarez, I noticed that catchphrases such as 'separation anxiety' came into my mind, as if to wrap up her trouble. But I didn't use them because I sensed that they were an easy way for me to escape the helplessness that I, like her, felt in the face of the confusion and pain that she brought to the session. I worked with the remnants of her experience stored in her unconscious as a noise and a physical sensation of paralysis. My association to a suicidal patient put me in touch with the persecutory trauma and gave me a way in to understanding Mrs Alvarez's fear of paralysis as a fear of something dreadful that happened before happening again. It reappeared in various versions in her narrative as she recovered repressed memories of traumatic events in childhood. Receiving the flow of associations in the countertransference allowed me to experience the impact of the persecutory object and to work with the patient on dealing with it: for the only way to deal with the bad persecutory object is eye to eye.

REFERENCES

Scharff, J. and Scharff, D. (1994). *Object Relations Therapy of Physical and Sexual Trauma*. Northvale, NJ: Jason Aronson.

Winnicott, D. W. (1963). Fear of breakdown. In *Psychoanalytic Explorations*, ed C. Winnicott, R. Shepherd, and M. Davis, pp. 87–95. Cambridge, MA: Harvard University Press.

Chapter 6

Persecutory objects in the body of self and other in Munchausen by Proxy

Kent Ravenscroft, MD

THE DYNAMICS OF MUNCHAUSEN BY PROXY SYNDROME

When persecutory objects and damaging parts of the ego have to be evacuated to protect the self, they may be projected into a part of the body that is then misidentified as the literal source of the badness. These parts of the self then seem to inhabit the body in a concrete way. Efforts to detoxify them take the form of desperate attempts at securing medical intervention to remove the offending body part. Many visits to doctors, repeated hospitalizations, and even multiple surgeries attest to the determination to be rid of the problem, and at the same time to get much-needed attention from physicians seen as godly. We recognize this as the disorder called Munchausen syndrome (Asher 1951). When the person repeatedly hospitalized is a child, we are dealing with the parent's projection of persecutory objects into the child. We recognize this disorder as Munchausen by Proxy syndrome (Meadow 1977). Whether the patient is an adult, or an indirectly affected child, the spurious symptoms are hard to diagnose, require heroic efforts at investigation, and lead to interventions that leave a sad trail of disfigurement and disability.

In Munchausen syndrome, the patient is almost always a woman. The woman uses her body as a container for projected badness, but her body does not detoxify the badness. Instead the body encapsulates the badness within her as an illness, and she yields her body to the doctor with whom she forms an ideal union to root out, attack, control, punish, or kill the disease which is attacking her body. The woman enlists the doctor to enact a sanitizing, morally sadistic attack on the embodied sick parts of her self. The power, authority, and charisma attributed to the physician as well as complex feelings of competition or resentment towards him are inextricably linked to gender politics and the history of women patients.

In Munchausen by Proxy syndrome, the patient is almost always a mother. The mother projects her badness not into her own body but encapsulates it in her child's body. She could not metabolize her badness and the child's body cannot contain it either. Afraid that she cannot manage the child alone, she begs the hospital doctors and nurses to step in between her and her child. She provokes their curiosity. The child with all her bad parts, parsed out and concretely embodied in his sick body parts, poses such an overwhelming challenge that even all the doctors and nurses are unable to figure out how to put him back together again. The mother challenges them to take over the care of her child and at the same time enlists them to carry out a sadistic attack on the illness on her behalf and with her blessing.

In this chapter I will focus on the hospital care of children whose mothers earn the diagnosis of Munchausen by Proxy. In the hospital environment the mother plays out her drama of longing to be seen as the perfect, helpful mother, the enduring support for her sick child, and a woman deserving of pity and extensive effort. I will examine the personal, social, and family history of one of these mothers to illustrate how the mothers' persecutory objects are formed and why they emerge in the perverted form of ultimately hurting their children while apparently trying to get help for them. I will conclude with a review of my use of countertransference to understand and detoxify the situation of Munchausen by Proxy syndrome.

It has not been easy to understand the dynamics of the internal object relationships of women who suffer from Munchausen by Proxy syndrome because they are secretive and deceptive and do not readily seek treatment for themselves, instead posing as perfect mothers. They relate to their children insincerely, the real object of their relationship with their children being to get access to a powerful, previously unattainable person, the doctor, who in fantasy can heal the early trauma of these women who frequently report feeling unwanted or uncared for by their fathers, even though the main problem tends to lie in the mother–infant relationship (Schreier and Libow 1993). The child is a vehicle for gratification of a fantasy by someone more significant than the child – like a fetish for the person with a sexual perversion. The mother who is lacking a secure identity and a separate sense of self is compelled to lie about her child to create a fantasy that is less unbearable than reality and that becomes real by involving other people (Greenacre 1958). All the sickness and confusion emanating from her persecutory objects are projected into her child and delivered into the healthcare system. Doctors and nurses spring into action in identification with the mother's concern. They overfunction to avoid resonating with her basic insecurity and confronting their own doubt and guilt. The neglected woman hungers to remain in the exciting medical world even at the expense of her child.

Some mothers bring in a well child with simulated or fabricated symptoms. Others poison their infants, repeatedly suffocate them, or withhold medications to make their children sick. Some mothers are newly fabricating only under stress or in altered states of consciousness; some are experienced, proficient perpetrators; and others at the end stage become callously, brazenly, and defiantly abusive. There are significant differences between these mild and severe versions of acting out on the child's body in terms of the degree of murderousness expressed, but the underlying dynamics are similar.

Some mothers locate the greatest danger outside the child, for instance in the form of an estranged father who threatens to take the child away from her or even murder him. Some locate the danger as a malevolent force inside the child's body. In either case, because something worse is about to happen, they take risky actions supposedly to keep the child out of harm's way.

Example: Erratic blood sugar levels and pancreatectomy

A 6-month-old baby girl was brought into the emergency room by her 27-year-old single mother because of a grand mal seizure. The mother was the only one to have seen this. The baby had already been in the emergency room twice and in the hospital once for treatment of fever and dehydration. The mother had a growing sense of the baby as sickly and troublesome. The mother had had grand mal seizures herself which were treated with dilantin until she was 15, when they finally stopped and she went off medication. Her pregnancy with this baby caused a new and frightening grand mal seizure. When the baby was admitted, it was found that the infant had a very low blood sugar, which was felt to be the probable cause of her seizure.

A long and complicated hospitalization ensued, during which the infant's blood sugar level bounced all over the map, sending the staff on a rollercoaster ride lasting several months. The baby became a legendary challenge to the paediatric staff and specialists. Periodically, they found extremely high levels of insulin in the baby's blood by which they were alarmed, mystified, and fascinated, since at other times the insulin level would be normal and stable for days, only to plummet or soar, the baby being found sweaty, lethargic, or comatose. Hopes dashed, staff pursued this elusive illness and the hospitalization went on. Mother was by now a well-known, beloved, and admired medical celebrity throughout the paediatric floors, respected for her quiet patience, private suffering, and support of staff and other families.

After multiple tests and procedures, and a particularly serious relapse, it was finally decided that the baby must be suffering from either a rare insulin-secreting tumour or a hyper-functioning pancreas. Radical exploratory pancreatic surgery was urgently needed. Mother received this frightening news readily with her usual trust and even enthusiastic relief. The next day the surgeons removed 95% of the baby's pancreas but found no actual tumour. As a result, they temporarily created a severely diabetic infant, assuming that the remaining 5% would over-function and make enough insulin for the baby. At first, to their surprise and horror, the infant's blood sugar rose to levels indicating she was severely diabetic. But then, shortly thereafter, to their relief and then concern, they discovered that her sugar began to fall precipitously. They were astounded when post-operative insulin lab results came back not low but so high that no human organism could possibly have produced them.

These impossible insulin levels finally aroused suspicion of foul play, and the nurses were alerted to watch the mother carefully. They noticed that no crises ever happened when she was away from the hospital. The mystery was cleared up when a child life worker saw the mother with a syringe in the play-room, and a sample of fluid taken from the baby's intravenous line came back with extremely high levels of insulin where there could not be any. When confronted, the mother denied having anything to do with it, and later said she suspected a staff member must be responsible.

On the strength of this evidence, the infant was placed in protective foster care and the mother was placed in jail. After several hours of interviews in jail, she admitted that she gave the child insulin – stressing that it was only one shot given after, not before, the surgery and thereby disavowing responsibility for causing the mutilation of her baby's pancreas by the surgeons. Once the child was in protective care, all her medical symptoms cleared up rather rapidly due to re-growth of her remaining pancreas – a testimony to infant adaptability. However, after a year of psychotherapy, the mother was still denying that she had anything to do with the insulin injections, and the baby was placed for adoption.

Only when the mother is able to admit to her role in harming her baby is there any possibility of detoxifying her internal persecutory object and allowing mourning to take place. Without that, the child is not safe with her.

Example: Bleeding leads to removal of stomach tissue

A 19-month-old boy had had 18 hospitalizations for breathing problems, urinary tract infections, diarrhoea, vomiting, dehydration, blood infections, seizures, failure to thrive, medication, and complications involving his medical equipment, and a diagnosis of an extremely rare, newly discovered enzyme deficiency disease thought to account for everything. He often spent only a few days out of the hospital before readmission because of taking a turn for the worse. More ominously, his mother's previous child, who had a similar condition and a similar history of repeated hospitalizations, had died suddenly just after discharge under unexpected and confusing circumstances. Following the death of that child, autopsy was refused and so bowel obstruction and sepsis were presumed as the causes of his death. This unexpected death occurred only five months before this boy's conception, and he was given the same name as his deceased brother.

Despite an exhaustive medical diagnostic evaluation, including some non-invasive and other more risky invasive procedures, transfusions, and operations, no primary cause for any of these problems was documented, making this very sick boy a continuing medical mystery. The fabulous diagnosis of a rare enzyme deficiency fell flat when the replacement therapy proved no more effective than anything else.

During his final series of hospitalizations, he had a naso-gastric tube inserted through his nose to his stomach and another tube directly into his small intestine through his abdominal wall for suction, bypass, and direct feeding. He had a large permanent indwelling catheter inserted directly into a large vein leading to his heart for intravenous feeding. Now he developed an ominous new symptom, which kept the staff deeply involved and preoccupied. He bled from his nasogastric tube and rectum periodically. The staff thought in passing of Munchausen by Proxy syndrome, but found the symptoms and signs so serious and so impossible to create, and the mother so good, so supportive, so involved, and so caring, that they dismissed it. They went on to do an exploratory operation and removal of what they thought was an ulcer causing the bleed-ing. The report came back as normal tissue, and the bleeding began again.

Careful monitoring revealed that the mother was removing the boy's own blood from the indwelling venous catheter, and injecting it through his tubes into his stomach or small intestine to cause the appearance of serious bloody vomiting and diarrhoea. She had been causing the bleeding, and perhaps many of his preceding medical problems. More ominously, we have to wonder if she caused the death of her previous son. This time, her actions were discovered in time. The baby's bleeding stopped immediately after the visits with her were restricted. The staff were able to remove all medication, tubes, and catheter in a stepwise fashion, and the boy began to flourish nutritionally and make rapid behavioural and develop-mental gains. From that point on there was no recurrence of illnesses.

THE MOTHER, HER CHILD, AND THE HOSPITAL STAFF

Munchausen by Proxy patients always have a specific psychotic core to their personality, whatever the surface personality pathology or diagnosis. I am using the term psychotic in the sense that object relations theorists use it to denote a primitive split-off repressed aspect of personality (Bion 1967). Through remarkably powerful projective identification, the mother is able to solicit caring for the child and herself and induce her doctor to pursue something in her body or in her child's body that is felt by both to be sick, bad, dangerous, malignant, pernicious, and insidious. She is able to inveigle doctors into a relentless investigation of the illness so as not to give up or abandon her damaged child – until she swings from idealization to denigration of her doctors. She is remarkably effective in exploiting the particular physician–patient relationship and the valencies of the medical profession, taking advantage of physician eagerness, vulnerabilities, and blind-spots. In doing so, she shows a willingness to distort truth, reality, and trust so as to exploit and manipulate the caring role of medical professionals. Those healthcare workers who deny the extent of their narcissistic investment in being altruistic, powerful, and helpful are particularly vulnerable to affective stimulation by a supposed victim like this kind of mother (Meloy 1988). The mother rationalizes her actions by saying that she is doing, or causing to be done, something less damaging to the child psychologically and physically in order to save, protect, and rescue the child from something more damaging and dangerous, usually thought of as lurking within the child's body, but sometimes localized in some malevolent person or circumstance outside. The mother is operating in the paranoid-schizoid position, warding off persecutory anxiety. The internal saboteur is at work corrupting her morality and her reality-testing.

Compliance and intimidation

The mothers seem devoid of hostility. They are described as saints championing the cause of saving their child, inspiring their idealized doctors to heroic levels of indefatigable pursuit of a serious but elusive illness, justifying invasive or risky diagnostic and therapeutic procedures. The doctors are caught up in self-blaming perfectionism, feeling that they should be able to diagnose or cure the disease, and that any failing or fault is in them. The mother seems so patient, so trusting, so supportive around doing whatever is necessary, bearing the uncertainty so well, understanding the waiting and the endless procedures, tolerating the recommendation of risky painful procedures, generally not getting impatient, angry, critical, aggressive – unless the doctor loses curiosity and gives up on his investment, or the child begins to get better and discharge is suggested. Then the mother may get irritable, critical, angry, and demanding. More ominously, she may fabricate more illness to induce renewed compliance from the doctor, control his proximity, and ensure his devotion. If the doctors are confused, frustrated, angry, bored, hopeless, or abandoning, the mother feels threatened and provokes a new symptom to rechallenge and restimulate their interest. She knows what to do and how to do it in order to bring everyone back into line.

These mothers break boundaries, befriend staff, take over medical roles, do procedures, read charts, get results, know medical facts and figures picked up by overhearing conversations and asking questions, and they sometimes even know the literature from reading in the hospital library and on the Internet. They know results sooner and sometimes know techniques better than young doctors and nurses. Their knowledge makes nurses and especially doctors uneasy. They capitalize on differences in opinion, they utilize splits in the staff, and they manipulate the system. They are at once compliant and intimidating.

When the Munchausen by Proxy behaviour is in evolution, the mothers' dynamics, their internal experience, and their internal object relations are still fluid, their distorted maternal behaviour appearing only under certain stressful circumstances. Mothers may carry out their acts of suffocation in an apparently playful fashion or in an impulsively passionate way. They may progress to a methodical, dispassionate method of dispatch. In the end stages of the syndrome, mothers are compulsive, callous, ritualistic, and automatic in their behaviour towards their children.

When they are not in a regressed state, the mothers seem ideally affectionate and engaging, at least in public. In private, however, end-stage mothers commonly do not to play intimately and do not relate warmly to their children, but this behaviour is seen only by the hidden camera. In altered states of consciousness during moments or periods of severe pathological regression with reversals and collapses of projective identification and loss of self–object boundaries, they may poison, infect, bleed, or suffocate their children. Over time massive secondary gain cements the ritual and the routine, and propels the mounting compulsion to repeat – and even escalate – the behaviour desperately. At times the balance of the internal object relations shifts and a new part of the mother emerges to continue the abuse in a state of manic defiance and triumph, but with the new motive of getting herself caught in anticipation of primitive surrender to archaic punishment.

THE GAINS OF ILLNESS

By making the child sick, or getting the physicians to think the child is sick, the mother's lost ideal family, or her alienated, abandoning, and rejecting family, may rally around the sick child and around her. By having a sick child, she herself is hospitalized by proxy and can receive the care she craves without asking for it for herself, and with the added benefit of becoming special, depended on, and indispensable. This immense gain traps her in a web of deceit and punishable lies, fraud, or criminal abuse. As she reaches the point of no return, she has to cover up the traces and lie low. There are quiet periods, lulls in the action, when the child seems to be getting better, and everyone seems to relax. But as soon as the staff see improvement and recommend discharge, the mother feels a double threat. At the external level, she fears the loss of the secondary gain. At the internal level, she faces the threat of getting close to the original unbearable situation, and the collapse of her psychic retreat. Pressure builds towards a compulsion to repeat the perpetration and so externalize the central drama to maintain her precarious psychic and social equilibrium.

The personality functioning of the mother fluctuates between the neurotic and character-disordered pole and the psychotic pole. Under threat of social and psychic pain, she begins to lose her self and object boundaries. She suffers a collapse of her mechanism of projecting into the real baby her malignant murderous impulses towards her baby-self. Her manic defences ruptured, she runs the risk of imminent catastrophe and annihilation.

If the baby recovers enough to be returned home to the mother's independent care, the mother loses her idealized, but perverse, deceptive, and dependent partnership with the unwitting physician and staff. The pernicious, cancerous, malignant, and murderous aspect of herself that has been evacuated out of her and then encapsulated, sequestered, and localized in the illness, in the sick baby, can no longer be maintained there. The doctor's persecutory pursuit of the illness that gave shape to her life, her complaints, and her deeds ceases. Then he is felt to abandon her and her baby to the nameless, shapeless, disembodied dread.

When the physician and the hospital staff abandon the mother and her infant to the full unbearable intensity of the exclusive mother–child relationship, the mother's badness escapes from its encapsulation within the good child's bad illness. No longer held at bay by the idealized mother–doctor pair, her badness now spreads to contaminate the whole child. If the child does return home, the mother soon feels desperate. She can't stand being alone with the child, can't tolerate being the sole caregiver, and ends up pushing the child away, foisting the mothering off on someone else, or attacking the child. The mother seeks revenge on the child and triumph over her physician.

At a deeper level the mother begins to feel the good child turning bad, menacing, and tormenting. The child now embodies the mother's murderousness and becomes an unbearably threatening monster. Finally, the mother reaches the point where she feels compelled to erase this tyranny. She may once more do toxic things to her child and not seek medical help any more, now creating illness directly and no longer by proxy. Sometimes she goes on to commit the murder of this child, or even to commit serial perpetrations over time, and serial killing of other siblings or subsequent infants. The persecutory object that must be projected at all costs compels her to get pregnant soon after killing the previous child. The pernicious cycle begins all over again.

Example: Blood in the urine

Mandy was a 6-year-old girl who was healthy until age 4 when she had a seizure. Mandy's older sister, aged 9, had a seizure disorder successfully treated with medication. Mrs Smith herself was on medication for seizures. So it was not surprising when electroencephalography indicated Mandy's need for seizure medication, and that problem was eliminated. During her hospitalization for seizure investigation, however, Mandy was unexpectedly found to have blood in her urine. After an extensive evaluation, including cystoscopy, Mandy was placed on antibiotics as well as seizure medication, both conditions cleared up, and she was discharged well.

Repeated bouts of bloody urine over the next two years responded well each time to antibiotics administered in the out-patient follow-up clinic. But their continual recurrence finally resulted in another hospitalization. The nephrologist explained to Mrs Smith that kidney biopsy might be needed, but that since it carried some danger to her child, it would not be done at first. Extensive preliminary tests of the genito-urinary system revealed no cause for the urinary bleeding. The nephrologist was delighted to tell Mrs. Smith that there was no need to recommend kidney biopsy, and so he proposed simply discharging her daughter to his out-patient clinic for continuing close follow-up. Mrs Smith, previously idealizing and compliant, became uncharacteristically angry. She insisted that her daughter was seriously ill and needed further studies. The wonderful doctor had let her down.

Before the child was discharged, blood appeared in the urine again, and the child had to stay in hospital for closer follow-up. Mrs Smith seemed to have the patience and understanding of Job, enduring further extensive testing and uncertainty and encouraging the doctors and nurses not to give up on her daughter. She was so medically knowledgeable, helpful, and supportive that the in-patient and out-patient staff found it impossible to get angry with the situation. Baffled but deter-mined not to admit defeat, they pressed on despite irritating inconsistencies. Mother thrived living on the ward, sleeping in, ingratiating herself to staff, and endearing herself to other young patients and their parents. The ward seemed to have become a haven from her disappointing marriage and the depressing outside world where custody proceedings were under way. Lawyers and physicians alike found her unbeliev-ably self-sacrificing, amicable, and fair, and with a notable lack of anger in the contentious court setting. So, when she became angry at the nephrologist, an alarm bell sounded, and the staff went into a state of heightened vigilance.

The staff soon discovered that only urine samples collected by the mother were found to have blood. The kidney specialist began to suspect the mother was causing the symptom. He cross-matched the blood in the urine with the mother's and child's own blood. The lab result proved that the mother had been putting her own blood in the urine specimens all along. The staff were furious on behalf of the child who had been made to suffer at their hands.

The psychological impact of the denouement on the previously unsuspecting caretakers always unleashes explosive and polarizing emotions. This makes continued responsible management of the patient extremely difficult for doctors and nurses, and later for protective service workers, lawyers, and judges – all of whom frequently get caught up in profound ambivalence, uncertainty, and adversarial encounters at every level. The persecutory object once located in the child is now unleashed in the ward. Doctors and nurses feel cheated and humiliated, their dedication exploited, and their healing intentions foiled. They feel guilty of omission when some of the abuse occurs when the child is under their care. They feel guilty of complicity through abuse by their own hands when they have to do invasive medical interventions. The necessary defences that permit them to hurt the patient in order to do good are exploded and their fears of doing damage run amok. The consulting psychiatrist meets with the child, the mother, and the ward staff to help them contain and work through the situation.

Understanding the mother

Mrs Smith had been 21 when her elder daughter was born. Three years later, after an ectopic pregnancy and a miscarriage, Mandy was conceived. Despite a pregnancy threatened with pre-eclampsia and toxaemia, Mandy arrived safely. But her birth was followed by another ectopic pregnancy, a third trimester miscarriage, and a full-term stillbirth.

In mothers with Munchausen by Proxy syndrome, there is an increased incidence of real and factitious obstetric complications associated with maternal ambivalence towards the foetus and unresolved grief over perinatal bereavement due to miscarriages, still births, and sudden infant death syndrome (Jureidini 1993). Pregnancy and childbirth facilitate the transition from the self-focused hostile behaviour of Munchausen syndrome to the externally focused Munchausen by Proxy syndrome. There is increased risk to both foetus and newborn from poorly repressed hostile impulses in the mother.

Mrs Smith's health was failing, her mental health was deteriorating as she took the losses of her failed pregnancies and bore the guilt of so many deaths, and her marriage was falling apart. Her husband had found her socially and sexually appealing early in their relationship, but he had become disillusioned because of her prudish, obsessional, anti-sexual manner, her disgust with his sexuality, and her disappointment in him as a hoped-for nurturer. Selfish, uncaring, and eventually unfaithful, he was no comparison to her adored father or her revered doctors. She became quite depressed. Her somatic symptoms increased and she worried about having an undiagnosed medical illness. She left the marriage, and took the children with her. Then the children became the parents' only neutral zone of communication and shared love, and even with them they seemed to form split allegiances. As the marital schism widened and the fear of internal malignancy grew in the mother, and then shifted to the daughter, concern for their daughter's health was the only thing that linked Mr and Mrs Smith in their increasingly cold war.

Mrs Smith was able to acknowledge her involvement in causing Mandy's ill-health. She allowed her parents to take custody and she accepted family-supervised visitation for herself for a year. While Mandy was separated from her mother, the signs of the so-called disease disappeared. Mrs Smith accepted treatment for herself, and the child was eventually returned to her. No more blood appeared in Mandy's urine.

CHARACTERISTICS OF THE MOTHERS

The outcome is rarely so good, many cases going unrecognized because of medical disbelief or unfamiliarity with the syndrome. Nevertheless, Mrs Smith is fairly representative of mothers with Munchausen by Proxy syndrome. She showed a powerful tendency towards splitting and projection, hysterical conversion, hypochondriacal problems, marital difficulty, a history of complicated and failed pregnancies in her own life, and enmeshment with her family of origin, and an unresolved oedipal involvement with her father covering a deeply ambivalent attachment to her mother. Also relevant are her visits to many different doctors and her repetitive idealization and denigration of physicians. Finally, like 10% of women with Munchausen syndrome behaviour she progressed to a full-blown Munchausen by Proxy syndrome provoked by the birth of a child, especially one produced after reproductive failure.

Compare the narrative of Mrs Smith to this description by Rosenberg (1987) of the Munchausen by Proxy mothers. Typically the mother spends a lot of time on the hospital ward with the child and exhibits a remarkable familiarity with medical terminology. She may have a history of symptoms similar to those she fabricates in the child. She may be friendly with, and even comforting of, the hospital staff, and yet her behaviour may be peppered with episodes of tearful frustration over her child's chronic illness and anger at the medical staff's inadequate vigour in pursuing her child's elusive problems. She may insist that she is the only one for whom the child will eat, drink, or swallow medicines. In some children, the diagnostic possibilities become, with time, limited to those of the rare type. The medical chart is laden with multiple subspecialty consultations, but rarely is an organic diagnosis made unreservedly. When the illness fits no known diagnostic profile, the doctor thinks he is discovering a 'never-before-described' disease.

Well versed in medical systems, the mother will seemingly stop at nothing to gain access to doctors and the inner circle of care in hospitals. Often there is a repetitive compulsive and escalating pattern to their surreptitious abuse. Hidden hospital surveillance cameras, used to document suspected maternal abuse, reveal that mothers carry out the abuse calmly and carefully in a premeditated fashion – even when they know they are under suspicion and are being watched. They are generally not overtly psychotic and not in a dissociative state when they harm their children. When confronted by physicians who suspect they are inducing illness, or even when confronted by documented proof of their abuse, the mothers tend to deny it vigorously and persistently. Some mothers deny their role in harming their children years after conviction in court, and others only gradually come to acknowledge it over the course of many years of therapy.

THE TRANSGENERATIONAL TRANSMISSION OF TRAUMA

To understand the formation of the persecutory object projected into Mandy, we need to study Mrs Smith's family history to see if there has been transgenerational transmission of trauma.

Mrs Smith's own mother had developed uterine cancer before conception and was receiving radiation treatment to her abdominal pelvic area when it was discovered that she was

pregnant with the foetus that would become Mrs Smith. Told
that the baby (Mrs Smith) might be deformed, her mother was
advised to abort. The family felt strongly that they wanted the
child in spite of the doctor's advice. Not only did Mrs Smith's
mother survive her cancer and the stress of her pregnancy but
also the infant Mrs Smith was normal at birth. The continuing
family legend was that this was a miracle and that the doctors
were fooled, proven wrong, and thereafter perceived as
dangerously untrustworthy. A narcissistic climate of special-
ness and denial of loss coloured the family's view of people
who had survived in spite of all the odds and in spite of the
opinions of experts. A sense of fragility was conveyed to Mrs
Smith during these early years and both she and her parents
became overprotective of her and concerned about her body.

As a young girl, Mrs Smith was deeply ambivalent about her
mother and close to her father. She and he had a mutually
idealizing relationship that persisted in her adulthood. They
projected into each other satisfying and exciting objects. In a
family interview they beamed and glowed in mutual admiration of each other. She compared her husband to her father,
found him wanting, and constantly searched her environment
for idealizable maternal and paternal surrogates who she
nevertheless felt were destined to let her down.

Mrs Smith sensed something morbidly wrong deep inside
herself. She had a deep sense of internal defectiveness that took
the form of dysfunction or disease shifting among different
organs. She sought medical care for multiple sclerosis, dia-
betes, eye problems, seizures, urinary tract infections, and a
suspected brain tumour. After having a child, her sense of
defect gave rise to illnesses localized in various systems of her
child's body. First as a woman Mrs Smith suffered from
Munchausen syndrome and then as a mother her illness took
the form of Munchausen by Proxy.

Mrs Smith had split aspects of her self-image and projected
them into the two children. Like her, both children had a
seizure disorder controlled with medication, but she saw the
older daughter as resilient and Mandy as succumbing to a
terrible disease process. This view of Mandy began in pregnancy when as a foetus she was associated with causing pre-
eclampsia and toxaemia (high blood pressure with risk of
seizures and stroke). Mrs Smith's pregnancy with Mandy and

its threat to her life recalled to mind the threat of uterine cancer and pregnancy experienced by her own mother when she unexpectedly conceived and carried Mrs Smith in her irradiated womb.

Mrs Smith's hopes for sympathy and nurturance from her husband were dashed. She found herself fundamentally disappointed by him. Her despair and disgust for him permeated their sexual life and led to his favouring their older daughter. Mrs Smith gradually withdrew from social life. She lost her old friends and became more absorbed with her own bodily concerns and presumed medical problems. She became intensely preoccupied with her children who learned to pay extremely close attention to her every word and glance. If Mrs Smith merely narrowed her eyes when they were bad, they would respond dramatically. She never had to yell at them to achieve compliance.

Around the time of her stillbirth, when Mandy was two, Mrs Smith became worried about eye problems and developed an idealizing relationship with her ophthalmologist. She constantly talked about him as her 'white knight', her rescuer. She became involved with him socially, and so did her father, who actually took to calling him 'son'. Towards the end of the marriage, mother finally became depressed, lost weight, and had more somatic complaints. Disliked by her father, and sexually and socially rejected by Mrs Smith, Mr Smith felt humiliated and despairing, but it was Mrs Smith who finally executed the separation, taking her children with her. This is when Mrs Smith developed a growing conviction that something was more seriously wrong with her insides – perhaps even cancer in her 'lower regions' like her mother had actually had.

Her tales of physical frailty and serious undiscovered illness played upon the sympathy of her doctors. She constantly felt they had not examined her well enough or cared for her sufficiently during these years of suffering and uncertainty – except for the ophthalmologist.

As her belief about an undiagnosed destructive process, possibly located in her sexual organs, grew and her despair of doctors discovering it heightened, she began to experience an increasing worry about something terribly wrong with her daughter. She described this shift in her focus away from her medical problems to those of her daughter in almost the same phrases as her medical preoccupations about herself. Her depression lifted as she began to feel that the hospital staff were rescuing her and her daughter from some dreadful and malignant process. When the hospital doctors finally confronted her with the presence of her own blood in her daughter's urine, Mrs Smith seemed more bewildered and hurt than angry. Once she had confessed, the intense medical drama abated, the temporary marital reconnection fell apart, and her mood shifted back into depression. Forced to give up her proxy link with her husband, the hospital, and all the medical attention, she exuded a forlorn, lost, empty feeling.

My hypothesis is that Mrs Smith's mother (Mandy's grandmother) repressed her fear and hatred of her foetus (Mrs Smith) because she felt so threatened by the uterine cancer diagnosis and so guilty about the effects on her foetus of the recommended treatment by irradiation. Faced with a dreadful choice between bringing her foetus to term and preserving her own life, Mandy's grandmother nobly chose motherhood. The dilemma got repeated in the next generation through repeated miscarriages and a stillbirth, and then a pregnancy in which mother (Mrs Smith) and foetus (Mandy) were both threatened with toxaemia and pre-eclampsia, and yet Mrs Smith, like her mother, chose motherhood. Mrs Smith's reproductive stresses and failures reinforced her fears of having something dangerous and malignant in her lower regions, representing her repressed fear of being a baby-murderer. The imagined malignancy within her body then got projected into her child's body, which she then manipulated through fabrication of illness to induce physicians to rescue, repair, and unwittingly mutilate her daughter as she basked in the medical limelight within her secure and idealizing hospital cocoon.

USING COUNTERTRANSFERENCE TO DETECT AND UNDERSTAND THE PROBLEM

My understanding of the deeper aspects of these cases has been informed by my countertransference reactions when interviewing and confronting these mothers and by my study of the reactions of healthcare professionals, protective service workers, and lawyers to whom I have consulted. The fact that a child's life is at stake raises

the level of my anxiety baseline. Civil or criminal charges are usually
pending and that means facing an adversarial legal process that
requires proof, not clinical impressions. But the signs and symptoms
of Munchausen by Proxy syndrome are unusual, unclear, and
complex. I have to deal with immense ambiguity and uncertainty. I
am consulting to physicians and nurses who are in a state of disbelief or perceived failure. I am confronting the highest values of the
caring profession and of motherhood. I am calling into question a
mother's use of the medical system. I may be accusing an apparently
good mother of monstrous child abuse. I may be recommending
taking a child away from a mother, which involves doing grave
psychological harm to a child and a mother in order to avoid a
greater supposed harm being done to the child by the mother.

I come to represent parent, doctor, and judge rolled into one.
For all these reasons, I find myself caught up in a situation rife
with powerful projective identifications. Almost every time, it's like
being in a mind-bending pressure cooker. I often have moments of
doubting my own sanity and judgement as the mother casts her
projective spell into me and I fall into her web of deceit. I may feel
guilty, forget the facts, and doubt my perceptions. I may wonder,
as the hospital staff do, how this person who seems so good and
caring and who loves her child so much could have done this
dreadful thing. Since she clearly loves and cares for the child so
much, how could I do such harm to her and her child by separating
them? If she denies her part in the story, her actions seem
unthinkable. If she partially confesses, but disavows any future risk
and promises never to do anything again, she may seem truly
repentant, and I may feel disarmed.

Example: Confrontation with a non-repentant mother

A single mother was in hospital accompanying her seriously
dehydrated son who was thought to have a stomach ulcer. He
had to have an indwelling intravenous catheter to carry
electrolytes, nutrients, and medicines directly into the blood-
stream. He had to be fed by a nasogastric tube that put some
food into his stomach and a J-tube that bypassed the stomach
and the duodenal sphincter to get the nutrition directly into the
jejunum. The child kept bleeding from the bowel. Repeated
invasive investigative procedures and surgeries to stop the

bleeding were to no avail. Eventually the staff suspected the problem was being created the same way it had been in the case I described earlier. The mother had been withdrawing the boy's blood from the valve in the indwelling intravenous catheter where medicines and nutrients were normally injected. She then injected his blood into his nasogastric and jejunal tubes to fake the appearance of massive bleeding. She denied the accusation against her and when her father heard it he was totally disbelieving and outraged. It fell to me to ask her about it and to explain that if she could acknowledge what she had done and tell her father about it, then the child could be left with him. If he still believed she wouldn't do such a thing, he couldn't protect the child from her. Then her child would have to go to a foster home.

Pinning me with a penetrating eye, she insisted, 'I didn't do it. You're trying to force me to confess to something I didn't do. You're going to injure my child and me forever, and YOU will have to live with the horrible guilt that you destroyed us for the rest of your life.' At that point I felt so monstrous and horribly guilty that I doubted my sanity and could hardly hold onto my knowledge, memory, and conviction. With the ambiguity of the situation, and with the superb medical staff so deeply divided, I worried that I might indeed be committing a horrible error and doing irreparable harm. In this particular case, the mother never did admit she had been doing it, but from the day she was separated from her son, all his signs and symptoms began to clear up, without any bleeding, seizures, gastrointestinal distress, or urinary problems. Referred by me to a woman therapist the mother developed a psychotic transference reaction. She became abusive and physically threatening towards the therapist, then accused her of abuse and physical assault, and finally terminated treatment.

In this case I went through agony and doubt, as usual. I always come close to believing the mother because she is so compelling. I become nearly crazy with uncertainty and guilt and worry that I might be wrong. Then I have the telltale experience. I suddenly shift in her eyes and mine from an idealized saviour to a monstrously dangerous, damaging abandoner, and murderer of the sacrosanct maternal–child bond. I experience a gut-wrenching, guilt-provoking internal attack. I feel torn up. I worry and I lose sleep. I have become the recipient of sudden massive projections. This is what everyone who is caught up in their web of projection and deceit goes through. And this countertransference sequence, in microcosmic detail, contains within it the best, most sensitive, and most accurate guide to what is going on inside the secret inner object worlds of these mothers.

THE WEIGHT OF THE PERSECUTORY OBJECT

The doctors and nurses are indeed given to feeling the full weight of the fear, bafflement, and confusion the mother feels when left alone with her child. But the bits of her experience are bizarrely multiplied and exaggerated as they reverberate among the staff. Through splitting and projection, concrete psychotic embodiments of fear proliferate among the staff like shifting patterns in a kaleidoscope. At the point of confrontation, robbed of the staff as an apparatus for deflecting her fear, the mother feels overwhelmed by her infant or child who suddenly becomes a huge monstrous thing – no longer a person – threatening the mother's sanity and life. She becomes flooded with annihilation anxiety.

The therapist or consultant working alone without a hospital staff has to be open to the full range of unbearable experiences in order to fully receive and contain the split-off aspects of the mother – both the loving, caring, nurturing, idealized aspects and the monstrous, claustrophobic, self-hating, rejecting, abandoning, murderous, and denigrated aspects. We have to learn to tolerate psychotic levels of affect and anxiety, a sense of catastrophe, and frightful levels of dread and doubt in order to contain and integrate what the mother is projecting into all the participants in her enactment. Only by bringing the parts of the woman together in relation to us can we hope to help her achieve integration and recovery of the missing maternal capacity.

Deep in their internal object worlds, the mothers have buried an aspect of their frightful relationships with their own mothers. This leaves them with a sense of the internal object and the self as bad, malignant, defective, dangerous, suffocating, abandoned, and rejected. The women and their infantile anxieties were not held and contained by their mothers. Moreover, they were recipients of intrusive projective identifications from their mothers, amplified by their own annihilation anxiety, panic, and terror emanating from rage and destructiveness at their uncontained and uncontaining mothers. The mother's father may have been overly distant, absent, or narcissistically overly close. Her parents' relationship may have been close or distant. Whether the mother's father mitigated or magnified what went on, both as an independently functioning parent and as the partner of his wife, the disturbed internal object relationships always centre on the mother–child relationship.

As a consultant given authority, my decision to rupture the mother–child relationship, my responsibility for risking psychological damage to the child and mother, and my guilt comprise a scenario that re-enacts precisely the compulsive drama of unmanageable risk and annihilation that the mother so deeply fears and denies. When I move towards attributing responsibility to the mother for her monstrous acts, she then gets close to unbearable awareness of her internal world and its fears of attack and loss, and she moves immediately into a redoubled state of offence through projective identification. She attacks by reprojecting these mother-murdering, child-murdering, parent–child-destroying impulses into me. She accuses me of all the heinous crimes that she cannot tolerate in herself – psychological crimes by and against her parents, experienced and repressed by her since childhood.

The psychological disaster these mothers are trying to avoid is one of sliding down the slippery slope into the psychotic claustrum (Meltzer 1992) where they are trapped alone with an ill child totally dependent on them for care. They are phobic of this terrifying situation. This is the situation created by separation from spouse, alienation from family, or discharge from the hospital. The mother comes face-to-face with the monstrous, murderous part of herself as she feels simultaneously overwhelmed and persecuted by the child from the outside and overwhelmed, attacked, and panicked from the inside. Years of individual psychotherapy are needed to help the mother recognize her persecutory objects as internal to her self, and then to tolerate, contain, and eventually detoxify them.

REFERENCES

Asher, R. (1951). Munchausen syndrome. *Lancet*, i: 339–341.

Bion, W. (1967). Differentiation of the psychotic from the non-psychotic personalities. In *Second Thoughts*, Marsfield Library, pp. 43–64. London: Karnac Books.

Greenacre, P. (1958). The relationship of the imposter to the artist. *Psychoanalytic Quarterly* 27: 359–382.

Jureidini, J. (1993). Obstetric factitious disorder and Munchausen syndrome by Proxy. *The Journal of Mental Disease*, 181(2): 135–137.

Meadow, R. (1988). Munchausen syndrome by proxy: The hinterland of child abuse. *Lancet* ii: 343–345.

Meloy, R. (1988). *Psychopathic Minds. Origins, Dynamics and Treatment.* Northvale, NJ: Jason Aronson.

Meltzer, D. (1992). *The Claustrum: An Investigation of Claustrophobic Phenomena.* Oxford, UK: The Clunie Press for the Roland Harris Education Trust, No. 15.

Rosenberg, D. (1987). Web of deceit: A literature review of Munchausen syndrome by proxy. *Child Abuse and Neglect*, 11: 547–563.

Schreier, H. and Libow, J. (1993). *Hurting for Love: Munchausen by Proxy Syndrome.* New York: The Guilford Press.

Part 2

The practice of detoxifying persecutory objects in assessment, psychotherapy, and consultation

Chapter 7

Working with murderous projection and internal mutilation

Michael Kaufman, MA, LPC

The Oedipal myth is not only a tale of incest acted out by a son towards his mother but also one of a father's hatred and murderousness towards an infant, and a mother's complicity (Abse 1987, Fairbairn 1944, Scharff 1992). From this point of view, Sophocles' Oedipus trilogy illustrates the transmission of trauma from Laius and Jocasta to their son Oedipus. An internal bond to a persecuting object is established in the child, and it determines the nature of significant adult relationships. To illustrate this, I will describe my work with a woman whose persecutory object had profound effects on the transference and countertransference. Therapy focused on transforming her persecutory object and the bonds that tied her to it.

A WOMAN WHO RECEIVED MURDEROUS PROJECTIONS

The patient is a middle-aged woman I will call Lin. She was suffering from anxiety with dizziness, vertigo, and fainting; fears of rape and murder; and depression with social isolation, insomnia, loss of appetite, feelings of worthlessness, and guilt over the death of her late husband. She also showed startle reactions and hyper-vigilance; constant apologizing; manic pressured speech; and over-identification with damaged people and animals.

One of Lin's friends sent her to me. He said that her second husband had died recently, and now her therapy had fallen apart at the worst time, leaving her in a precarious state. He said Lin's situation was desperate. When Lin called, I was so haunted by the urgent quality in her voice that I adjusted my schedule so I could see her within 24 hours.

THE FIRST SESSION: PRESSURED AND DESPERATE

The next morning I went to the waiting room to find my new patient standing there waiting for me. I could immediately sense that she was too anxious to sit down. A woman of about 50, she wore no make-up and had colourless grey-blond hair. There was an apparitional quality about her, as if she could not allow herself to be physically or psychologically present in the room. She wore blue jeans and layers of shirts that concealed her figure.

Once inside my office, Lin announced that she was not doing well. She told me that her husband had recently been injured in a car accident and had died in the hospital. To make matters worse, this was the second time she had lost a husband. Her first husband, she reported, had been murdered. She believed that her second husband's death had been her fault. I sought clarification on this point and learned that she blamed herself for not doing enough for her husband while he was under the hospital's care, even though she had gone to extraordinary lengths to provide for him.

Lin's speech was pressured and desperate. Her body twitched restlessly. She kept dropping her water-bottle and her car keys, and each occurrence seemed to startle her anew. As she spoke, she frequently craned her neck in a manner that never seemed to relieve her tension. She spoke in one continuous sentence, allowing few openings for a comment from me and certainly no dialogue. Nevertheless, I felt that my presence as a witness was important to her and my attention as a listener created order and meaning for her in the midst of her flooded universe. Only at the end of the session did she finally stop to ask me what I thought.

I learned in this first session how much guilt and blame Lin felt for all the harm that had befallen those who were close to her. After describing the deaths of her two husbands, she described the failure of her previous therapy, which had ended badly after five years. She felt that the multiple traumas of her life had overwhelmed and damaged her therapist, and now she felt abandoned, rejected, confused, and overwhelmed by anxiety and despair. When I managed a brief comment about how much she had suffered, she immediately drowned me out by telling me instead how much her mother had suffered both as a child and as an adult. Lin also informed me that she herself was childless, and that she had had eight miscarriages. Her misery seemed unending and her narrative uninterruptible, killing off any therapeutic dialogue. I wondered how else murder might be represented in the therapeutic relationship. At the conclusion of the session I briefly addressed her sense of guilt over her husbands and her therapist, linking it to her feeling that she had not taken care of her mother adequately, even though she might not be solely responsible for the misfortune that befell her and her loved ones. After my comment, Lin felt momentary relief, but she soon experienced a rush of guilt at the thought that someone else might be to blame.

Background

Lin said that her father was a high-ranking military officer involved in covert operations connected with protecting the country's interests overseas. She had heard that his unit identified dangerous enemies, gathered information about their habits, and carried out planned assassinations. My reaction to this information was to wonder if I was placing myself in a dangerous situation by knowing too much. Lin grew up in the Far East, the second child of four and the only daughter. Her father was extremely possessive of her love and showered her with jewellery and dresses from childhood onwards. When she reached puberty she began to be interested in boys. In high school, she met a boy, and she told her father she wanted to go out with him. Her father flew into a rage. He went over to the boy's house, screamed at him, and threatened his family. This experience ended Lin's wish to date.

Lin's mother was a self-indulgent military dependent who idealized her husband and his line of work and basked in the glory of his position. She was openly jealous when he favoured Lin, their beautiful only daughter. She left Lin to take care of the house and look after her brothers, while she maintained her social position in the overseas community as the wife of a powerful man. Repeatedly, Lin was told by her mother that she would make a terrible mother.

Lin applied for and received a scholarship to an American college and left home to study in the United States, much to the satisfaction of her mother who got rid of a hated rival. At college on the West Coast, a law student attached himself to her and soon she married him, interrupting her dream of returning to Asia to work with refugee children.

Eight months later her husband was murdered in his motel room while he was out of town on an internship. Perhaps he surprised a robber, perhaps it was a case of mistaken identity, but the killer was not found and the crime has remained unsolved. Lin has fantasies that her father had her husband murdered.

Lin moved to the East Coast and transferred to the college where her first year room-mate was now studying. While at this school another graduate student attached himself to her obsessively. 'He wouldn't leave me,' she said, 'and so eventually I married him. He wanted that. I knew it would be bad when he screamed at me just because one of the papers I wrote for him had a couple of errors in the footnotes. But I didn't say a word. I retyped the whole paper and that was before there were word processors. I did it perfectly.'

Lin worked tirelessly to promote her husband's career, although he was seldom satisfied with her efforts. She felt that she was a bad and inadequate wife. She regarded her series of miscarriages as further proof of her badness and murderousness. His death during trauma surgery for injuries received in a car accident precipitated her breakdown. She was incapacitated by guilt, anxiety, and depression. She kept going over the details of that husband's death to confirm or rid herself of the fantasy that her father might have arranged to do away with her second husband as well.

PERSECUTORY OBJECTS IN EARLY DREAM MATERIAL

The following dreams from the first year of three-times-a-week therapy provide insight into Lin's inner world of persecutory objects tied to her tortured, wounded self.

Dream 1 (second week of therapy). A toddler is tied by a rope to the bumper of a car and dragged along because she refuses to get in. A man is driving the car. A woman is riding in the car and she wouldn't do anything to help the child. Lin picks up the child and unties her. The child is damaged.

Dream 2 (fourth week of therapy). Lin goes to the dentist. The dentist drills a molar, exposing a deep cavernous pit.

Dream 3 (eighth month of therapy). A man puts his arm around Lin's waist. He has a crushing grip. She screams in pain. The man is smiling as if he were helping and supporting her.

Dream 4 (ninth month of therapy). Lin is in an auditorium with another woman. Some brutal males come in. They are communists like Stalin. A man who is a monster puts his hand under Lin's chin, forcing her to look into his face. The women attempt to leave, but are accosted when no one comes to pick them up. Lin and another woman hide in the women's restroom, where they discover another woman who has been attacked. She cannot stand upright and her eyes are vacuous, like the walking dead.

These four dreams provide a framework for understanding the inner world of the self and its persecutory objects in a patient whose parent was trained to eliminate enemies of the nation. Lin's history and her dream life demonstrate the impact of a murderous, violent object that has been introjected during development. Confusion results when murderous phantasies arising from Lin's own sadism are coloured by her real experiences of the sadism of her father. This confusion is mirrored in my own countertransference feelings. I am aware of a reluctance to describe specific reactions to the case, which run in parallel to Lin's reluctance to speak of her father. I can remember many nights when I left my office and looked up and down the street, apprehensive of the cars that were driving by or were parked at the kerb. At times it felt as if I were living in a *film noir*. The thought that I too could be knocked off and that the crime would be unsolved was often in my mind – and still is from time to time, but with less intensity.

In the first dream, the self is represented by the toddler who has been damaged by a cruel persecuting man. The self is tied to this persecuting object that controls her aggressive drive (represented by the man who drives her car) and thus compromises her development. The self is unprotected by the maternal figure in this dream who cannot help her to integrate her drives in a mature way. In this dream, Lin was bringing her damaged self into therapy. But she was unable to discuss or associate to the dream. The very act of articulating any of these early dreams flooded her with anxiety, overwhelmed her with despair, and led to psychosomatic reactions that included vertigo. At the beginning of treatment she could not utter the word 'father' at all, and the one time I said 'father', she nearly fainted from fright and panic, as if she had been internally attacked by a murderous object.

The second early dream captures the way in which the therapy is exposing Lin's psychotic depression, represented by the cavernous pit in the molar. This depression had been covered over by her hypomanic activities in the name of her husband's career, her depression having meant that she could not allow herself to experience her own ambition or self-interest.

The third and fourth dreams emphasize the sexually sadistic aspect of Lin's persecuting objects that accost, stimulate, and terrify the self. In the third dream, the self is held in the grip of this object, just as in the first dream it had been tied to this object by a rope. This internal object relation left Lin in a state of heightened vigilance and fear. For three and a half years she was unable to look at the couch in my office since it implied sex and murder to her.

EARLY CONTAINMENT OF PERSECUTORY ANXIETY

Therapy for a woman living with this level of persecutory anxiety needs to address her fears and create a sense of safety. Simultaneously, the therapist must focus on her sense that she does not deserve to feel better, an issue of diminished self-entitlement. Therapy must provide a container that is not overwhelmed by the patient's anxiety and persecutory terror (Bion 1970). A tie to a dependable object must be developed through repeated good-enough experiences within the therapeutic context (Winnicott 1971).

The first thing I did to contain Lin's anxiety was to help her tie her fragmented experiences together to create some meaning and order. In a calm and gentle voice I would say, 'These are feelings that have been inside of you for all of your life but you never knew this – now we are working at getting them out of you. You have never had a real sense of yourself – and now we are working at finding that self. You never felt the right to exist for yourself – and now you are claiming that right.'

Especially in the beginning, it was critical to offer myself as a dependable object both within and outside of the therapeutic hour. I gave Lin permission to telephone me when she felt flooded with anxiety. I undertook to tolerate my resentment and find the patience to be there for her when she was fragmenting from anxiety and her ego was disintegrating. It was essential to respond to the needs and limitations of Lin's terrorized self in this way. I acted as an auxiliary part of her ego during these calls, remaining a good object with the capacity to think when she could not.

The most demanding aspect of containment, however, has been the task of managing and metabolizing the intense countertransference engendered by working with Lin. From the beginning, it was necessary to hold onto hope in sessions in which Lin was filled with despair. I had to believe that we could survive the attacks of her murderous objects. This meant that I had to contain my own paranoia and believe that it was not likely that anyone was going to kill me. I was also challenged by feelings of frustration and impatience, as I worked at listening and responding emotionally even while feeling shut out hour after hour. Such feelings caused me to feel hostile at times, thus compromising my capacity to function in a helpful manner. I had to work hard to detoxify my own identifications with the patient's persecutory objects so as not to react with sadistic sarcasm.

My reactions to Lin's violent objects presented a special challenge. The anxiety that these objects created in me threatened the therapy by eroding the boundary between my inner and outer reality. At such times, I was in danger of losing my capacity to think about Lin's experience. This could have led to a dead end such as had occurred in her first therapy. Lin might have again found herself in the position of having to take care of her therapist from a false-self position, burdening her with anxiety and guilt, and robbing her of the experience of a dependable object that was available for introjection.

Providing a containing presence for Lin also meant not blocking her out defensively or becoming bored to death when I was subjected to her manic run-on speech. To remain present as a thinking and concerned therapist, I had to draw on my sheer will to understand. To cope with my aggression, I thought of myself as asserting my curiosity, my 'epistemophilic instinct' (Freud 1909, p. 245; Klein 1928, pp. 190–191). Only in this way could I find something in me that felt alive, that could go on being despite the onslaught of her verbal violence. Most sessions were made up of one run-on paragraph with a slight pause in the last few minutes preceded by the question, 'What do you think?' It seemed that making a statement about the meaning of what Lin had brought in was essential, but it took a lot of patience to wait for an opening. I was helped to understand this when Lin told me, 'In my family you did not speak when my father was around. Only my father did and he only shouted.' I noted her use of the pronoun 'you' meaning everyone, but it felt as if she meant that I should not speak around her when she was going on like her father.

SIGNS OF TRANSFORMATION

Dream 5 (after three years of therapy). Lin is with a group of children who are in hiding in a house. They are hiding from men who would torture them to death. Horrible native men come, with instruments of torture. On the wall, she taps out a message for help, but no help comes. The children are tortured to death. Watching this she screams and cries.

This dream marks a major transformation in Lin's inner world. While the horrible objects continue to persecute the self, Lin is now beginning to become capable of communicating her terrifying experience. In this dream, the communication is not yet verbal, but it is in a language of tapping like Morse code, which indicates a movement towards thinking in words and towards reciprocal dialogue. Lin is not as strongly identified with the victim-self represented by the children. By turning, even in despair, towards someone who might hear her on the other side of the wall, she is developing a potential psychic space in which she hopes to find a helpful other with whom she can communicate. After this dream, Lin's run-on monologues began to give way to reciprocal exchanges with me. I was now able to address her fear that I would not respond to her cries for help. I could now refer to the ways in which her experiences in therapy were different from her experiences in childhood and adult life.

As Lin became more capable of representing her trauma, she began to share with me some of the thinking function that I had been carrying for her. She began to metabolize her destructive and despairing emotions and to link symptoms, feelings, and experiences. Slowly, she began to translate her tapping language into words, so that there could be a shared experience and a therapeutic dialogue, rather than the monologue that attempted murder of my mind, a way of reversing and yet repeating her perceptions of her terrified childhood. Aspects of her damaged and wounded self shown in extreme feelings of worthlessness and guilt were also modified through this new kind of communication. I provided support for her trying the new behaviours that were always accompanied by anxiety episodes. When these changes occurred I would acknowledge them and support Lin's effort to take into her mind an expanded and more vital view of herself. The work of understanding continued and was not destroyed by bad objects.

After this dream, many things now could be put into words. The madness of the patient and her family – their rage and their craziness – had to be named repeatedly. Lin's fear that I would be assassinated by her real father or by her murderous internal objects had to be named and explained. In a family where murder was a real possibility and was sanctioned as a valuable, professional activity for the good of the country, the real must be named and its horror acknowledged. Psychological death leaves the possibility of recovery, but physical death ends it.

One day my car was not in its usual parking space. Lin came into my office and in a startled voice said, 'Oh! you are alive. Thank goodness.'

This comment led usefully to thinking about the meaning of this fantasy that I would not be there, as a transference to me dictated by her history and her inner world. This piece of work in the transference led to a significant modification of her murderous internal objects and reduction in the projection of those objects into the environment. Her symptoms – flooding of anxiety with dizziness, vertigo, and fainting; paranoia about rape and murder; despair and depression; insomnia; loss of appetite; extreme dependency on the shadow of the object (her dead husband); social isolation; feelings of worthlessness and guilt; startle reactions and hypervigilance; constant apologizing; manic pressured speech; and over-identification with damaged people and animals – all improved. Lin's persecutory objects were gradually losing their toxicity.

EVIDENCE OF DETOXIFICATION (AFTER THREE AND A HALF YEARS OF THERAPY)

The following clinical material from consecutive sessions in one week illustrates Lin's growing ability to think about herself with less interference from internal persecution.

From session 1

Lin says, 'I had a long, terrifying dream last night. There are boxes of rope – like vipers, coiled fibres and strands that are interwoven. It is very scary. It is all down in the basement – in the dark recesses of my mind. This is part of not being able to breathe. I don't mean to exaggerate, but it was like enslavement in my family. They had us so confused. They made knots out of our lives. The liberty I now have for myself, the sanction to develop myself, and connect up parts of myself, is such a contrast to how we grew up.'

There is a silence of about 30 seconds. I notice that this is the first silence in three and a half years.

Lin continues, 'My parents were so . . . awful . . . it makes me so ill. None of us was allowed to have freedom. It really was a prison. It was always like this on my father's side. His mother married a brute who was like her father. Her sister married another monster who beat my male cousins. On my mother's side, her sister married a pig who was after the daughters, and she tried to kill herself. My mother is a mean person, a bad person. I acknowledge it more and more. It is one heck of a screwed-up group of people.'

There is another silence, perhaps 40 seconds.

Lin says, 'I'm not pleased at seeing the wicked mother.'

I say, 'Are you mad at me for helping you to see this?'

Lin says, 'I'm sorry. Maybe I can salvage something good. What is productive about this?'

Noticing that Lin looks much more together, even saner today, I say, 'Your mind won't feel so persecuting to you and you won't feel that you are persecuting me so much.'

Lin replies, 'You said if I can see her more realistically I won't feel so destructive. I see the whole family as very extreme, perverted. But how do you know I'm sane?' Lin returns to the topic of her dream. 'In the dream I am cleaning out the basement of our house. I'm in the basement. Cleaning and clearing out the basement. I come across nice fabric with figures on it – Chinese babies – a tapestry with cushioning to it. It is soft. I give it to a Chinese woman and she puts it on her abdomen. It is like a pregnancy. A mean and vicious man appears. He yells savagely, "No, no!" about there being a baby. I find jewelled hair combs, ornaments, and pins for a woman's hair. They are beautiful. I give them to my sister. She rejects them. Then there are the four boxes of fibrous rope, thick rope that had been used. I turn to get help. I am frightened because I didn't know if the woman and the baby were alive. I ask my friend Tom for help. He is like you – he's helped sort things out for me. His wife was jealous of that. Tom is a kind, sweet person, but masculine.'

This dream shows the persistence of her fears of attack and death, but they are now in a form she can describe – attack against a vulnerable woman, rejection of feminine beauty, and ropes for binding her and keeping her in place. For the first time she includes a helpful figure, Tom, a good man who might help her despite the jealousy of the avenging woman. This figure stands for the therapist in the positive paternal transference.

Session 2

Lin begins, 'I had nightmares again last night. I am in the ladies' restroom and men come in. I had another dream. People are dying. I feel targeted, pursued, abused, and battered. The wind squalls.' (Outside the wind is actually howling.) 'I haven't been afraid of the weather. It is all so upsetting. It all feels so violent. I would rather be with a woman therapist. It all seems so venomous. I try to think of something good. You said the ropes could become something positive, providing connections. I feel so threatened. I have no mother.

'I thought my cousin wasn't beaten and oppressed like her brothers who as kids were running for her Dad, who was a heroin dealer. A real pillar of the community! But then she married an abusive man just like him. She had to leave him in the middle of the night with her child, her purse, and her dog. All these mothers knew full well what was going on and did nothing to intervene. My mother worked in tandem with my father to keep us in their prison. There was nobody to help. It is so sad. As you said, I have to build an infrastructure to replace all this so that I can console myself.'

I say, 'You are telling me about how vulnerable and unprotected you feel.'

Lin says, 'More than that, I feel invaded and abused. I feel victimized. I don't like that word. These feelings are reminiscent of my childhood.'

I say, 'Not just reminiscent, your feelings *are* your memories and they re-create your childhood all the time.'

Lin insists, 'I never wanted to feel this. The anniversary of my husband's death is coming up – four years. I can't believe it. I'm still attached to him. It wasn't a murder or a suicide. Do you think I enabled him to prey on me?'

I reply, 'He had a violent temper and he expressed it in lots of places in his life.'

Lin says, 'He did. I hope he has found some peace. What if I give myself recognition for constructive things I did? I know I was critical to my husband's functioning. This is something I can't say about my father. My husband wanted to be a good person, though he had a brutal side. I stayed in that relationship and it wasn't good for me. I'm still dominated by his presence in another way. I'm trying to establish a personhood. I'm going through the debris to get an area that is clear. It's like you said, I'm going through my house and clearing some space. Therapy is the first step.

'I don't know why I still long for a mother, given how terrible mine was. I always wanted to help poor children, refugees. That's a way to help myself. Maybe it was a greedy need, but like you said, I could have chosen a less noble way. And I supported my husband 100%. But what have I done lately?' She laughs. 'I accept more nurturing and support from you now.'

There is another silence.

'I knew it was important for me to get here today. I'm sorry to burden you with so much. Anyway I think that my security and safety with you has to do with establishing a feminine identity. There I am in the ladies' room! That's my fear – if I'm identified. This is hard to tell you. It's shame about being a woman. I'd rather tell a woman that.'

In this session, Lin moves into another important development. She begins to rehabilitate a maternal object that could be associated with a positive identification of herself as a woman. Having worked through the transference to me as the potentially murderous father who has to be shut out, and then admitting me as a helpful man, she now arrives at the possibility of telling me things she prefers to tell a woman. She longs for the missing maternal object and begins to find it in me despite my gender.

Session 3

Lin complains, 'My muscles are so contracted that I am sore all over. I want you to be a woman. I know this is about forming a feminine view of myself.

'I had an exhausting dream. Part of the dream is in daylight and part in the dark. I am annihilating Coke bottles – throwing them into a coliseum-like pit. Throwing them as brutally as possible. There is a spray of glass with a prism-like effect – all the colours are visible. I start smashing then while it's daylight. Then it's dark, and I'm still destroying. I finally leave and go back to my car, but it's not my own car, it's my husband's Chevy Blazer.'

Laughing, she begins to associate to her dream, 'Maybe I ran out of energy or ammunition. My husband never actually had a Chevy. I think of the Landrover we had for a long time until he totalled it. He had several accidents, forcing this other car off the road and blaming the other driver but my husband was charged. What was so sick about our relationship is that I was the one who met with these people and gave them the money. He used to get speeding tickets. I took care of them. I took care of everything for him. There is so much. I don't want to go into his violence – no, *my* violence.'

I say, 'You're sorting out whose violence it is, and how much of it is yours. Violence in a dream is at a different level of destruction than actual accidents, speeding tickets, and rages.'

Lin says, 'Once he was with one of his friends rushing off to a football game. He almost ran me over. He had to stop and check me, and he was enraged he would miss the kick-off. I wasn't in a rage, but his friend was. I just said it was my fault that I didn't get out of the way fast enough, but his friend was so mad at my husband that he could never be around him again. Another time he backed into my car when it was standing still. He was full of rage, but, yes, I have plenty of my own rage.

'Anyway, in the dream I go back to the Blazer and the police arrest me. I've done a terrible thing. There is mayhem. There has been so much destruction.

'It's *my* dream, not my husband's. These are parts of me. Those Coke bottles. Those bottles are like an icon of my generation. The bottles are like a woman's figure. My husband would drink Coke only from those bottles. It was incumbent on me to find those bottles. I had to go scour the town. When they stopped using them, I had to search for them for the sake of his sanity.' She laughs. 'My sanity. It was a symbol. He would get angry and blame me if I couldn't find them. There were cases of these bottles. I'm smashing these bottles.'

I say, 'You're helping us to break into these images and get at their meaning.'

Lin was also breaking up the way she let herself be used as her husband's denigrated object.

Lin says, 'I was trying to oblige, that is what a good wife does. Right. He never appreciated what I did. He was so angry. I don't have him to express my anger now.'

I ask, 'Tell me more about the bottles you're smashing.'

Lin says, 'My husband wanted to suck on the bottles. I think of the shape, shame, and anger. The glass reflects images and parts of myself. Mirrors are made of glass and I have not wanted to look in the mirror. Literally and figuratively. Breaking it down into its basic components, glass is made of sand, which comes from the ocean. Visceral parts, deep parts, un-industrialized countries – you need power to bring it all together. I want some sense of power in what happens to me. I always think of helping people less able than me. I want to help poor children. This is hard to say. I have never experienced innocence.'

One day, talking about her house, Lin reported that she was afraid that bats would get into her attic. I interpreted that her sexual feelings frightened her and this interfered with her capacity to think. She replied lightly, 'So, I get it. If I allow myself to feel sexual I won't have bats in my belfry.' The reduction in the sense of persecution creates space for thinking, room for sexual and humorous thoughts.

RECLAIMING THE SELF FROM THE VIOLENT OBJECT

In these sessions, Lin is no longer overwhelmed as she once was by anxiety and depression. She is now able to think about her inner world and separate what happens inside her from what happens outside. This could not occur until there had been a reduction in her internal sense of persecution. Murderous persecutory objects have been modified so that the sense of self can now take in nourishment in therapy and in her life. Unlike Oedipus, who was unable to modify his inner destructiveness, Lin is transforming her inner landscape into one in which new life can take hold.

Years of terror induced Lin's violent and stimulating internal objects. The toxicity of these objects has been reduced to the point that Lin can now think about her internal world and experience her sexuality without being overwhelmed with fear. While this therapy is far from over, there have been many levels of change in Lin, both in her sense of self and in her objects. Like Lin, I have been changed by working with these intensely persecutory objects. I, too, have had to sort out the real dangers from my countertransference fantasies.

Lin gives a vivid demonstration of the impact of the persecutory object on her life. This object seeks expression in her bodily symptoms, her view of herself as deserving victim and guilty perpetrator, and in the unravelling of her relationships in her intimate life and in her previous therapy. The psychological holding and containment provided in the countertransference survived Lin's attack and provided the necessary condition in which she could come to terms with her history and her self. She has made great progress in detoxifying her objects and reclaiming her self.

Fairbairn (1944) wrote that the story of Oedipus was not centrally explained by the boy's urge to murder his father and replace his mother being natural consequences of the infantile neurosis. The enactment of his Oedipal wishes has to be set in the context of his suffering during the first act of that mythic family's drama. Long before Oedipus murders his father, his father tries to murder him as an infant, his mother complies with his rejection and abuse, and he is abandoned, maimed, and left on the hillside to die. Lin's experience of her father as aggressive and domineering was augmented by awareness of his professional capacity for skilfully planned assassinations. She experienced her mother assassinating her self-esteem as a woman by contemptuously telling her she would be a bad mother, while regarding Lin's father's work as good. It is the traumatic early deprivation that sets the stage for frightened, murderous internal object relations such as Lin harbours.

What does a child do who is bereft of a loving internal couple, inhabited only by the murderous couple that Oedipus and Lin share? Children cannot bear to think that their parents are bad. Lin unconsciously does the only sensible thing she can do as long as she is dependent. She decrees that the parents are good, and she is bad. Then she has the hope that if only she can be good, the parents will become good to her. She has no choice. At least if she makes them good in her eyes, there is the hope she can please them and gain love. However, if the child's world is bad, '[T]he only prospect is one of death and destruction' (Fairbairn 1943, pp. 66–67). If the parents are bad, she lives in a universe of bad objects, hopeless about being treated with love and feeling afraid of destruction.

Lin began her treatment with a history of dependent, abusive relationships. She soured her previous therapies because of her adherence to persecuting objects, an addiction so severe that fantasies of murder permeated both the transference and countertransference. The security of the therapeutic relationship yielded a steady erosion of the fixed relationship between anti-libidinal self and object, between internal saboteur and persecuting object, and a slow transformation of the murderous paternal object, then of the compliant and contemptuous maternal object. Finally, Lin began to find a new object in the therapist and to find herself as a woman who is not, in her own mind, murderous.

REFERENCES

Abse, D. W. (1987). *Hysteria and Related Mental Disorders: An Approach to Psychological Medicine*. Bristol, UK: Wright.

Bion, W. (1970). *Attention and Interpretation*. London: Tavistock.

Fairbairn, W. R. D. (1943). The repression and return of bad objects with special reference to the 'War Neuroses'. In *Psychoanalytic Studies of the Personality*, pp. 59–81. London: Tavistock, 1952.

—— (1944). Endopsychic structure considered in terms of object-relationships. In *Psychoanalytic Studies of the Personality*, pp. 82–136. London: Tavistock, 1952.

Freud, S. (1909). Notes upon a case of obsessional neuroses. *Standard Edition*, 10: 153–257.

Klein, M. (1928). Early stages of the Oedipus conflict. In *Love, Guilt and Reparation and Other Works 1921–1945*, pp. 186–198. London: Hogarth Press and the Institute of Psycho-Analysis, 1975.

Scharff, D. E. (1992). *Refinding the Object and Reclaiming the Self*. Northvale, NJ: Jason Aronson.

Winnicott, D. W. (1971). The use of an object and relating through identifications. In *Playing and Reality*, pp. 86–94. London: Penguin.

Chapter 8

Treating persecutory anxiety in an adolescent boy

Leslie Johnson, PhD, LPC

The scene opens in a hospital room, where a teenage boy, his head bandaged, tosses in bed unable to sleep. His attention is drawn to the faintest of sounds – soft labial bloops and bleeps that grow louder and more rhythmic. Then, over the edge of the bed sheet, two toy cars and a tiny teddy bear come marching towards him: toys on parade. Fascinated, the boy reaches out to them, only to have them disappear, together with the music. Suddenly the silence is rocked by thunderous rhythmic noises. The toys are marching back, having grown to monstrous size. They break down the walls, burst through the door, wreaking havoc. Worst of all is the teddy bear: It crashes into the room, rears up against the ceiling, and then literally begins to crack up. Cracks streak across its eyes, face, and body. White liquid spills from the cracks and then the giant teddy falls to pieces, milky liquid gushing forth. Swept off the bed by the torrent, the boy cuts his foot on a splinter of glass. Instantly, the sight of blood restores the toys to nursery size. 'Ooooow!' they whimper as the scene ends, 'that huuuurts!'

This remarkable scene, drawn to my attention by a teenage patient, comes from *Akira*, a classic Japanese film that tells the story of a schizophrenic breakdown cloaked in the guise of science fiction. It focuses on the quintessentially trusty transitional object (Winnicott 1958) but turns into a rogue teddy bear. What does it mean when the transitional object of comfort cracks up and goes on a rampage? What happens to a person when the teddy bear becomes a persecutory object? What has gone wrong in the sphere of early dyadic relations if there is no internal teddy-bear object available for soothing and falling asleep? Clinically speaking, how is one to treat a person who lacks an internalized self-soothing object, so that the transference is inevitably experienced as persecutory?

These are the kinds of questions that have arisen for me in the treatment of Marty, the adolescent patient who introduced me to *Akira*. None of these questions occurred to me when I began to treat him, but eventually I realized that the film, and in particular the scene of the rogue teddy bear, uncannily foreshadowed the development of the therapeutic process over the next two and a quarter years. With Marty, I was to suffer the vicissitudes of his persecutory object before I could begin to think about it. I learned about Marty's persecutory object by becoming it, and by feeling persecuted by it.

I will present the treatment of Marty as it has unfolded in five phases distinguished by shifts in the transference and countertransference. Following this clinical section, I discuss issues of aetiology, the conceptualization of Marty's persecutory object, and a summary of the steps I have taken to detoxify it. A postscript provides an update on the case.

A BOY WITH PERSECUTORY ACOUSTIC OBJECTS

Marty is the only child of a Jewish couple. His mother, herself the only child of Jewish refugees from Italy, trained as a musician but never had a career. Marty's father, a physician, grew up in an Orthodox Jewish family where he felt oppressed by his father. Marty came to therapy at their insistence. He was musical and highly intelligent, but his grades were slipping, he was depressed, had no friends, and had given up swimming at which he was outstanding. His parents worried that all this would damage his college prospects. Marty's mother obsessed about her son's insomnia. She complained that he had never liked to sleep, even as a baby, and she described futile strategies, such as stroking his eyelids, to put him to sleep.

Anxious about being pregnant with a boy, Marty's mother had bathed him *in utero* in classical music. After his birth, she continued to swathe him in a surround of voice and music. Marty, who claims to remember his first year of life, reports that she always read to him while he played, and that he developed a 'dual-track' capacity to 'hear every word' while attending to his own business.

Father, devoted to his profession, was more than typically absent, leaving mother and son inseparable. Mother breast-fed Marty until he was two and a half. Weaning was a nightmare, with Marty ever clamouring for a feed and pounding on the door behind which she would barricade herself. Toilet training followed shortly thereafter.

FIRST TREATMENT PHASE (MONTHS 1–9): CONTROLLING THE THREATENING THERAPIST

Marty struck me as both babyish and overbearingly arrogant. Already a handsome 14-year-old who promised to be tall and well-built, he nevertheless reminded me of Baby Huey. His head seemed too heavy for his neck, and he had the habit of letting it fall onto the back pillow or arm of the sofa. His face seemed pasty-puffy and too soft, despite his good looks, while for all his athleticism his body seemed floppy and flaccid.

During the first treatment phase a pattern emerged that prevailed for about nine months. Marty would come in, flop onto the couch, yawn, and force himself to speak. He had three themes: cartoons, computer games, and especially music. These were not, however, topics for conversation. They were more like occasions for masturbatory performance. Thus, hands held out in front of him, he would pantomime computer games or imitate the keyboard virtuosity of his rock heroes. His music invaded my mind, and I grew to hate it. I felt excluded and my mind became numb. When Marty condescended to speak of something else, he showed withering contempt for peers, teachers, everyone in the world. Certain that this included me, I felt incompetent, stupid, and stultified.

As much as I felt persecuted by these hours with Marty, they also persecuted him. His need to control the sessions was fuelled by deep uneasiness in my presence. Often he expressed suspicion about female authority figures and sometimes he became paranoid. Once he could not refrain from opening the drawer of the table beside my chair, to be sure there was no microphone inside. Sometimes he asked me to shut the blinds completely. Only once did he allow me to see him cry as he recalled the death of a pet. I felt a welcome surge of empathy – only to have it thrown back in my face.

'Imagine,' he blurted out, 'how you would feel if this were a cage and some giant eye or finger were poking in at your window?' I was appalled by the perception of our relationship implied by this grotesque image, his sense of the huge disparity in our size, and the magnitude of the threat I seemed to pose for him. For all my good intentions, Marty suffered a totally persecutory transference – to my furniture, to my room, to me.

I had been working too actively, pressing him to be, not my teddy bear exactly, but a fantasy patient who would comply and make me feel helpful. My mind, with its structured conscious and unconscious systems, was for Marty an invasive object, just as his mother's had been in his infancy, and he could scarcely tolerate its presence or pressure. He gave me a glimpse of his baby self, cowering like a tiny bird with a giant maternal Cyclops at the window. I was chastened by this image, and began to detoxify the maternal object by letting him find his own way to use me.

SECOND TREATMENT PHASE: WAKING UP (MONTHS 10–20)

The onset of the second treatment phase was marked by an unprecedented event: Marty asked me to see *Akira*. Astonishing as this now seems to me, I got very little out of it at first. It seemed to be just another cartoon, only more manic and violent. The aesthetics of the movie – the fast cutting, the psychedelic graphics, the sheer primary process of the thing – confused, assaulted, and threatened me and inhibited my thinking. As for Marty, he dwelt only on the technical aspects of the animation. Unconsciously, however, I feel sure that both of us knew what we were watching.

Apart from a general impression of mayhem and, especially, the image of the rampaging teddy bear, I remembered very little. *Akira* soon faded from the sessions. Nevertheless, it had an epoch-making effect on the countertransference. It boosted my morale that Marty had asked something of me: perhaps he believed I had something to give. By insisting that I see the film, he had taken a risk, betrayed a need. Trust had flickered in the transference, and I rose to the occasion, feeling more alive and alert. In short, after *Akira* I began to wake up to how he needed me to be.

Marty also began to use therapy differently. Entering the second year, he could sometimes sit still and talk about his frustrations.

Feeling persecuted by school and peers, he reacted not only with contempt, but also with a hatred so corrosive that it seemed to exhaust him as much as it did me. He was deeply affected by the Columbine massacre and frankly identified with the perpetrators. I began to hear descriptions of computer kill games, which Marty regarded as a safety valve for people like him: 'Better to kill a pixel than a person.'

This phase also marked a change in Marty's musical interests. He had been amassing music software and now was devoting himself to electronic composition. He championed so-called 'industrial' rock and 'ambient' music, revelled in the noise of machines, and thought that becoming a robot or a cyborg would be a good thing. Music was everywhere, but shifts were occurring in the transference and countertransference. For one thing, Marty didn't just talk about this music. He brought in a Discman and bade me listen. Week after week, I submitted my ears to acoustic attack, worrying that it would damage my hearing. Marty relented and turned the volume down. He would select the program, hand me the headphones, and watch as the fearful din passed into my head. He was enacting sexually charged omnipotent fantasy in the transference. Only he knew the lyrics and he wouldn't recite them or bring the album notes to the sessions. We weren't equal players, but at least there was something mutual about it. It gave him pleasure to make 'ruthless' use of me in this way. I even earned the dubious distinction of being told that I resembled Marilyn Manson!

Marty's insistence that I see *Akira* was a key unconscious communication. He used this film to show me his persecutory object (the rogue teddy bear), his persecuted baby self (the insomniac patient), and also the kind of soothing object that he needed me to become (a baby teddy not a rogue). In this phase of detoxification, which continued into the third phase, I became a wide-awake eye and a wide-open ear, the better to register Marty's narcissistic rage. Subjecting myself to acoustic attack, I allowed Marty to repeat, this time upon my sensorium, the invasive trauma of his infancy.

THIRD TREATMENT PHASE: CRISIS OF SLEEPLESSNESS (MONTHS 20–24)

Eight months into the second year things took a turn for the worse. With father permanently unavailable, mother had begun to make behavioural demands on Marty. At first, he regressed, becoming surly and insulting. He kicked in a door, and even kicked her. Mother kept calling to complain that he wasn't getting better. To protect the treatment, I briefly invited her to attend the first half of one of Marty's sessions, where she could air her grievances openly and where I could witness first-hand their remarkable *folie à deux*. In the meantime, I consulted with her therapist. Mother pulled back, but not without posing yet another threat to Marty and to our work.

Having responded well to an antidepressant, she prevailed on Marty to try Prozac. Although offered as the milk of mother's kindness, the Prozac had a toxic effect, provoking a manic, paranoid-schizoid reaction. Medication was discontinued, but not before Marty used my emergency number several times to stabilize himself.

Towards the end of the second year, there occurred an ominous shift in my countertransference. I knew, from Marty as well as from his mother, that he was sleeping very poorly. But now, much to my surprise and anguish, so was I. Marty's insomnia had gotten into me. At night, I could picture him in bed glued to his headphones, studying his music, falling asleep to it. Meanwhile, tossing in my own bed, my sleepless mind worked like a computer in overdrive, permutating, combining, sifting and re-playing a whirl of details and impressions from recent and not-so-recent sessions. As my anxiety mounted about Marty's mental state, Hegel's famous phrase resounded in my ears: 'The owl of Minerva spreads her wings only at the falling of the dusk' (Hegel 1817–1818, p. 7). I remembered the rogue teddy bear in *Akira* and I felt that psychosis loomed.

I knew that Marty knew something different was afoot but he wouldn't talk about it. He bragged about his 'dual-track' mind, withdrawing and eluding me as I asked him to consider medication. Finally, Marty agreed to return to his psychiatrist, who corroborated my fears. But the blunting effect of the new medication was intolerable and he discontinued its use, declaring, 'I'll get through it on my own.'

This phase marked a crisis of identification in which I became deeply identified with and toxified by Marty's cardinal symptom, his inability to sleep. The persecutory object had broken through my stimulus barrier, so that I could have a mini-experience of cracking up, which I could stand because, unlike the sensorium of the infant Marty, my adult mind was already structured. But the effort was exhausting, and I could scarcely have done it without the benefit of consultation and containment by colleagues and friends.

FOURTH TREATMENT PHASE: MAPPING THE SOUNDS OF THE PERSECUTORY OBJECT (MONTHS 24–26)

There was a ray of hope. One of the analysts with whom I consulted during the crisis suggested that I try a technique from music therapy. Whereas before, when Marty would discuss his music, I limited my interventions to the verbal register, now I employed a graphic technique as well. With a large drawing tablet on my lap, I declared my need to learn more about how Marty makes his music. I would slow him down, insist on understanding how he creates his effects, and transcribe it all onto paper. A typical drawing would illustrate the composition of a rhythm loop (a several-second repeating unit) consisting of sounds pasted together electronically to produce a rhythmic percussive beat. I drew a big circle and divided it into little sections, each one labelled by its sound or sound-source – a water droplet, a snatch of computer code from a kill game, scratches on glass, a tongue clicking – and connected them by lines and arrows. I used this graphic technique for almost two months, with significant modification in the countertransference and transference.

In the first place, I began to sleep again. For me as well as for Marty, each drawing offered an image of bounded anxiety, of fragmentation visually contained upon the page. Even though I expressly avoided the content of the songs so as not to stir Marty's paranoia, I still learned a great deal about his use of acoustic distortion, the importance of acoustic texture, and the tension between fragmentation and cohesion in the compositional process. Thus I felt safer because I was gaining insight into the psychic function of Marty's music-making. The graphic technique allowed me to contain and metabolize his psychotic anxiety.

As for Marty, initially he was leery of my new technique. The fact that I was now using a writing implement changed my status in his mind. It signified that I was a thinking other, less controllable through omnipotent projection, and it represented my alliance or coupling with a paternal, analytic principle, in relation to which he feared exposure. Suspicious that the dangerous psychic contents condensed and encrypted in his music might leak out or escape his control, he made me agree to let him have the drawings eventually. Soon, however, he was reassured by my explicit focus on his creative methods. This left him in the position of knowledge and therefore power. Moreover, sharing a task that he found interesting calmed him down. Five weeks into this phase, near the end of the hour, he told me a dream which indicates how his transference to the total situation was changing.

The dream

Marty is in the country, walking in dead grass of a pale but not unpleasant colour. He comes to a lake. The shoreline is indented to form a little pool, where a fish is swimming in circles. When he returns later, the fish is dead, floating on the surface as if asleep. When next he returns, the dead fish is floating vertically, like a buoy. He wonders at this.

He enters a long shed with a low ceiling like the one in this room, dimly lit by holes in the walls. In the middle stands a long table on which metal shelving is stacked. The shelves are arrayed with aquariums filled with water and plants. Reaching into one, he lifts and swishes a plant, listens to the lapping sound, then restores it to its place. Slowly he circles the table, surveying the aquariums as if through the viewfinder of a camera. He hears a few seconds of music, about the length of a rhythm loop.

Leaving through another door, he expects to enter the room of an earlier dream. Instead, he exits into a misty river landscape in shades of blue, green, and brown, with gentle hills in the distance.

My first response to the dream was a feeling of wonder that he had been able to sustain such an organized, developed image, and gratitude that he had felt safe enough to divulge it. I felt that I must not show too much interest or I would scare him away.

Marty associated to the dream, gravitating characteristically towards its dissociated element, namely, the camera. He specified that the framing perimeter of the viewfinder was always visible as he circumnavigated the table, and commented that the angle of vision kept shifting from table level to ground level or overhead shots, but it never took the perspective of 'normal' vision.

As he spoke, I had time to consider the process of internalization that had occurred. The shed was indeed our therapeutic workroom, while the frame of the viewfinder and especially the orderly array of aquariums represented the hard work we had done. The few bars of music alluded to our musical focus. In size and shape, the aquariums reminded me of my drawing tablet. Taken together they represented the series of drawings which had helped to contain his persecutory anxiety.

I decided to risk a question: 'What had you thought to see behind that other door?'

Marty was forthcoming. 'In an earlier dream,' he explained, 'the door led into a room that was a huge aquarium, filled with plants and monsters, where people fell in and were eaten.'

'Ahh!' I murmured, 'That aquarium was more dangerous.' But I had pushed my luck. This was the first time Marty had dwelt so long on a dream, and he had never before put a dream into play between us. He quickly put me in my place.

'No it wasn't,' he snapped. 'There was a glass wall.'

It was still much too terrifying for Marty to think about that other aquarium, and far too dangerous for him to let me think about it. It was one thing to allow me to transcribe his methods of composition onto paper, but quite another to allow his dreams to be probed by my mind. Nevertheless, after this session I felt a stirring of hope in the possibility that, like the delicate plant in the aquarium, something good could survive and grow in the therapeutic relationship.

After the crisis I began to wrap my mind around Marty's. My drawing tablet enabled me to hold his chaotic parts by mapping them. Marty could see that the destructive music of the persecutory teddy bear was containable on the page, and as he introjected this containment, he calmed down, as indicated by the aquarium dream. Detoxifying Marty's persecutory object involved the provision of two containing spaces: one to contain the sadistic attacks of the teddy-bear self, and another womb-like space in which the regressed self can rest and grow.

FIFTH TREATMENT PHASE: THE FRAGMENTING EFFECT OF SEXUAL DESIRE (MONTHS 27–28)

My optimism didn't last long. A girl named Cheryl had recently appeared on the scene. Overwrought by the sexual fantasies which she aroused, Marty exhibited renewed signs of a psychotic process and I had to take further measures to contain him. Negotiating first with his mother and then with him, I undertook the delicate matter of changing the frame from one to two sessions a week. In the twenty-seventh month of therapy, we began to meet twice weekly. Here are process notes from the last session before the increase. Cheryl's effect can be seen.

Marty shambles in and collapses onto the sofa. But today he isn't sleepy. He sits up and watches me, alert and silent. I feel challenged and interested.

'You start,' he teases, smiling.

His opening gambit strikes me as a novel departure, so I decide to start fresh as well. I ask, 'Who's the guy on your shirt?'

Marty is delighted. 'It's De Niro!' he exclaims, 'Armed to the teeth!' He impersonates a famous scene from *Taxi Driver*, where De Niro talks to himself in front of a mirror.

I recall his description of the movie last year – something about guns, a girlfriend, a prostitute. 'What an incredible scene,' I murmur.

Marty shows me how De Niro concealed guns underneath his shirtsleeves. At the press of a button they popped into his hands. He falls silent.

I wait, then mirror his opening gambit: 'Now it's your turn.'

Marty rehearses the usual hypochondriacal complaints, then again falls silent.

Gently, I ask, 'Any new songs?'

'Yeah,' he replies, 'but we don't have to do those drawings. There are other things to talk about.' Then he declares, 'I have trouble talking with girls.' This is what he came to talk about today, and as he tells his story, a strong affect saturates the room. He tells me that yesterday after school Cheryl drove him home. In the car she said that she wanted to hug him, but that he wasn't very huggable. He told her he wouldn't mind. When they got home, Cheryl asked to be invited in, but he didn't have his key!

'Oh my God!' I groan sympathetically.

He shakes his head: 'I felt like such an ass.'

'I think you like her,' I venture. He agrees, but explains that she has a boyfriend, a college guy with a car. So it's hard to compete.

'He's so stupid!' he exclaims with characteristic contempt.

Counteracting his sense of inferiority, I say, 'Well, there you've got him beat.' I feel admiring of his honesty as he proceeds to convey his state of mind when he's with a girl.

First he describes the 'huge distance' that seems to separate him from others. He feels so far away, and there are so many thoughts in his head, but when he tries to talk it comes out in 'shorthand' and people don't understand. He mentions an Italian girl he once kissed when he was drunk.

I ask if he'd felt distant from her.

'No,' he explains, 'that doesn't happen when I'm drunk: it's different from being stoned.'

'Yes,' I reply, linking to an earlier session, 'pot takes you out of yourself.'

He nods, as if he appreciates that I've remembered. Then he admits, 'I'm kind of a misogynist . . . I can't help hating cute little bitches.' Cheryl, he explains, isn't one of them, although it makes him mad when she pretends to be weird by dyeing her hair green. He adds, 'She likes me because I'm weird, because I'm a freak.'

Moved once again to protect his self-esteem, I ruefully observe how hard he is on himself. Immediately I sense that it's a false move, motivated by my own need to defend myself against craziness. Marty is dead earnest and I have to face his weirdness with him. 'Do you really think you're a freak?' I ask softly.

'Yes,' he replies, 'Cheryl *acts* weird, but I really *am* weird. My mind is weird.' Falling silent, Marty gazes at the ceiling.

This gives me time to examine my countertransference. There is a vague tension in the pit of my stomach, and I have a sharp sense that he is fighting back tears. Surveying his sprawled-out body, I notice that the cuff has ridden up above the combat boot on his outstretched leg. The skin is exposed, and I see that his calf is hairy. I am becoming aware that I am in the presence of a sexually mature male.

Marty returns to the problem of his weirdness with girls. 'It gets sort of manic,' he says, 'like nobody's driving. It's like everything is high. There's this straight road, and – no hands on the wheel.'

'Ah,' I reply, realizing that this manic state is conflated with sexual arousal, 'so it feels good.'

'Yes,' he nods, 'but afterwards you crash.' He offers another image: 'It's like there's an eye, a centre, and two inches away everything is swirling around very fast, and you're two steps away from tears.'

I ask him, 'Does being with Cheryl cause this feeling?'

'Sometimes,' he answers, 'but it can also be self-created.'

By now I recognize my own feeling of arousal and ask quietly, 'Is something like that going on now?'

'Yes, kind of.' Smiling at a private thought, he says, 'Today Colin complained that what he really needs is a hot babe. I told him, "Sure, dream on."' Then Marty takes up a new image. 'It's like there's a cupboard with things on the shelves and you shake it, but it doesn't have a door so everything falls out, falls into fragments, and there are pieces all around, chopped up and broken. But your mind can single out one of them and think about it.'

I feel sad. I dread psychosis. I ask if he feels as if his perception is fragmented.

Interpreting my question as implying a limitation, he informs me, 'Even though the pieces are broken, there's a sense of power, and,' he pauses, stroking the arm of the sofa, 'no pain.'

At this point, there floats into my mind the cutting incident of last week. I notice the band-aid on his arm.

As if on cue, Marty looks up and adds, 'It's like this when I cut.'

'Yes,' I say, 'I was wondering about that too just now.'

'It's all mental,' he boasts, 'like in martial arts. Once I punched a locker, two feet from a kid's head!'

Feeling horror and fascination, I ask, 'It didn't hurt?'

'Not at all.'

'And it doesn't hurt when you cut?'

'No,' he replies confidentially, 'it's like cutting a sandwich.'

I am horrified at my concordant state of dissociation, as the image of a hero sandwich rises in my mind.

Marty continues, 'Cheryl asked about the cutting. She said, "At least don't commit suicide until I've fucked you."'

I raise my eyebrows, commenting drily, 'That was quite a thing to hear.' Madness and sex, I think to myself, don't mix.

Very much as if 'nobody were driving,' Marty leans over the arm of the sofa, smiles, and recites a song they listened to. It describes an incestuous tantrum, a frenzied longing to fuck and to breastfeed, to break out of the cage.

I have a sinking feeling that Cheryl will drive him mad with her sexual antics. What can I do? The session is winding down. My feeling of arousal is still strong.

Suddenly Marty's tone changes. 'I don't want a second session a week,' he announces emphatically. 'It's not necessary.'

He abruptly reaches for the footstool, pulls it between us, gives it a slap, and says, 'It's like chess! We need one of those clocks that face both ways, with two buttons!'

Taken aback by this quite unprecedented playfulness, I struggle to keep up. 'Oh!' I respond, quickly associating buttons to sexual touching and to the gizmos De Niro uses to release his guns, 'You mean, three minutes for you and three for me?'

'Yeah!' he laughs, but his mirth soon vanishes. 'I'd rather talk to a friend,' he protests. 'I don't like the idea of paying for a friend to talk to.'

Again I think of the De Niro movie and decide to interpret: 'You're telling me that it seems to you that coming here is like going to a prostitute and paying for your time with her.'

Listening closely, he nods, and then offers a final metaphor for his difficulty. 'I know a lot, but not about people: it's like algebra and I can't solve for x.' He traces an equation on the arm of the sofa to illustrate his point: 'There's x on one side, and all these factors jumbled up on the other, but it's a mystery how to figure it out.'

I nod and reply, 'You're saying you don't know how to figure me out.' He nods and I continue. 'I seem mysterious, and you don't know what kind of a person I am.'

'But I don't want to come twice a week,' he pleads, 'I can talk to myself. I can have dialogues in my head.'

'The thing is,' I reply, 'I'm not a prostitute, even if it some-times seems like that to you. I think that you worry about parts of your mind. You do need help, not a prostitute, but another mind that can think with you about this weird equation. And when our two minds can think together, you'll feel closer to people, including girls.'

At that moment, the microwave in the corridor goes *cha-ching*!

'Did you hear that?!!' he bursts out, laughing.

I also laugh: '6:00 on the nose!' As he rises to leave, I add, 'See you next week.'

He does a double-take: until this moment he's been con-vinced there will be a second session this week! Leaving the room, he looks back in and says, 'You know, I'm really angry right now.'

'I hear you,' I say, 'but our session is over.'

In describing his feeling of elation with girls, Marty reveals that Cheryl scares the wits out of him, and so transferentially do I. The sex object that I become for him here is not undifferentiated from the persecuting mother. This is why it feels as if we are in a deadly chess game, why he needs his De Niro t-shirt, and why he dreads the second session. He puffs up with anger at being conned into showing his terror before it's necessary. But this only happens at the threshold, when he can escape from the mysterious sphinx that I have become.

Marty cannot withstand the shake-up of sexual arousal, which threatens to fragment his mind like the tumbling contents of a shaken cupboard. Though sexually mature, his cupboard, in his own words, 'doesn't have a door.' In the ensuing weeks, incited by chat-room talk with Cheryl, Marty hardly slept at all. He talked about an Internet site that shows a man drilling a hole in his own skull to relieve the pressure. Now that he was talking sex with a girl, Marty thought that my drawing technique – by which I had hoped to nudge him from presentation of his preoccupations in music to thinking about his problems – was stupid and naive. I would have to move with him into new ways of working appropriate to the new developmental phase. Working with his feelings of persecution that accompany sexual urges, I will need to emphasize the reality of himself, the other, and the possibility of two people sharing the same space without one of them having to be obliterated.

DISCUSSION

Marty suffers from profound narcissistic disturbance. His anxiety is massive, ranging from fear of punishment to terror of invasion, fragmentation, and annihilation. His inner world is impoverished and dominated by the earliest object relations, displaying a pathological organization (Steiner 1987) of predominantly obsessional and manic defences. The self that inhabits this world cannot rest because there is a striking lack of an internal soothing object and, concomitantly, a weakly developed repression barrier. Instead of a soothing object, there is an overindulgent part-object representation of the breast. And there is, to judge from the many ways in which it is projected inside and outside the transference, an unusual persecutory object that, especially since the onset of puberty, has come to stalk Marty's mind.

THE AETIOLOGY OF MARTY'S PERSECUTORY OBJECT

I began to reconstruct the origins of Marty's persecutory object when I found myself suffering from insomnia. I felt as if I were the sleepless teenager in the scene from *Akira*, unable to achieve an internal relation with a soothing object, while Marty became identified with the monstrous teddy bear who crashes into my mind and keeps me from sleep. This persecutory dynamic highlights a key element in the transference: the fact that almost every session opens with a performance of sleepiness. Marty really is sleepy, but transferentially, all the time he is blaming me for keeping him awake for yet another hour of therapy. He projects onto me a persecutory mother who won't let him sleep.

This persecutory mother was a reality in Marty's early attachment. She always obsessed about his sleep hygiene, but whereas she harboured the belief that he never liked to sleep, in actuality she dreaded that he would die if he slept. She had an unconscious need to keep her baby aware of her. Thus, she invaded his sensorium with music and her ubiquitous voice reading, and even stroked his eyelids – to keep him awake. As a result, she frustrated his ability to learn to self-soothe and she interfered with his need to forget and then rediscover her as a soothing internal object.

Schooled by mother's reading voice, he learned to split his perception amongst competing stimuli. I am amazed at his ability to discriminate between sounds and to hear them simultaneously. Now he exploits this capacity musically, teaching himself to be a master and connoisseur of chaos. But this capacity to split has drastically compromised Marty's ego functioning. In order to survive annihilating anxiety in relation to the invasive mother, part of the self split off very early, while he constructed another self in compliance with his mother's narcissistic use of him. I think of Marty as split between an embryonic or baby self and something like the milk-besotted teddy bear in *Akira*.

The teddy bear as a narcissistic object in Marty's inner world points to the lack of secure introjection of a soothing object. To judge from his chronic insomnia, the teddy bear is not something he *had* so much as something he *was*. I see him as having been his *mother's* teddy bear, during a symbiotic phase that was uninterrupted for too long because his father was absent, and for many years there was no contact with any relative or even any close friend who might have held Marty differently and thus enriched his inner object world. I think of the rogue teddy bear as originating in his mother's unconscious fantasy and existing in Marty as a foreign body. It is an *interject* – not an introject but another person's project, an 'object projected into a self by the other which interrupts and momentarily disorients the self, which can proceed only insofar as it accepts the interjection' (Bollas 2000, p. 129). Because the paternal phallus has been weakly structured in his psyche, sadistic protest at weaning and toilet training went unchecked. Mother got a taste of this when Marty pounded on the door during weaning. His persecutory object can thus be thought of as a sadistically animated teddy bear that tries, as in *Akira*, to break down the door.

In daily friction with the world, Marty projects his sadism outwards, identifying it with all who threaten the grandiosity of the teddy-bear self. He meets these threats with characteristic hatred, arrogance, or contempt. But the teddy-bear self is also an internal persecutor that wages war against the frustrating breast, the parental couple, and the paternal phallus in violent fantasies de-repressed by industrial rock. In the aquarium dream, the dead grass and the fish floating dead in the indented pool represent sanitized attacks on the mother's body and the parental coitus.

There is a pervasive persecutory anxiety that the phallus, obliterated to maintain incestuous merger, will reappear as a punishing object. Such an object was the fantasied microphone, which Marty had to assure himself was not hidden in my drawer (or 'drawers') recording evidence against him. Likewise, at first Marty suspected my drawing technique, as if my pen were a dangerous phallus that could discover the fantasies encrypted in his music.

The teddy-bear self was less persecutory during latency, when his mother functioned as Marty's auxiliary ego. But with the onset of puberty, it has become a terrible liability. It can only 'grow' in an undifferentiated way, swelling with milk until it bursts. Marty may not know he is his mother's teddy bear, but he certainly knows he's a mama's boy, and this fills him with shame and self-loathing. He feels persecuted by his own body because it is identified with the foreign body of mother's projected object. The episodes of cutting express an urgent need to cut through the milk-engorged teddy bear to release his flesh-and-blood self. To continue the parallel with *Akira*, it is as if only the sight of blood can dispel the hallucination of the rampaging teddy bear.

THE FUNCTION OF MUSIC IN MARTY'S PSYCHIC ECONOMY

Marty has to bring his music into his sessions because it has literally been a matter of psychic life or death for him. In his songs, he presents and represents both his endopsychic perception of fragmentation and his creative attempt to stand outside of and to contain the madness. In terms of persecutory anxiety, this music serves a threefold function. It is a persecutory object; it asserts omnipotent control over other internal persecutory objects; and it conjures the mirage of a refuge from persecution.

Marty's music is meant to be scary to others. The thunderous, crashing sound, the fascist march tempo, and the incidental surprise noises devised to startle and scare re-create the sense of the father's phallus come to disturb the aquatic paradise on which he is fixated. His songs are acoustic objects that rely on amplification, distortion, and reverberation to penetrate the mind. He can specify where in the cranium an effect is meant to resound. The violence of the music lies hidden in the compositional technique. Marty showed me that he can do *anything* with a sound: stretch it, squeeze it, mix it up, chop it up as tiny as he pleases. A rhythm loop involves the fragmenting of hundreds of sound sources, many of them linked metonymically or metaphorically to some hitherto persecuting or frustrating object, part-object, or combined object.

There is also a psychotic trend in Marty's music-making. The technique of infinitesimal fragmentation and distortion tends towards the obliteration, in the acoustic realm, of the boundaries and definitions of the secondary process. Any sound can be morphed into another and all can be fused into a kind of primary process plasma. Marty can submerge himself in ambient sound as if it were the amniotic fluid in his mother's womb. At such times, he revels in sheer aural sensation, floating in it rather than relating to or with it. This regressive trend is captured in the water of the aquarium dream, where the aquarium is a transferential representation of my room-mind-womb. When Marty retreats into ambient sound of his own devising, he creates for himself a blissful womb free of persecutory objects.

DETOXIFYING THE PERSECUTORY OBJECT

Marty's case is still a work-in-progress. With so much persecutory anxiety, operating at all levels but primarily at that of narcissistic object relations, there was little space in which we could coexist as separate psychical origins at play. The paramount task has been to create a safe space in-between, which when introjected can permit new kinds of object use and, eventually, self-transformation.

Update

I have continued to try to modify Marty's persecutory anxieties by clarifying them in terms of the difficulty he has in conceiving a safe space where two people can coexist mentally, physically, and sexually. Shifts in my countertransference indicated that we were beginning to coexist as separate entities in my consulting room. Once Marty's mind slowed down, not always darting away from me like a minnow spooked by the movement of thoughts in the waters of my mind, I noticed that I could think of what was going on and what to say while he was still in the room, rather than long after he had gone. I heaved my first sigh of relief when Marty declared one day at the beginning of a session, 'I don't want to be schizophrenic.' I could enjoy being with Marty. Once after a session, I actually recognized an old tipsy, fond feeling that can only be called a 'crush'. More recently, I have found myself feeling that I could and should defend myself from one of his contemptuous attacks. These changes signify that I am more like myself with him, and that to me he seems less like a baby.

I note corresponding changes in Marty's transference. He uses the room more freely. The transference to the total situation is less persecutory: There is now space to grow. Though often sleepy, he is much less floppy. He will move from the couch to the chair, and occasionally he will use the drawing implements. On our many music-listening days, he sits next to me, and even holds the album notes for both of us to follow. He brings music to communicate with me and show me what he is feeling, and we talk about it seriously. I still hear more industrial rock than I would choose, but we also listen to an innovative German group who play on Moog synthesizers. This points to a trend towards the integration of Marty's chronically fragmented psychic contents.

Changes in Marty's experience of space have entailed changes in how he perceives me. I was amazed one day when he picked up my beret and put it on. He has also asked me to put on my wide-brimmed sun hat, observing that his mother would not look good in it. In keeping with this differentiating trend, he has begun to use my name. I let him make a phone-call one day after a session, and he told a friend that he was 'at Leslie's'. There is now a new object in his inner world who has a good head and whose difference requires a name. I welcomed this evidence of the function of secondary process.

Finally, ten days ago Marty spontaneously lay down on the couch, declaring that it was 'more professional'. Since he stayed there, I joined in the play of 'professional' therapy, moving my chair to the analytic position. Eventually he turned around and sat up, but not before he had allowed himself to experience a new kind of silence. I had time to recognize and savour it as well. In this bit of play, Marty confirmed my understanding of the origin of his persecutory anxiety and the goal of our work together. He is developing, in Winnicott's words, the capacity to be alone, to relax, even perchance to sleep, in the presence of another. In the therapy process he is inventing the teddy bear for himself, instead of having to be one.

REFERENCES

Bollas, C. (2000). *Hysteria*. London and New York: Routledge.

Hegel, G. W. F. (1817–1818). Die Philosophie der Recht. Trans. T. M. Knox. In *Great Books of the Western World*, Vol. 46, pp. 1–152 , ed. R. M. Hutchins. Chicago: William Benton for Encyclopedia Brittanica, 1952.

Steiner, J. (1987). The interplay between pathological organizations and the paranoid-schizoid and depressive positions. *International Journal of Psycho-Analysis*, 68: 69–80.

Winnicott, D. W. (1958). Transitional objects and transitional phenomena. In *Collected Papers: Through Paediatrics to Psychoanalysis*, pp. 229–242. London: Hogarth Press and the Institute of Psycho-Analysis.

Chapter 9

Containing anxiety with divorcing couples

Carl Bagnini, CSW, BCD

Instead of being treated as a developmental challenge from which recovery is possible, divorce may be experienced as an unmanageable persecutory object, both for the partners of a broken marriage and for their couple therapist. Divorcing spouses or partners may torment and persecute each other with their hurt, ambivalence, and lost hope. Then the couple relationship appears devoid of any good, and yet the partners with their deep unconscious attachment pursue the 'forever' dream. Fused by hate, loss, disappointment, and betrayal, the partners are unable to detach or differentiate. They insist on defending themselves righteously against the accusations of the dying marriage and the disappointed spouse. In a symbiotic partnership or a long marriage with children, the unconscious terror of ending and aloneness prevents exploration and resolution.

Couple therapists may agonize over raging couples that struggle over whether to stay together. Emotion-laden sessions are the usual in working with couples on the brink. Their disturbances press hard on us, as we experience the insanity of love gone wrong. Divorce is a painful outcome for us too, even though we are more individuated then the partners in the couple relationship. We can use our training to help us deal with loss and dread, and we can think ahead. We can contain our experience, and yet we may long for the moment after they exit the office, so that we can begin our recovery. It is so difficult to help them let go.

Termination anxiety accompanies work with a terminal marriage, and it affects the therapist and the couple. Fear of the end of a marriage brings harshness to the therapy process. Angry protest precedes acceptance, which cannot be arrived at without going through a mourning process. Mourning the lost marriage is difficult to do with the spouse who is about to be lost, and with the couple therapist who is also about to become a lost object. The pain is often too great for the couple to stay with the therapist they originally chose as the one they hoped could help them save their marriage. Couples in a divorce mode seldom stay long enough in couple therapy to grieve their loss so as to move on to individual lives with confidence and understanding of their vulnerabilities.

In cases of divorce, loss of love brings with it a cruel and persecuting superego. Unprepared for dealing with the demise of their wished-for marriage, a couple feels pain and persecutory anxiety. Suddenly the parting spouses have to learn skills that they did not expect to need. They need therapy to adapt to dashed expectations and prepare for the future. Some couples feel so damaged by the time they get to the therapist that they cannot undertake the therapy task. Others can work to detoxify the malignant projective matrix as they mourn the loss of the good and bad parts of the marriage and re-own the parts of the self that had been projected into the spouse.

Some couples arrive for treatment obviously at the brink of marital dissolution. Their verbal attacks are dramatic, unrelenting, violent, and sometimes irrational. Yet, surprisingly, hard work sometimes salvages the relationship. Other couples are rational and cooperative. They seem to respond well in therapy, only to reveal that they are one step from indifference, a death knell for marriage. Detachment of affect implies an emotional separation of long duration without a formal notice. Love is indeed gone.

Some couples present for therapy when one spouse emphasizes the other's vulnerable personality. The individual identified as sick is placed in the therapist's care for the day when the complaining spouse vacates the home. Other couples initially appear to be very much intact, with just a few problems to be worked with, but when one spouse begins to change for the better, a deeper malignancy emerges. The unfamiliar new behaviour disturbs the projective identificatory system of the marriage and the marriage deteriorates, despite the therapist's Herculean efforts.

When there is individual growth in one spouse's ability to relate and be intimate, the other spouse experiences an unwelcome jolt in the system. The integrity of the unconscious object relations set of the marriage has now been disrupted. An unexpected new good experience in treatment creates a deep disturbance, as there is now the possibility of reliable dependency. Massive schizoid defences are mobilized against it. When one spouse becomes self-directed and self-defining, the borderline spouse is torn apart with envy and attacks the possibility of integration. Further individual breakdown then sabotages movement into the depressive position. In other couples, the spouse who longed for improvement in the partner, and finally gets it, cannot accept it because of resentment at how long it took. Sometimes change is too little or too late. Sometimes hope is too painful to bear, for fear of renewed disappointment.

CLINICAL ILLUSTRATIONS OF DIVORCING COUPLES

The older woman being left

Anne called in deep distress. She told me that she had been married to Bob for 35 years, and that they are the parents of three successful out-of-the-home children. Three weeks ago, she said, Bob announced that he wanted out of the marriage. He seemed so much in a hurry to get out that she wondered if he had someone else.

Now, on the phone, Anne is close to being out of control. She tells me she is frightened, desperate, clutching herself to hold herself together, her entire existence at stake. All her life she had been taken care of by Bob. They have done everything together – child-rearing, business failures and great successes, and now this, an earthquake. She needs help. She says she is willing to do anything to save the marriage and will come in immediately. She is sure Bob will be motivated to come in to 'help her get therapy for the marriage'. Anne shows no awareness of the implications of stating Bob's motive in this way. I schedule an emergency appointment for Bob and Anne to see me that evening.

As they talk in my office, I see that Bob is self-assured, in control, calm and articulate. Anne is wide-eyed, high-strung, painfully tearful from the start, obviously in shock. Bob restates what Anne related on the phone: he is there for her, he wants to help her through this, but he has reached a decision and wants to move things along as soon as possible.

'Why so fast?' I ask.

'Because I am 56 years old and I don't want to waste time. I do still love Anne, and I know she is a good person, but I don't want to be married to her any more.'

This sounds as if Bob is simply dealing with a solution to his personal anxiety over ageing, as if it has nothing to do with Anne or the quality of their marriage.

So, I inquire about prior marital problems in this long marriage. Anne tells me that she had an affair 12 years ago. When Bob had found out about this he had felt persecuted by the images of her involvement with another man and had become violently disturbed. They went together for counselling. After only two sessions they left with the advice to try and get past it. They tell me they never spoke of it again. I note that they are talking about it now with me, in the first session of this, the next treatment opportunity. I ask how they could avoid talking about such an important sign of trouble since then until now. Calmer now, Anne volunteers that there was no sex in the affair: she got to the motel but she couldn't go through with it. Sex wasn't the primary motive for her. I nod for her to continue. Bob is staring at her. She looks away, then at Bob, and tells me sadly that he never believed that she didn't have sex. Bob says he thought that she must have had sex with her lover because she didn't initiate sex in the marriage. Anne firmly blocks the discussion of problematic sex, defensively pressing the point that Bob was so tired with work problems that she thought he needed to sleep. Avoiding this for now, I ask if they differed on other issues, or needs in the marriage, and any other disturbances they never got past.

They continue telling me about their roles in the marriage – he the financial provider and protector, she the home-based provider and child-rearing parent. Anne tearfully relates that she has no other skills, that she is nothing without Bob! He answers with a limp reassurance that she will be okay, because they can sell the house, and the settlement should be quick and easy. I am thinking to myself that he hasn't heard her at all. I ask Anne if she is ready for difficult discussions or decisions. She responds that the room is spinning, this is so fast. I intervene saying to Bob that if he insists on going this fast harm may be done and a backlash may follow. He nods, saying that he can see how upset Anne is. I ask if there is anyone else in his life that he might be in a hurry to join.

I look at Bob, waiting for him to answer my loaded question. He doesn't look at me. He doesn't answer. Anne says she received an anonymous phone call telling her Bob has a woman in Dallas, but Bob says that the call must have been from a business enemy trying to make trouble. In the face of uncertainty about any hope of reconciliation, I ask if they could agree to a slowing down of the separation process to give time for thinking about what led to their current crisis, whether Bob wants a new relationship, and how they can adjust to the changes.

Bob says he will come if it will help Anne, but he insists that he wants out of the marriage. He remains calm, self-contained, and adamant. I tell them that 'coming to therapy for Anne' will lead to ending the marriage. Anne says she wants to come back anyway to understand what is happening. I close the session by mentioning that 35 years together means that much has transpired and needs to be reviewed, and that each of their futures depends on learning as much as possible about themselves in the intimate and sexual relationship of this marriage. We could determine whether they could accomplish this together, or not, in which case individual therapy would be a good option.

I wanted to assess if this was going to be marriage therapy or divorce therapy, a consult to determine individual therapy needs, or no basis for therapy at all. Based on Bob's attitude, I felt little optimism that they could use couple therapy to recover their marriage, or that Bob would accept individual therapy, but I hoped to slow him down a bit. Bob experienced this offer of sessions as an opportunity for relieving himself of a guilty burden and then getting on with his life. Anne saw it as an opportunity to prevent the fragmentation of her self, and perhaps to change Bob's mind. My approach offered time, space, and a holding environment in which Anne might be able to confront the enormity of her plight, or at least reduce the immediacy of her impending loss, and Bob could review his decision without panic. There was still a chance that I might be allowed to help them detoxify the persecutory effects of Bob's lack of sexual desire, Anne's old affair, and the threat of divorce itself.

Guilt and fear complicate the decision to divorce. A spouse may worry that the spouse being left will break down, or become so livid that violence could ensue in the form of suicide, or destructive legal attacks. Here the persecutory superego exerts its wrath over the lost love object (Schecter 1979). The ego is under attack. Previous holding that was good enough in the long marriage is insufficient to sustain a more benign adjustment to its termination. The dependent wife cannot rely on her husband any more except to the extent that he provides for her financially. If the husband was the ego-ideal, the wife being left can no longer count on association to him to maintain her self-esteem.

When the fears of loss of income, loss of companionship, loss of social standing, and loss of self-esteem are intense, narcissistic clinging of one spouse to the other may last for months or years. Even after a legal separation and divorce the persistence of this phenomenon cannot be underestimated.

The baby as saviour

> Dick and Sue had been unhappy in a childless marriage of 24 years. They had been in marital therapy for two years without improvement in how they felt because they had little in common to work with towards reconciliation. Termination of the marriage and of treatment seemed inevitable. Sue no longer loved Dick. Nevertheless, she insisted that he give her a baby, even though significant marital problems had not been worked through, including her infidelities, his difficulty in providing financially, and their problems with intimacy and sexuality. Dick refused to provide her with the necessary sperm.
>
> Within three months of moving out, Sue showed up unannounced at the couple's former residence to tell him that she would return to the marriage, if he would relent and give her the baby she required. Dick's life was beginning to take shape, while Sue's was bogged down in continuing anxieties and insecurities, and a desperate longing to have life from the man she could not love.

Partners who cannot love each other may put all their hope into a baby. Unmetabolized aspects of the couple's projective identificatory system get projected into the foetus. In the case of Dick and Sue, the foetus remained a battle ground of longing and withholding like the marriage itself. Sometimes a couple may proceed to have a live child who becomes the receptacle for unmanageable parts of the couple relationship. The child is then treated as the elusive but cherished part or as the hated, rejecting aspect of the frustrating spouse. This is obviously a burden on the child of unhappy marriage or of divorce and induces problematic behavioural changes that become autonomous. It is also a burden on the couple whose efforts to deal directly with their marital or post-divorce relationship are diverted to responding to the needs of their child.

At the ex-spouse's service

Tony had moved out of the home he had shared with his wife Alice. After the separation, Tony continued to be available to help Alice prepare and physically set up her art shows, work for which she had had no motivation during the marriage. Alice looked well, she was working out for the first time in her life, she was productive, and her outlook was improved. In contrast to being dependent when she was married, Alice was now on her way to an independent new life without Tony.

Tony's disillusionment with his marriage had led to a long-term affair with a younger, livelier, and more self-directed woman. This had increased his withdrawal and further fuelled Alice's depression. Their relationship had clearly been unfulfilling over many years and Tony's decision to end the marriage was final.

Although there was little evidence of love and devotion between them from the earliest days of the marriage, Tony continued, for some time after the separation, to cling to Alice in the role of her assistant. Guilty about leaving her and curious about how she was doing without him, he wanted to help and feel needed.

Couples like Tony and Alice are fearful of individuation. The spouses look after each other, but without passion or growth potential. When one of them leaves, it may be difficult to give up the parental caregiver aspect of the former marital role. Even after divorce, the couple may continue to share the unconscious long-term assumption that the only form of couple is one consisting of an anaclitic, infantile dependency, the parent and child roles oscillating between them. If the abandoned wife copes, the husband who separated from her can't believe that she doesn't need him as before. Her individuation is felt as a psychic injury to him. This may lead to an unhealthy return to the marriage in a caregiver role so as to be reassured of the value of the self.

The young woman's folly of forgiveness

Rachel, a 36-year-old woman in a three-year marriage to Saul, eventually separated from him after two years of marital therapy. She realized that she had married him mainly to keep her parents happy. Her mother was physically and emotionally abusive (and so was Rachel's sister) and her father was deeply depressed. Her parents' relationship was readily destabilized by any stress and so Rachel acceded to her father's request that she ignore and forgive the ongoing emotional and physical abuse heaped on her as a child by her mother and older sister, so that her protests did not cause trouble between her parents. As an adult, Rachel continued to protect her parents at the sacrifice of her own needs by marrying Saul because he was a nice, cute, Jewish accountant who was adored by her family and whose presence kept her parents calm.

Soon Saul neglected Rachel's needs and withdrew from her demands as her father had done. The neglect and withholding of the past were repeated. Her fantasy marriage quickly evaporated. As she got closer to divorce, physical symptoms emerged as if the clamour of protest in her body could no longer be quieted by her association with Saul. Although not an abusive person, Saul nevertheless represented the abuse that Rachel had not been allowed to protest.

After the separation there was tremendous pressure on Rachel to forgive Saul, to see only his good points, and to re-unite with him. On the one hand Saul asked Rachel for forgiveness (both a stunning reversal of the childhood pattern in that he asked for this for himself only, and yet a repetition in that yet again Rachel is required to forgive to keep the peace), but on the other hand he continued to manipulate her emotionally and to side with her parents who obviously pre-ferred him to her. The therapist was also pressured by phone calls from the mother requesting him to bring the therapy to a happy ending, by getting the daughter to give up her crazy ideas and forgive her husband, and by extension give her parents absolution. Keeping her marriage would require Rachel's constant forgiveness, and she was no longer willing to subordinate her needs in favour of others.

This case illustrates the way that the family's projective matrix may exert a malignant effect on a couple. Marrying to earn a parent's love and staying married to keep both parents together are heavy burdens on a marriage. Marital therapy allows reworking of family dynamics so that the spouses can move out of the projective matrices of their families of origin, deal with the persecutory objects internal to the psyche, and develop autonomy. Only when a spouse is separate from the projections of the past and recognizes the separate other in the spouse can love flourish.

THE PERSECUTORY CHALLENGE TO THE THERAPIST

Few situations are as challenging or persecuting for couples and for therapists as the issue of divorce. It draws into the consulting room our personal value system concerning monogamy and our theories about what makes or breaks a marriage. When faced with the possibility of the end of a marriage, our countertransference may be concordant with the feelings of the children. We may be angry or afraid as if our parents are failing us, or we may grieve for our failure to keep them together. The painful prospect of being involved in a great loss stirs us to the core. Our psychoanalytic paradigm is no insurance against this. Simply tracing each spouse's unconscious precursors of marital conflict and making the individual's unconscious conscious are not sufficient as therapeutic approaches. We have to analyze the interpersonal situation of the couple relationship. Working with here-and-now realities in marriage is as important as dealing with past traumas, neglect, and failed attachments that have influenced pre-marital life and mate choices. Such issues as hope, subculture, religion, devotion, will, loyalty, and spirituality need to be included when we are exploring couple resilience and potential for reworking the relationship.

We ask couples to what extent there is a narcissistic preoccupation with the self and its right to be served by the spouse. Is personal sacrifice seen as a restriction of individual needs and strivings? To what extent are communal issues, or the needs of the group, including the family, a major concern for one or the other spouse? The proper balance between the needs of the individual, the marriage, the nuclear family, and the families of origin is central to the future of the marital institution itself. In one case keeping the family together was the driving force for the husband to remain married, due to his ethnic and cultural values. The wife was not of his background and could have taken the action leading to divorce, but she had accommodated to his views about family values. Shame was a powerful motive for maintaining this loveless marriage.

The literature abounds with discussion of the effects of divorce on children of different ages, the legal ramifications, the economic impact, the problems of remarriage and blending families, and the reactions of extended family members and friends. Not so available to us especially in the psychoanalytic literature are the interpersonal and intrapsychic aspects of marital dissolution, the shared object relations that must be deconstructed in a divorcing process, and discussion of the therapist's role in the process of growth and recovery.

The psychoanalytic literature lacks details of these phenomena because of the clinician's pain in studying and staying with the lingering process of marital dissolution. Therapists need concepts to contain the potentially devastating effects of the fallout of a failed relationship, but there is scant information in the literature. The lack of theory follows from an avoidance of admitting to and thinking about the therapist's affect in terminations of all types (Martin and Schurtman 1985). With little preparation from psychoanalytically informed training, we are challenged to think our own way through and keep our egos intact when feeling persecuted during such difficult work. Suffering is to be expected in termination. In dealing with the regression inherent in the divorcing couple, we find ourselves quite alone when we need the most support.

Being so close to couples puts us uncomfortably close to their loss and sense of failure. We may feel like ejecting them from treatment under pressure from our internal objects if our losses resonate with the couple's loss. Each of us has personal and professional feelings that colour the extent to which we can approach the object relations of divorce. We may not have mastered all these feelings, but we can work with them if we feel supported. Too few analytic therapists come together to discuss and explore these issues, and so there is not a good containing environment in which therapists can find help with processing their experience.

LOSS AND MOURNING IN DIVORCE

Since divorce is a form of termination, an understanding of loss and mourning may be of help in contemplating the end of a marriage and the end of a couple's treatment. In his paper 'Mourning and melancholia' Freud (1917) described the process of acceptance of loss at times of grief:

> Each single one of the memories and situations of *expectancy* which demonstrates the libido's attachment to the lost object is met by the verdict of *reality* that the object no longer exists; and the ego, confronted as it were with the question of whether it shall share this fate, is persuaded by the sum of the narcissistic satisfactions it derives from being alive to sever its attachment to the object it has abolished.
>
> (Freud 1917, p. 255)

In her paper 'A contribution to the psychogenesis of manic-depressive states' Melanie Klein (1935) wrote that the loss of good objects is a major threat to our security and fear of this loss is the source of great pain and conflict. Alteration in the external circle of family objects produces insecurity in the internal objects. Threats to good internal objects leave the child feeling filled up with bad, persecutory objects and fears of annihilation of the self. Depending on the nature of the internal objects children and adults can experience manic and depressive responses to anxiety, related to phantasies and affects associated with the internalized mother, and coloured by whether she was experienced as helpful or revengeful, loving or angry.

During our development as therapists we have internalized objects based on experiences with our mothers, teachers, therapists, and former clients. These internal objects have attributes that may be dangerous and unpleasant or consistent and helpful. Dealing with divorce in couple therapy, we are faced with mainly the more dangerous and unpleasant ones. We experience sorrow, distress, and feelings associated with failure such as low self-esteem arising from perceptions of ourselves as unhelpful objects.

Any leave-taking re-awakens losses and mourning issues. Even the cases that we wish would leave treatment cause us pain, since we feel persecuted by our own hate of a particular couple or divorcing partner. We feel guilty to be relieved of the burden of some couples. We are alive, witnessing a death, even though a necessary one if the individual spouses are to develop by beginning anew. If so much of marriage is dependent on a search for lost objects, then when that marriage breaks up, it becomes another lost object compounding a previous, and perhaps deeper, loss. What was never achieved in the marriage cannot be recovered in the divorce.

During the divorcing process, infantile loss and the painful layering of reactions to frustrated hopes are experienced again. Conscious and unconscious attachments are severed for a second time. No wonder couples often fly into manic attempts to salvage what they can. The denial of psychic reality allows the attachment to persist in the face of tremendous difficulty. In despair, a spouse may become depressed with suicidal feelings, while the other may act out through extramarital flight. Murder or suicide end growth for spouses dramatically, but more commonly unresolved grief cripples future growth in an ordinary way. Defences including omnipotence, avoidance, even idealization may continue to prevent total collapse and assuage one spouse's terror of the depressive position.

HATRED, SPLITTING, AND AMBIVALENCE IN DIVORCE

If hatred of the object and splitting instead of ambivalence dominate the separation process, hate will not then be available to the self for use in differentiation, separation, new realistic boundary setting, and mourning loss. Instead, the hated spouse or therapist takes on an entirely bad persona, in order to preserve the self as good. This is a precarious bargain since the distribution of all-good and all-bad can shift, and then suddenly it is the self that feels bad. Splitting in which only good or bad can be tolerated at one time leads to destructive actions alternately towards the self and the formerly loved partner. While these dynamics frequently accompany divorce to some degree they usually resolve over time to a more mature state of ambivalence. In object relationships dominated by persecutory superego functioning that has not been resolved in therapy, the therapist notes with regret that the primitive and punitive affects will continue to affect individual and family development long after the divorce is final. This knowledge propels us to keep divorcing couples in therapy long enough for them to learn as much as possible about themselves and the nature of the relationship they created so that mistakes in fit are not repeated. Sensitivity to the clients' capacity to endure this type of soul-searching is essential so that we judge correctly the moment when enough is enough. Otherwise the result will be abandonment of treatment, rather than a mature integration of the feelings of love and hate, with resolved grief over past losses and hope for an easier future.

WORKING WITH THE THERAPIST'S SELF

If we have too much anxiety about endings and too much grief about losing divorcing couples from treatment, we may rush them into premature endings; on the other hand, we may deter them from making the decision to end the marriage by re-hashing marriage dynamics so as to avoid blaming ourselves for abandoning the couple. We may have difficulty letting the spouses leave each other and us if our self-esteem is insecure. Our professional competence is shaken by termination due to unanticipated divorce if we are not always prepared for that eventuality, even though we should be because we know that it is not our responsibility to save marriages or to break them up. We simply help couples learn, and they are ultimately responsible for the fate of their relationship. Yet, in the throes of flawed couple relating, we may be drawn into an attempt to improve holding so that we do not face the narcissistic injury of not being able to help the couple hold on to their commitment. We may seek object constancy in the face of object sorting and splitting in the couple. In this phase of therapy, the splitting may be a necessary part of dissolution of the marriage partnership and we must learn to accept it.

The loss of a meaningful relationship with one couple can cause a crisis of confidence in our professional life. We may obsess over the case. Have we done all we could? Do we ever know for sure? We may turn against ourselves through self-deprecation, self-abasement, or depression. We wonder, question, analyze our reactions, and if necessary seek consultation to ensure that we maintain an impartial sensitivity to the needs of both the divorcing partners.

Divorcing couples force us to work on ourselves, grow in maturity and acceptance, face loss, and confront reality. We do not always welcome the variety of experiences that we have to contend with in the pursuit of a therapeutic ending. We are forced to revisit the unworked through parts of our internal world as the loss of love reaches its emotional peak. The struggle between the benign and persecutory elements in the object relations of divorcing clients evokes our own struggles. The couple's shame, guilt, and low self-esteem resonate with our own. The divorcing partners may regress and attempt to kill off what was once loved, and that may include annihilating us. We learn to accept and forgive ourselves when some marriages, and some treatments, fail.

Comfort with the therapeutic process of the divorcing couple is at best a momentary accomplishment. Detoxifying the persecutory object of divorce is not an easy matter, but it can be achieved by containing the persecutory superego affects, understanding termination anxiety, and metabolizing the attacks on love as the couple leaves the partnership with each other and with us.

REFERENCES

Freud, S. (1917). Mourning and melancholia. *Standard Edition*, 14: 243–258.

Klein, M. (1935). A contribution to the psychogenesis of manic depressive states. *Love, Guilt and Reparation & Other Works, 1921–1945*, pp. 344–369. London: Hogarth Press and the Institute of Psycho-Analysis, 1975.

Martin, E. and Schurtman, R. (1985). Termination anxiety as it affects the therapist. *Psychotherapy*, 22(1): 92–96.

Schecter, D. E. (1979). *The Loving and Persecuting Superego*. Presidential Address, William Alanson White Psychoanalytic Society, New York, May 23.

Chapter 10

Recovering from projections as a group co-therapist

Hilary Hall, MA, LMHC

A therapy group became a persecutory object for me when it persisted in projecting its aggression into the co-therapists, my husband and me. We were married three years ago. Our marriage was – and continues to be – the topic of much discussion in the group. The group idealized him as lively and helpful and viewed me as depressed and unhelpful. In the grip of this projective identification, I felt that our containing capacities were seriously threatened and that my sense of competence and value was difficult to maintain. My account as the female co-therapist of this group describes the process of containing a persecutory object and working in the countertransference towards detoxifying it for myself and then for the group.

The therapy group that I am referring to is a slow-open group that has been meeting for 12 years. It comprises two men and six women varying in age from 40 to 71 years. Two of the members have been there from the beginning and six others have been in the group from four to eight years. They meet once a week for one and three quarter hours. They struggle with preoedipal issues including self and object constancy and they function predominantly from paranoid-schizoid positions.

Dependency and fight/flight basic assumptions marked the early history of this group. Members were often angry with the leaders for not telling them how to do things. They complained that the group couldn't function adequately because the leadership was so minimal. Someone was always threatening to leave. The role of being the abandoning object rotated among the group. As new members have come and gone, group members have tried to understand how they might be contributing to driving others away.

During the past two years, a major theme of the group has been its tendency towards inactivity and unresponsiveness. A member brings up a topic, few people respond, and the member feels dropped. This has been analyzed many different ways without much change in the behaviour. When the group did seem to get up and running, still one or two members did not participate. This resulted in efforts to get the silent members to speak. When pressed, whoever was quiet during a particular group (and it might be any one of the group members) inevitably said the discussion was irrelevant, hard to follow, or just a waste of time. At these times, the persecutory attack fell on the group itself.

Last year, a man with a history of severe bipolar depression joined the group. Showing manic defences at the time of entry to the group, he became an enthusiastic, highly verbal new group member. The group members seemed to make him the container for activity, liveliness, and affect in the group, but then resented his leadership and attacked him for trying to enliven the group. He stayed active for six months, but then left abruptly. When he was gone, the remaining members restarted the same old struggle of how to keep the group from becoming flat and lifeless.

Before I continue to describe the current problem in the group and its effect on me, I will give some theoretical background to thinking about the group processes from an object relations point of view.

OBJECT RELATIONS THEORY AND GROUP THERAPY

Object relations theory holds that within each person, internal representations of experiences with others are built up from infancy. The self is constructed in relation to these. They may be conscious, or unconscious, object relationships representing the self's experience of the other person. We bring these traces of past relationships to present interactions with significant others through projective identification, the mental mechanism for unconscious communication that accounts for how one's internal world manifests itself in the interpersonal world (Grotstein 1981, Scharff 1992).

Unconscious object relationships are vividly demonstrated in group therapy where many combinations of personalities provide multiple versions of the various internal object relations sets in the group. Exploring this in group psychotherapy leads us to an understanding of each patient's internal object relations structures and how to effect change.

In addition, each person also brings to the interpersonal experience of group therapy an internal couple (Scharff & Scharff 1991). The internal couple is an unconscious, internal version of the parental couple and it is the basis for imagining what couples are like. This combined internal object conveys a fantasy of two adults relating closely and excitedly to one another and an image of the self as an outside observer – simultaneously a dyad and a triad. The internal couple has an important place in the developing child's internal object relations (Scharff and Scharff 1998). We can recognize the mental image of this internal parents-in-a-relationship, both in the patient and in ourselves as therapists (Scharff and Scharff 1998). As group members engage in serial dialogues and creative work pairings, we see coupling (including our own) having its effect on individuals (including us) and on the group as a whole.

These internal couples are readily detected in the transference and countertransference when there is a co-therapy team, especially when the team is a married couple like us. Group members may re-enact scenarios from times when they felt shut out of their parents' relationship or when they joined with one parent and excluded the other. The re-enactments include experiencing the group co-therapists as helpful or hurtful, loving or hating, appropriate or inappropriate, or myriad other views based on perceptions of and reactions to the parental couple at different developmental stages. In the group I am describing, my co-therapist and I experienced our couple relationship under strain from group behaviours and comments that felt like attacks. The group interaction had the effect of dividing us. The members devalued our couplehood, ignored our leadership, and sometimes joined with one of us to exclude the other.

From time to time the group operates like an infant in the paranoid-schizoid position and at other times it functions in the depressive position (Klein 1964). In the paranoid-schizoid position, the earliest developmental position, the defence of splitting predominates and the group lives in a world of discrete events with no continuity, experienced as all or nothing, good or bad, and nothing in between. Group members have little ability to have empathy for one another, or even to think about the experience of the other person. Only the present is held in mind, disconnected from past experience and future expectations. Because of this, the group cannot appreciate itself as a whole object. When a group is in the paranoid-schizoid position, each group member projects a part of the inner world into another group member who unconsciously identifies with it and feels subtle pressure to act in keeping with the projection. The original projector then takes in and identifies unconsciously with what has been projected into the other.

Group members in this state of mind have a tendency to forget one or the other extreme of their experience, especially in regard to persecutory feelings (Akhtar 1996). In the paranoid-schizoid position prevalent in the mind of the group that was so troublesome to me, the members used splitting as a defence against the pain of ambivalence and envy induced by recognizing the group as a whole object. They used another system of defence called psychic retreat, a pathological organization of the personality that allows the patient to defend against anxiety by avoiding contact with other people and with reality (Steiner 1993). This manifests as a feeling of being cut off and out of reach, with little spontaneity or aliveness of affect. These defensive organizations may be idealized by the group, but are often experienced as persecutory because they contain tyrannical, perverse, persecutory elements.

When a group moves into the depressive position, the members develop the capacity to see and tolerate the mixture of positive and negative aspects in themselves and others. They can maintain a connection to the past. They have a capacity for symbolic and abstract thinking, empathy and concern for each other and for the therapist, and maintain a complete view of the group as a whole object. As the group proceeds over time, it continues to move back and forth between paranoid-schizoid and depressive positions.

It has been difficult to help this group move into and maintain depressive position functioning because of its avoidance of loss and mourning. We tried to do so by establishing a good holding environment, developing the capacity for containment, and keeping a whole object in mind (Akhtar 1996). To give good holding, we maintained a respectful demeanour and provided reliability, consistency, and clear boundary setting (Winnicott 1958). We contained experience by taking in, tolerating, and metabolizing the affects in the group so that the members could re-own them in a more manageable form (Bion 1967). We recalled contradictory versions of experience to build up a whole object for the group to contemplate.

But the group remained in the paranoid-schizoid position during its early years. Even when it became able to function in the depressive position, it tended to revert. As a result, both of us often felt persecuted by the group's projections. In the group that I am describing, my co-therapist and I can be thought about as experiencing both concordant and complementary identifications with the group's persecutory states (Racker 1968). We felt bad, inept, attacked and ignored, identifying with the persecuted parts of themselves – concordant identification with an aspect of the group's self. At other times we felt angry, anxious and frustrated like the persecutors, identifying with those who had persecuted them – complementary identification with a projected part of the group's objects.

Group members' past experiences with faulty holding and containment showed up in the group's transference to our providing a therapeutic space and to our ability to process experience, respectively. The group transference was predominately negative. Although members voiced that they came to the group for help, they often experienced interpretations as making them feel bad, as if they had done something wrong. Then the therapists seemed to have done something wrong. We were often seen as confronting the group in a hurtful way, to be destructive and manipulative, not for benevolent reasons. In spite of this, a core group of individuals stayed and drew benefit. They slowly began to have some success at working as a group and being able to move towards the depressive position, thinking about and speaking to the group dynamics as well as to their individual ones.

THE DEVELOPMENT OF THE GROUP TRANSFERENCE TO ME

My co-therapist and I began to notice that the group interacted differently with each of us. When I made an intervention to the group, I was ignored. If I commented on being ignored later, I was usually still ignored. If my co-therapist made a similar comment, he was responded to, usually quite energetically. Even when this phenomenon was pointed out, the comment was dropped unless it came from him. As we began to stay on this topic and its possible meanings, the group members voiced the complaint that I was too unemotional and too cold. They said my comments were based not on feeling for them, but on using the mind to think, which was said to be too much work and too medicinal. I felt that the processes of linking, thinking, and working which I represented were being attacked in order to destroy awareness of the distinction between internal and external reality (Bion 1967).

The group's behaviour could also be seen as an attack on the process that brought the group members, my co-therapist, and me together, thus preventing their joining with me, and preventing the linking of the co-therapists. He and I were split into two different aspects. He was seen as emotional, giving, playful, and fun-loving, while I was seen as depressed and withholding. I felt resentful that he was having all the fun while I was becoming more and more withdrawn. Several outspoken women said that I seemed selfish, only interested in the group for what I could get for myself, and not really interested in their concerns. They saw no point in pursuing the topics I raised because these were only pertinent to me, not them.

At first, I felt myself recoil from the hostility I felt in many of their comments. I wanted to stand up for my worth and my acceptability. I wished I could remind them about times in the past when they'd valued me but I didn't want to be defensive. I felt confused, anxious, and self-conscious. I became less able to respond. I began to think of myself as indeed depressed, silent, and apart from the rest of the group. I wanted to join in and show them that I really wasn't depressed but I felt unable to connect mentally with anything they were talking about. My face felt frozen in a partial smile, as I tried not to look so depressed. I realized I felt attacked and wanted to withdraw, but with considerable effort I maintained my focus on the group process.

At one session, a male patient I work with in individual treatment came to my defence and expressed his appreciation of his individual work with me. I appreciated his attempt to rescue me as a whole object but I felt even more uncomfortable, as if I was so ineffective and meek that my patients now had to stand up for me. A few others said that they appreciated the way I seemed to keep the group on track, even though I was not as lively as the male therapist. I tried to reassure the group and myself that I welcomed all their reactions and that they provided useful material for us to use to understand the group. I knew that the full expression of the negative transference focused on me was an important movement in the group. They were finally able to verbalize feelings that had been operating silently for a long time.

WORK WITH MY COUNTERTRANSFERENCE

I wanted to avoid discussing the unpleasant doubts, insecurities, and persecutory and depressive feelings that came up for me in the group because I thought they were evidence of my personal problems. Working on them in therapy was useful, but revealing my reactions with my co-therapist/husband in a safe supervisory situation has been essential to regaining my perspective on the group. When we processed our ideas about what was happening in the group, I revealed that I was angry, envious, and defensive that my co-therapist/huband was getting to frolic and play while I was stuck down in the dumps! He observed that I was quieter and more serious in the group setting than he knew me to be as an individual therapist presenting my work in our seminar group. This discussion gave me the distance that I needed to sort out what the group was putting into me versus what I might be importing into the group.

THE INTENSIFICATION OF THE TRANSFERENCE

In subsequent weeks, with the transference focused on me and actively addressed by both therapists, the group showed more energy and affect. The group discussed what it might mean to its members to have a depressed, withholding female therapist, and a frolicking male therapist. The group associated to its feelings about mothers who were subdued by more powerful fathers; females who were repressed and repulsed by their sexuality; and depressed mothers too withdrawn to respond to their children. I was told that I might do better with my own group somewhere else and that maybe then I would be able to be livelier.

I said that I thought the group was trying to kill me off by ignoring me and then sending me out to form another group. One person said that receiving my responses in the group felt like being hit over the head with a hammer. That was exactly the way I'd been feeling about the group for weeks! This realization helped me start thinking again.

RE-EVALUATION OF THE COUNTERTRANSFERENCE

I examined my state of mind more objectively. I had been seriously task-oriented, and at the same time seriously withdrawn. I was perceived as selfish. Might these two aspects reflect concordant and complementary identifications in my countertransference? The group members came from families where thinking about feelings was non-existent. Some of them had had strict, domineering, and angry mothers while others had had passive, withdrawn, and depressed mothers. They had either felt ignored and neglected or emotionally and physically abused. In a complementary identification I was identifying with their persecutory objects, doing to them what had been done in the past. At the same time a concordant identification in which I was identifying with their childhood selves left me feeling ignored, devalued, and abused.

I thought of my selfishness now as a concordant identification with the group's selfish wish to possess only the male therapist. Perhaps I was stuck there because of my fears of annihilation by their envy and aggression towards me for being his partner. I still felt horrible in the group, but at least I could now think about it. The aggression the members were expressing towards me was energizing the group and mobilizing me. When my co-therapist and I discussed the situation again, we realized that either way, depressed or frolicking, we weren't being listened to. The group couldn't be taking in our interventions because his were just 'play' after all, and mine were ignored.

My co-therapist and I were not being used as a couple; we had to be kept separated. If the child is forced to recognize the parental sexual relationship at a time when the child has not established a securely based maternal object, the parental relationship may be registered, but its reality defended against and denied (Britton 1998). This may result in an internal division of parental objects whose coupling must be prevented in one's mind so as to avoid feared explosion and disintegration. Perhaps this was the unconscious basis for the group's need to split us apart.

THE TURNING POINT SESSION

In the session that I am going to describe, I made the transition from feeling impotent in the face of my countertransference to becoming clear about how I could use it more productively. On the occasion of this session, my co-therapist had to be out of town without warning. Unexpectedly, I was running the group without him. My being there alone freed up the group somewhat and allowed me to think about and play with the members' shared perception of me as depressed. I got the idea that the group seemed to me to be operating according to the fantasy that if the group can split the couple, or deny the reality of the couple, a disastrous internal situation can be avoided.

The group had not met the previous week owing to a scheduled break. I had enjoyed the week off. As the group was reconvening, I was feeling anxious and self-conscious and also aware of feeling in a bind. I worried that I might be too active in this group without my co-therapist. I was concerned that overfunctioning like that would be selfish and manipulative. On the other hand, I did not want to succumb to being the depressed therapist either. I realized how influenced I was by what I thought the group members wanted me to be, the x in the group equation (Symington 1986).

The group session began with their asking me if my co-therapist was late, and my advising them of his unexpected absence. You will notice that my co-therapist was not referred to again, after the beginning of the group. Hanna, an often-depressed female member, said that she had been to the dentist during the break since the group last met and was much better, thanks to relief from an aching tooth. (I thought the dentist was a substitute for the therapists and the missed group.) Chuck, a 71-year-old male patient said that he was aware of missing the group. He told a long story about his apartment being broken into during the break. He had lost some cherished possession and now he was worried the burglars might come back and steal more things, especially his loaded gun. He had been eager to come to the group to relay his feelings of loss, anger, and anxiety about a repetition, and then realized that the group was not meeting that week. He went into detail about the lack of appropriate response from the policemen who came to investigate. (The group not meeting was like the neglectful police.) They hadn't seemed interested in his losses and his fears that the burglars would return to take more of his things. He

thought their efforts at fingerprinting were ancient and mean-
ingless, and they hadn't even found any of his fingerprints, he said.
(I think this refers to the group being useless.) So he had to play
amateur detective. Canvassing the neighbourhood for information,
he was told of a similar break-in two blocks away. When he related
this to the police, they thanked him for the information, as if it
never would have been connected to his situation without his doing
it for them. The group was responding with outrage and disbelief.

Dolores, a group member who works for the juvenile justice
system volunteered the information that a gang she had worked
with in town had been connected with these break-ins and two
teenagers were now in custody. (The group has been like a gang
breaking into the co-therapy couple.) Cindy said angrily that this
discussion seemed highly inappropriate. She thought there were
confidentiality issues here, but was unable to clarify whose confidentiality about what issue was at stake. Cindy, who felt the group
was acting inappropriately, and Dolores, who had said she was
working with the gang, both became defensive and argumentative.

The group struggled for some time with the idea that someone
had done something wrong, but where was the wrongdoing
located? I said that the discussion of events outside the group was
secondary to what was going on here in the room. I said that the
group was talking about whether they could get help from the
authorities in the therapy group or would have to help themselves
by gaining access to confidential material and privileged relationships. I said that the group was confused about who was committing what crimes because of preoccupation with what crimes
and special relationships were here in the room. I noticed that I
was not feeling depressed or withdrawn.

Tina who had not yet spoken and who is known for her insight
but also her tendency towards schizoid withdrawal, announced
plans for a picnic and bonfire being held at the nature reserve
where she works. I noticed that again someone was taking the
group discussion outside, but I let it go, for fear of being too active.
Many members admitted that they'd often thought about coming
out to Tina's park activities but they hadn't done so because of the
long-standing group prohibition against meeting outside the group,
except accidentally. This boundary was set in order to discourage
sub-groupings and pairings that might then influence the group
process destructively. I said that what stood out in this discussion
was their emphasis on the boundary as an imposed rule and a

deprivation, with no reference to understanding its meaning and relevance to the group.

Then I asked the group to think about the meaning of this discussion here and now in the group. Peter suggested that it was relevant to making the group more life-like, because not enough life outside the group gets talked about inside the group and that might be why the group is so dead at times. Others said, as they had before, that they can be spontaneous and alive outside the group, but they become inhibited in the group. I said that this didn't seem to me to be for lack of bringing in stories about outside events, but because of difficulty bringing in some parts of themselves to the group. I said that I was beginning to wonder if the group needed me to be dead, so that they could be livelier. This was met with deadly silence.

Suddenly Tina began to talk excitedly: 'Hey, here's an idea. If it's true that the group needs Hilary to take on all our depressed, dead, bad feelings, we could make a dummy representing her, and then we could all meet at the bonfire next weekend and sing and dance while we throw the dummy in the fire. That would kill off all that nasty stuff and we could move on!' I realized for the first time what the term dumbfounded meant. I was speechless at this unbridled aggression and shocked at the image of myself being burned at the stake.

At the same time, I was also extremely interested in this new development, both because Tina had actually heard my intervention and had responded, and because the group's hostility was being represented so clearly. I waited to see how the group would react. The group members were pleased with themselves, becoming more lively and present with each other. Did they not get the implications of what Tina was saying, or were they excited by the fantasy of the roast?

Cindy and Hanna who had contributed early on in this group had withdrawn. The group now focused on their lack of participation. Both of them said tearfully that they felt isolated and depressed, and were unable to feel any connection to the group. They then experienced themselves as bad because they couldn't connect with the others. Hanna said that it must be their turn to hold the depression for the group.

Chuck told a story about himself as a child at a family gathering in the middle of summer, where he had been forced by his mother to wear a heavy, woollen suit and had been so uncomfortable and distressed that he could only stand around watching from a distance the activities around him. Others tried to convince Cindy that Chuck's memory was an association to her experience, which she denied. We were near the end of the group. Without me containing the depression in the group, someone else had to take it on. I said that Cindy, Hanna, and Chuck were embodying the awareness that uncomfortable experiences and hostile, disconnected feelings cannot just be killed off, but are kept alive insisting that we can notice how they stem from depression and ultimately from underlying aggression.

RECOVERY FROM THE HATED INTERNAL COUPLE

I no longer felt depressed and my ability to think had returned. I could see what had been happening. The group had been attacking the co-therapy pair by splitting its internal representation of the therapists into one good/exciting object and one bad/rejecting object so as to avoid feelings about the couple. It had tried to get rid of and kill off parts of us, especially of me, as the bad mother who produced the deadness by her lack of holding and containment of their internal objects, especially those filled with aggression. It had been splitting its experience of itself into an outside group and an inside group so as to avoid the link between there and then and here and now.

The group members had attempted to detoxify the persecutory process by evacuating and projecting their own critical internal objects into me. That did not protect them because, through projective identification, they re-found in me the persecutory object of the bad mother. The group had succeeded in attacking my thinking in the group so thoroughly that I was unable to recognize my countertransference identifications and remained locked into re-enactments of the past. While persecuting myself for my boredom and depression in the group, I allowed the group to frolic with my co-therapist. When he and I became a couple again by being able to think about our experiences together, the group could begin to move out of repetitive old patterns, as could we.

Once we were able to talk about what was going on, the group members could begin to show parts of themselves that they might no longer approve of but had been afraid to let loose. As group members continued to verbalize and own their aggressive feelings towards me and towards the co-therapy couple, they did not need to kill off these parts of themselves and us. So they began to have confidence that the group could help contain these experiences, and that no traumatic situations would be repeated.

This group demonstrates in action the concepts of projective identification, envious attacks on thinking and linking, and the toxic effects of the persecutory internal couple that is filled with envy and aggression. Holding the affective experience, tolerating suffering, waiting for clarity, and subjecting the co-therapy experience to process and review led the integration of feeling and thinking about the experience.

In that group I no longer feel like the depressed group therapist. I may feel that way again in the future, partly because of my gender and my valency to resonate with the projection of the bad mother, and partly because of being married to my co-therapist. Being a couple with my co-therapist in marriage as well as in the group provokes envy and attack. Bearing uncomfortable feelings like these, thinking about the experience, having insight such as this, and putting it all into words is the therapeutic activity that enables the group to recognize and take back its projective identifications. Speaking in the group to that envy about my co-therapist also being my husband is the next step in detoxifying the persecutory object for the group and for myself.

REFERENCES

Akhtar, S. (1996). Object constancy and adult psychopathology. In *The Internal Mother*, ed. S. Akhtar, S. Kramer, and H. Parens, pp. 129–156. Northvale, NJ: Jason Aronson.

Bion, W. R. (1967). *Second Thoughts*. London: Heinemann.

Britton, R. (1998). *Belief and Imagination*. London/New York: Routledge.

Grotstein, J. (1981). *Splitting and Projective Identification*. New York: Jason Aronson.

Klein, M. (1964). *Contributions to Psychoanalysis, 1921–1945*. New York: McGraw-Hill.

Racker, H. (1968). *Transference and Countertransference*. New York: International Universities Press.

Scharff, D. E. and Scharff, J. S. (1991). *Object Relations Couple Therapy*. Northvale, NJ: Jason Aronson.

Scharff, J. S. (1992). *Projective and Introjective Identification and the Use of the Therapist's Self*. Northvale, NJ: Jason Aronson.

Scharff, J. S. and Scharff, D. E. (1998). *Object Relations Individual Therapy*. Northvale, NJ: Jason Aronson.

Steiner, J. (1993). *Psychic Retreats*. London/New York: Routledge.

Symington, N. (1986). *The Analytic Experience*. New York: St. Martin.

Winnicott, D. W. (1958). *Collected Papers. Through Paediatrics to Psycho-Analysis*. London: Tavistock Publications.

Chapter 11

Holding and containment during surgery for physical deformity

Marianela Altamirano, MEd

THE DEFORMITY AS THE LOCUS OF THE BAD OBJECT

A physical deformity may become the locus of a bad object. Children may come to hate the deformed part of themselves that makes them different from their peers and their siblings, and see it as something that is sent to punish or persecute them. Their fantasies about themselves and how others see them coalesce around this physical aspect that they imbue with badness. Some parents may unwittingly reinforce the sense of badness if they feel that their impaired or handicapped child is punishment for something they did or did not do. Others view the infant as a negative part of their own selves or evidence of a flawed marital relationship. Getting rid of the problem with surgery, however, does not get rid of the fantasies that surround it, because the children have become used to being the way they are. It takes time to recover and adjust to surgical improvement, especially when the deformity has been present for years because the family could not afford surgery. Not only that, the surgery to correct the problem can be experienced as a persecutory experience by children and families who are terrified of medical intervention.

In this chapter, we describe the detoxifying effects of sensitive psychological services to prepare and support the children and their families through the experience of surgical repair of the damaged or persecuting part of the body. Our team of psychologists asked to join Operation Smile, an organization manned by volunteer doctors, technicians, and nurses who operate on disadvantaged children with harelip, cleft palate, and other facial and orthopaedic deformities in countries with little access to plastic surgery. We hoped that our theoretical constructs taken from object relations theory and applied in this specific situation of field surgery could help the children, the families, and the surgical team. We proposed joining Operation Smile in Panamá because we believed that good psychological support could help the children and their families face the anxiety of anaesthesia and surgery, mourn the loss of the way the body had been, and then adapt to changes brought by surgical improvements.

We found support for our idea in the child analytic literature on working with children before surgery. Solnit (1984) stated that 'preparing children to cope with, adapt to and eventually to master the potentially traumatic experience is a vital application of the psychoanalytic theory of trauma and of theoretical propositions concerned mainly with the protective shield and functions of the ego beyond traumatic challenges' (p. 631). We made our proposal to the surgical team and they accepted. For the first time in these missions there would be psychological support for the children who were about to undergo surgery and for their families, and we would have the privilege of providing psychological services in this unusual setting. We felt we had a lot to offer, but we soon found out that first we had to learn how to work under these conditions.

FAILURE IN OUR HOLDING ENVIRONMENT

We set off in September 1999 to a place in the interior, about three hours from Panama City, where we expected to meet with a group of about 50 to 60 children during the pre-selection process prior to the upcoming mission. We planned to interview the parents to assess their levels of anxiety and provide a holding environment to the family as they faced the challenge of selection and possibly eventual surgery or rejection. We planned to meet each child in a play interview in which we would also administer the individual and family drawing tests with the aim of understanding the emotional state of the child and evaluating the child's developmental stage, self-esteem, body image, and intellectual capacity. We wanted both to present a programme that would support the children and their families before, during, and after their surgical intervention, and to do research into the impact of deformity and its repair on attachment and on family dynamics by addressing the following questions:

1   The deformities being mainly in the face, specifically in the mouth, how did attachment form when feeding was such a difficult and sometimes dangerous task, and gazing was so emotionally painful for the parent and others?

2   How was social development, and especially the onset of the smile, impaired by these deformities, and what implications had this for object relations development?

3   How guilty, rejected, and rejecting did these parents feel and how did their affected self-esteem interfere with the parenting process?

4   How could the baby internalize a good object when the deformity made every effort of the mother to feed him a battle between life and death?

5   How did the process of emotional containment occur when so much of the parent's psychological energy had to be used for providing physical support and holding?

We arrived a day before the surgical team so that we could be with the patients early in the morning and could start our pro-gramme before the doctors arrived. We were shocked to find over 130 patients waiting to be selected, with all kind of deformities, with their hopes for a better life placed squarely on this mission, and with their eyes pleading for support and understanding. There were far too many people and too little time. The surgeons would select a manageable number to operate on, but those not chosen needed us as much or more than those who would have surgery. There was no way to give our usual level of individual attention. The interview we had prepared for this purpose was too long, with a vocabulary too sophisticated for the families' level of education. Our tools were useless and our research agenda was hopelessly ambitious. Our well-organized plan for formal evaluation, testing our hypotheses about the value of psychological help, and answer-ing our research questions was not at all what we were needed for. These people were begging for holding and containment, not for research. Had we proceeded according to plan, we would only have added to the trauma. We would have introduced another persecu-tory object into the experience instead of helping the families to deal with the persecutory objects of deformity, the tantalizing possibility of cure, and the fear of surgery and anaesthesia.

So we would have to improvise a new plan in keeping with the social reality of the families, using our training and clinical experience to gain insight into their inner world. How could we provide what they needed when we returned for the four-day mission? We decided to work with the large group, using colourful images and a story-telling technique to prepare children and parents for the surgery. We selected toys depicting doctors, nurses, medical equipment and tools, soft dolls, so that the children could elaborate their fears through play. We decided to stay with the child patients before the surgery and right after it and to keep their anxious parents informed during the procedure in order to contain anxiety and so minimize the traumatic aspects of the experience. To this end, we attended surgeries at the city hospital so that we could get used to bearing the anxiety of the operating room procedures ourselves. Everything had gone smoothly in the city and we felt well prepared by November when we returned.

THE REVISED PLAN FOR HOLDING AND CONTAINMENT

We walked into a room full of the pre-selected children and adults who had been awake since two or three in the morning. They had travelled from remote places and had not eaten because they did not yet know who was going to surgery on the first day. The atmosphere was charged and tense. Children were crying and the adults were not interacting among themselves or with their children. We read the story we had written to the large group and then invited the children to join us on the floor to play. Most children participated spontaneously, mothers or fathers staying with the smaller ones. Little by little, children started to play more freely and to include us in their play. At the same time, parents felt more relaxed and started to interact with other parents. The atmosphere in the room changed from one that was charged with apprehension to one of anticipation filled with laughter and playfulness. As the team of supportive psychologists worked creatively with the exchange between the patients, their families and us, we saw unfolding before us a vivid demonstration of Winnicott's concept of providing a holding environment and Bion's concept of containment.

Winnicott (1960) described how the observable exchanges and play activities between mother and baby help the child to use mental processes. Using our presence, our narrative, toys, and visual materials, the children and their families struggled to comprehend and control a persecutory external process. We were creating the space for the external exchange to take place and we were providing a transitional space for internal exchange between fear, defence, and mastery. Through the children's play and the families' interaction with each other, all of them could find support for imagining and anticipating the process that they would have to face, now not so alone.

Bion (1970) described the mother's capacity for 'containment', a mental process in which she takes in her infant's anxieties (which he called beta elements) through projective and introjective identification and then metabolizes them through her maternal reverie so that they become thinkable (alpha elements) and therefore less disorganizing to the infant. We were receiving and handling projective identifications and anxieties from the children and their families. We took in the beta elements of their anxieties and transformed them into thinkable alpha elements and fed them back in an acceptable form.

In these exchanges we saw both concepts of holding and containment at work. We saw the child actively working in the space between mother and infant as Winnicott described. We saw the parents learning to do the psychic work of containing their children's anxieties, the process that Bion described. We felt good about our work and confident of our effectiveness, but we did not know what lay ahead.

Further revision of the modified plan

That first day, the surgical team began to operate. On the first day, 14 surgeries were done, 19 on the second, and 15 on the third. Close to the operating room there were many people: nurses, assistants, technicians, volunteers, students, and other employees. Then there was a major unanticipated complication. Reporters, news cameras, and administrative personnel arrived on the scene with the First Lady who had decided to visit the project. Because of this there was total confusion and chaos, quite unlike the calm and controlled scene at the city hospital where we had gone to learn about the process of surgery. We could not claim the time and space needed for implementing our plan. Two frightened children were given their intravenous infusion for the anaesthetic, surrounded by strangers who tried to calm them, but this only made the children more scared, and they cried and screamed in terror. The children returned from their surgeries, and when they awoke from the anaesthesia, they were still terrified.

At this point we were feeling angry and helpless. Our holding was again failing for these children because of unanticipated difficulties in this setting. We felt temporarily paralyzed by feelings of inadequacy, impotence, and guilt at not being able to help. Analyzing our reactions, we realized that we were too identified with the helpless children who had clearly been traumatized by the experience and we felt guilty because we had not been able to fill our role as good containers to protect them from persecutory experience. We galvanized ourselves into action.

We talked to the administrator of the mission and asked her to allow us to make additional changes to prevent further trauma. We asked her to clear the waiting room of visitors and we insisted that we needed to be with the patients before surgery and right after. We talked to the parents constantly while the surgery was taking place and we were with the nurses when they took the child back to the parents. At the end of the day, we visited the patients. The surgical team understood and appreciated our intervention, and the families were helped considerably.

THE NEED FOR EMOTIONAL ATTUNEMENT

These missions are planned to provide free treatment that will bring a better physical appearance to children and adults who have facial and other deformities that make them feel different, and sometimes unloved and rejected. The administration, the medical team, the volunteers all focused on repairing this physical part to change the lives of these patients in a miraculous way. However, since the physical aspect was so overwhelming and took all the energy, effort, and concentration of the surgical team, the emotional concomitants took second place or were completely overlooked. There was no space for relating to the current situation, much less for talking about how to recover from deviations in the course of early relationships.

Like the surgical team, the parents of these children were drawn to focus on the traumatizing physical abnormality and many of them then couldn't create a transitional space in which the child could grow and develop psychologically. Could Winnicott's object mother ever come into being if the environmental mother was so busy with externals that prevented her from providing a secure environment to her child? If these parents were too pressed to provide the holding, how could they be able to contain? For these children, both internal and external processes constitute a threat and the handling of anxiety is difficult for everyone involved, so the chance of undisturbed development for these children is minimal.

HELPING A BOY BRAVE SURGERY AGAIN

Hector is a 5-year-old boy whose left-hand fingers are webbed and therefore they do not have the freedom of movement made possible by the usual separation between them. His mother told us that he is disobedient, gets easily frustrated, and frequently responds with aggression. She mentioned in his hearing that she didn't want to have any more children since Hector was so difficult. Hector responded to this comment with loud noises and disruptive behaviour.

The first day of the mission, the day before surgery, Hector caught my attention because he was strikingly able to elaborate his conflicts through play. I sat close to him on the floor as he was rehearsing several medical procedures in his play. He had his doll baby die on the operating table and come to life again. I asked him why he was there. He showed me his deformed hand and said that he wanted it to be just like his other hand. He also said that he had been operated on before, but that his hand was still ugly. He seemed calm and I said that I thought that he was waiting happily for the surgery. He confirmed this and said that if his two hands were the same, children would not bother him any more. I thought that the surgery was the only way he thought he could get acceptance and love.

The day of Hector's surgery, he again seemed happy and calm. My colleague and I wondered if this might be the defensive way he handled his anxiety, but we were persuaded that he must have had a good experience the last time and so felt less scared of the unknown than the other children. We wondered if we had been exaggerating the children's need for psychological support. Hector walked hand in hand with the nurse into the operating room and commented on the clothing everyone was wearing.

Hector asked, 'Is my doctor rough?'

We said, 'No, he's going to take care of you and he is big and strong.'

He asked, 'Are you going to be there with me?'

We answered, 'Yes.'

'Good,' he said.

Our presence had been contributing to his confidence.

When Anna Freud (1952) investigated the effects of various nursing, medical, and surgical procedures on children, she concluded that the 'physically ill child has to renounce ownership of his own body and permit it to be handled passively.'

On the operating table, Hector was smiling and socializing with the nurses who were as amazed by his attitude as we were. Hector seemed well able to place his body in the hands of the medical team and to deal with surgery with confidence. He struck us as a resilient child.

The anaesthesiologist for Hector's case was not yet in the room, and so the one at the next operating table gave the instructions to the nurse. When she started to remove Hector's pyjamas, he got scared and began to cry softly. The anaesthesiologist arrived, gave the anaesthetic, and Hector went to sleep. One of the tubes connected to the oxygen tank kept getting unhooked and the anaesthesiologist kept fixing it. My colleague was worried that the balloon into which Hector was breathing was not receiving enough air for Hector. She and I were clearly feeling anxious on behalf of the sleeping child. The sheet over the rest of Hector's body on the operating table slipped, the child was uncovered, and the room was cold. We looked across at a second operation table in the same room, and felt envious that things were going more smoothly for the patient there.

The surgeon came in and explained the procedure to us, the main objective being to make the boy's little hand functional. He made the first incision with the scalpel and the child jerked his hand away. The surgeon said: 'His body is telling me that he is not ready,' and he walked away to wait for the anaesthetic to take full effect. He tried and had to wait three more times. For the first time, the possibility of something going wrong for Hector on the operating table and the possibility of his life being in danger came to mind.

The surgeon was finally able to start the surgery. He started with Hector's little finger and at this point my colleague left the operating room, explaining later that she couldn't contain the anxiety because there was nothing she could do for Hector. I stayed in the room and watched how they worked to free his little fingers. There was not enough skin to cover them, and they took a graft from the pelvic area, near the scar from his previous surgery. The assistant surgeon told me that hair grows in that skin. As an adolescent Hector would grow hair on his hand. I felt a bit upset thinking of how that might look, but my feelings were quickly eclipsed by my reaction to what happened next. At this point, a tourniquet on Hector's elbow to keep the operation site free of blood got loose and his hand started bleeding copiously. The surgeon was upset, nurses ran to the rescue, and in a few minutes they controlled the situation. The surgery proceeded.

I felt equipped to stay by Hector's side by having gone to observe surgery as part of my orientation prior to the mission, but I had not seen a surgical emergency there. This was new to me. It made me anxious and there was nothing I could do to help. I meant to stand by while all this was going on, but I felt anxious at what I was seeing and I had to leave the room. I pulled myself together and when I came back, they were finishing Hector's third finger. Finally, they completed the operation and the surgical team left the room. I left with them because Hector was still asleep, attended to by the nurses and the anaesthesiologist. I heard him coughing. I looked through the glass and saw that he was having difficulty breathing. I watched the anaesthesiologist putting the mask over Hector's face. I felt worried seeing Hector moving a lot. I felt terrified lest such a confident and pleasant child should die on that table.

I kept looking through the glass and when Hector's body calmed down I came back in. The doctor was trying to put on the boy's shirt, but had it backwards. I was able to be helpful in straightening that out. The surgeon took the boy in his arms and carried him still sleeping to the recovery room. I walked beside them carrying the intravenous drip and again I was glad to be doing something helpful. The surgeon left Hector to the care of the nurses. Hector was still coughing and tossing a lot, and so the nurses started to tie him to the bed because they were too busy to watch him individually. I asked them not to tie him down because that it would make him anxious when he awoke, and I would be there to watch him. They hesitated, but reached a compromise, and left only one foot tied down to the end of the bed. His mother and paternal grandmother were looking anxiously through the glass. My colleague was with them reassuring them.

Soon Hector woke up and sat upright in the bed. He looked straight at me. I told him that it was over, that they had fixed his hand, and that he was going to be okay. I pointed to the glass to show him where his mother and grandmother were waiting to meet him again in a few minutes. He was calm.

Next day we went to see Hector. He was dressed, and sitting on his bed. I walked up to him and knelt beside him. He said that I was his aunt and that my colleagues were all aunts. I joked that his family had grown while he was in the hospital.

Then Hector asked me, 'Can I have the piñata now?'

I asked, 'What piñata?'

He replied, 'I had a dream about you being with me in the operation room. I remember you came too and you were carrying my piñata and the other lady had my birthday cake. You were celebrating my birthday.'

I thought back to a paper I had read. In a preliminary investigation and analysis of dreams during surgical procedures, George Pollock and Hyman Muslim (1962) found that the analysis of a patient's dreams revealed the unconscious meaning of the surgical intervention and the ego's defensive and adaptive activities that were mobilized in the face of bodily threat. Hector's dream was of a reassuring nature. It was evidence of the ego's attempt to maintain a steady state of balance and to do so by using us as encouraging objects. In Hector's case, the mental process of elaboration of an external experience was possible both in the play ahead of time, and in the dream. This unconscious work promoted a later capacity to face the experience with confidence and recover quickly.

Two months later we saw Hector again for re-valuation. He was social and friendly but was uncomfortable showing us his hand. It was actually much better-looking and quite functional. However, he said that he didn't like it. When I showed him a picture of his hand before the surgery to prove how much better it was, he denied that this was a photo of his hand. His mother said that Hector was still being a very difficult child.

Thesi Bergman and Anna Freud (Freud 1952, Bergman and Freud 1965) described how frequently children view surgery as a mutilation that is a punishment for their own naughtiness and forbidden desires. I explained this to Hector and his mother in simple words and it helped her to see him as troubled by what he had been through rather than just bad. I showed the photo to Hector again and he accepted that indeed it was his old hand.

During the surgical procedure, when there was a failure in the holding environment, we felt helpless and anxious. Lacking experience in the operating room, our capacity to contain anxiety was annihilated. When we felt this, we started to put an emotional distance between ourselves and Hector. Then we felt guilty for leaving him alone to take care of our own distress and we returned to his side. Physical holding provided by our presence as helpers and emotional containment provided by our ability to process the experience have to go hand in hand in order for the child to be able to organize and internalize his experience. Winnicott's environmental mother and object mother have to coexist in us if we are to help the child to master the experience and continue to develop his inner world in a healthy way.

WHAT WE LEARNED

In subsequent missions of Operation Smile we applied our understanding of the mental processes and the emotional ordeals of these children and their families. We were more able to help them integrate their experience and foster their children's social, intellectual, and emotional development. Like the second-time mother who learns from her first baby, we went to the mission better prepared to help. We had learned to tolerate our anxiety about meeting the needs of a horde of damaged children and needy families, and had become used to surgical procedures and emergencies. Managing countertransference feelings of helplessness in response to the child's surrender to the surgical process contains the persecutory anxiety of child and family, and improves their treatment outcome and their adjustment to surgical improvement.

REFERENCES

Bergman, T. and Freud, A. (1965). *Children in the Hospital.* New York: International Universities Press.

Bion, W. (1970). Container and contained. In *Attention and Interpretation*, pp. 72–82. London: Tavistock.

Freud, A. (1952). The role of bodily illness in the mental life of children. *The Writings of Anna Freud*, Vol. 4, pp. 260–279. New York: International Universities Press, 1966.

Pollock, G. H. and Muslim, H. L. (1962). *Psychoanalytic Quarterly*, 31: 175–202.

Solnit, A. (1984). Preparing. *Psychoanalytic Study of the Child*, 39: 613–632.

Winnicott, D. W. (1960). The theory of the parent–infant relationship. In *Maturational Processes and the Facilitatory Environment*, pp. 37–55. London: Hogarth Press and the Institute of Psycho-Analysis.

Chapter 12

Persecutory aspects of family business

Michael Stadter, PhD

All mental health professionals know that both the workplace and the family can evoke powerful and primitive responses and inter- actions among their members. Family businesses combine the dynamics of the family and the workplace to produce uniquely intense phenomena (Levinson 1971, Gage 2002). To understand the complexity of family business we need a theory that bridges indi- vidual, couple, group, and organizational dynamics. Object rela- tions theory is a theory grounded in clinical psychoanalysis and intensive psychoanalytic psychotherapy (Greenberg and Mitchell 1983, Scharff and Scharff 1998) that has been applied to group psychotherapy, couple and family psychotherapy, and brief therapy (Ashbach and Schermer 1987, Scharff and Scharff 1987, 1991, Stadter 1996) and to the study of group dynamics in institutions (Bion 1959, Obholzer and Roberts 1994, Menzies-Lyth 1988). Concepts of family dynamics, power, authority, responsi- bility, containment, and processes of projective identification are particularly helpful in understanding the difficulties of family businesses.

Consider Shakespeare's presentation of the dynamics among three brothers in the royal family business – Richard, Clarence, and Edward, the King:

> Plots have I laid, inductions dangerous,
> By drunken prophecies, libels and dreams,
> To set my brother Clarence and the king
> In deadly hate the one against the other . . .
> Clarence still breathes; Edward still lives and reigns:
> When they are gone, then must I count my gains.
> *Richard III* (Act I, Scene I)

Few family businesses proceed to actual murder, but many involve strong and regressive forces and some are quite persecutory.

There are multiple definitions of a family business. For the purposes of this discussion, I define a family business as an organization (profit or non-profit) largely owned by two or more members of a family and where two or more family members are in management positions.

FAMILY DYNAMICS AND FAMILY BUSINESSES

In the workplace as in other settings, people interact at various psychological levels. One level involves conscious interaction that is task-oriented, rational, and good enough to be gratifying. Another level involves transference to figures from one's family of origin. For example, a man's supervisor may evoke reactions in him that are intensified by his unconsciously relating to the boss as if he were his father. However, in a family business the man's boss may actually *be* his father. A son or daughter may be treated like, or may act like, a child rather than like an adult employee. Siblings may replay their childhood roles. A parent-manager may avoid making necessary staffing decisions because he is afraid of seeming to show favouritism by appointing one son or daughter to a higher-level position than those of siblings. Unconscious re-enactments occur universally in the workplace through transference relationships, but when the 'real' family members are the actual participants there is an additional level of intensity to the interactions, not uncommonly reaching persecutory proportions.

Rivalry, guilt, envy, and hostility: Common affects of persecutory states of mind

Competition over power and resources, envy towards those who appear to be more favoured, hostility towards rivals or winners, and guilt over these attitudes are often prominent in the unconscious life of family members in the business. Family dynamics intensify such attitudes, which may be denied and if acknowledged, their impact may be disavowed. For example, one hard-charging CEO had no difficulty acknowledging his own ruthlessness and aggression towards non-family employees. He actually seemed proud of it. However, he denied that he treated his employee/son the same way. 'I don't do that, I love my son,' he thought. The son and other company staff, however, saw the aggressive pattern directed towards the son.

Family members in business together may try to promote the fantasy that they are or should be 'one, big, happy family'. This fantasy and the denial of the real interactions often cause damage to both the family and to the business. When family members can face uncomfortable feelings and states of mind, they can be freed to work and interact with each other more successfully.

Family businesses managed more like families than like businesses

Family members may try to deal with their family issues through workplace decisions and strategies. For instance, all the siblings may be given the same degree of status and authority despite their differing levels of competence and motivation. A father regrets that he neglected his daughter when she was young so he gives her a position as senior vice-president even though her experience and training make her ill-prepared for this position. A brother resents it that his younger brother was always the favoured son and he will even the score by keeping the younger brother in a lower-level position. A mother feels guilty because the family did not do enough for the son with severe learning disabilities and so she appoints him to a high-level finance committee despite his ignorance of this area. A father appoints two brothers to be equal CEOs of the company as a way for them to be forced to work together, an ill-advised remedy for the fact that they had never been compatible.

Trying to resolve family conflicts or problems through business decisions works to the detriment of both the family and the business.

The family business that can impair family life

The different roles that family members fill in the workplace – for instance, manager and subordinate, sales representative and manufacturing chief – complicate the already complex interactions among family members. Lack of separation and space between the family members can be problematic when they work together and live together. Workplace conflicts and discussions can spill over into home life and vice versa.

A husband and wife who came to me for couple therapy struggled with this issue. Charles was a lawyer in solo practice and Cynthia was the office manager in their six-person office. Working together proved to be a chronic and serious strain for their marriage. Cynthia hated Charles's style of management – authoritarian, like her father's style of parenting – which was not the way he was with her at home. Charles often felt that she should agree with him when conflicts arose among employees. Their marriage dramatically improved when Cynthia chose to leave the firm and Charles grudgingly accepted her decision. Then couple therapy helped them to deal with her guilt over leaving and Charles's feelings of abandonment.

Family dynamics in the organization resonating among non-family members

The powerful, unconscious forces of projective identification can induce non-family members to play out roles in the family's drama. This can greatly intensify the conflicts among these employees, and the effects cascade throughout the organization.

Two vice-presidents in an office furniture company, David and Diane, were referred to me because of their inability to work together. At the conscious level, they did have real clashes of opinion over company policy. Out of their awareness, their conflicts were exacerbated by their unconscious identifications with family members. David was identifying with the founder-CEO of the company who espoused a more conservative, low-tech approach to business and who was having difficulty turning over more responsibility to his son, the ambitious company president. Diane was unconsciously aligned with the son in promoting an aggressive business plan which involved more computer and Internet activity and which pushed decision-making down to lower-level employees. When the two vice-presidents became aware of how they were playing out the father–son conflict, they became able to work more collaboratively. Although they still had frequent conflicts, these struggles no longer had the previous level of primitive regression and aggression. If the father and son had dealt more successfully with their differences, this resolution probably would have had a further beneficial impact on Diane and David's conflictual working relationship.

Like non-family employees, organizational consultants may be drawn into taking roles in the family drama unconsciously. The enactment gives the consultant valuable information about the unconscious power of the projective identificatory system of the family business and offers a position of personal engagement from which to arrive at an interpretation geared towards change.

Different sets of rules for family members than for non-family members

In a mid-sized sporting goods company owned by a father and two brothers, one brother embezzled $35,000 to cover gambling debts. Even though this was the second time that he had stolen from the company, he remained in his position. The only consequences that the family imposed on him were closer supervision over his access to corporate funds and the requirement that he begin psychotherapy. A non-family member would have been fired and probably arrested.

In another business, a non-family member complained to me that he would never be able to reach a certain level of responsibility in the company, no matter how outstanding his performance, because he was not a member of the family. 'I'm not royalty,' he explained. The different sets of rules for family members (or the perception of different rules) can increase tensions in family businesses and decrease the motivation and commitment of non-family members.

Difficulties in succession planning in family businesses

Most owners of family-owned businesses want the business to remain owned and operated by their future generations. In one survey, 87% indicated that they wanted the business to stay in the family. Most new businesses do not endure beyond their first year and only about 30% actually make it into the second generation of family ownership and operation (Higgins, 1998). As for the other 70%, these businesses fail, merge, or are sold.

The founder of a successful business is typically a rather dynamic, highly assertive, maybe even charismatic individual who tends to create a dependency culture in the company with strong forces inhibiting other individuals, including those of the next generation, from taking leadership.

For instance, let's say a father wants to turn the business over to his son. At the surface of his consciousness, he feels that he is doing everything he can to pave the way for him, but the transfer of power doesn't happen. At deeper levels, the father may have unconscious fantasies that impede him from letting his son take control of the business. For instance, where the man relates to his company possessively and protectively as a mother would relate to her baby, the fantasy is at the pre-Oedipal level. Where the father is enthralled with his company as a lover or bound to it for better or for worse as a spouse, he may equate giving his son control of the company with loss of manhood or death of the self. Here the fantasy is at the Oedipal level. All of these unconscious fantasies could cause the father to sabotage all attempts to let anyone else take charge of his business. Clearly, the dynamic forces of parental possessiveness and the Oedipus complex can change a business succession into a life and death struggle.

As for the son, consciously he may be feeling ready to take control of the company and be eager to do so. Unconsciously, he may be feeling anxious and insecure about his ability to take over the reins. He may also feel guilty over his desire to take charge and move his father out. The son may see the father as holding him back by being hypercritical and infantilizing. He may also feel guilty for being angry at his father's behaviour. As for the father, he may be angry with his son for being ungrateful, for not doing it his way, and for not being strong enough. If these unconscious dynamics remain unexamined they can easily prevent an effective succession from occurring.

EXAMPLE: COM.COM, A FAMILY BUSINESS

The nature of the family and the business

At the time of the consultation, Com.com was a family owned business in its first generation of ownership. The company sold specialized computer hardware and software to businesses over the Internet. It had just begun its fifth year, it had 20 employees, and for the first time registered profits, but barely. There were four owners, Arnold, Ann, Bill, and Betty. They are all in their 40s and each has a 25% share in the company. Betty is the oldest and Ann is the youngest of three sisters. Ann is married to Arnold and Betty is married to Bill. There are three pairs in charge: Arnold and Ann (husband and wife), Bill and Betty (husband and wife), and Ann and Betty (sisters). Arnold is the President of Com.com in charge of managing operations. Bill is the Executive Vice-President and manages sales and marketing. Ann is the Office Manager and reports to Arnold, her husband. Betty is Sales Representative and reports to Bill, her husband. Interestingly and problematically, Arnold and Bill really report to no one.

In the first consultation meeting, the owners identified the following issues:

1 Tense atmosphere and lack of communication: Arnold and Bill literally had not talked to each other in two months.
2 Lack of decision-making: the conflicts were so severe that the owners were not able to make any major decisions.
3 Stagnation: The business was in a state of paralysis.
4 Survival: The owners wanted an opinion on whether the partnership could survive and, if so, how.

The consultation

I consulted with Com.com as part of a consultant team for Business Mediation Associates (Gage et al. 1999), a consulting group that specializes in working with family-owned and closely held businesses. The consulting model blends mediation, organizational consultation, and family therapy approaches and so calls for a multidisciplinary consultant team: a psychologist paired with a professional from the fields of law, accounting, financial consulting, or organizational development. My consulting partner in this case was Melinda Ostermeyer, an experienced organizational consultant with expertise in decision-making models and alternative dispute systems. This consulting model does provide recommendations and opinions, but it places greater emphasis on facilitating a negotiation process whereby the principals develop their own solutions.

The consultation unfolded in four sessions with the four owners and the two consultants:

Session 1:   (At a conference centre away from the office.) One half day meeting with the four owners as a group.

Session 2:   (One week later.) A full day meeting with the group and the partners individually.

Session 3:   (One week later.) One half day meeting with the owners as a group.

Session 4:   (Five weeks later.) One half day meeting with the owners as a group.

Session 1: The initial engagement

We met with the four owners in a preliminary meeting for three hours to see if they wanted to work with us and to assess whether we could work with them. Neither Arnold nor Bill addressed each other in the meeting but talked to each other through us or through their wives. They agreed to work with us but specified that due to financial constraints they could invest only two days. This is much shorter than a typical engagement. Even though we had misgivings, we agreed to do it.

As the preliminary meeting was ending, we reviewed the written contract for our consulting engagement. Arnold balked. 'I'd be willing to do this,' he said, 'but I'm not sure everybody else wants to do it. Do we have enough information?'

I intervened and said that they didn't need to sign today and that we could schedule another hour next week to decide whether to proceed or not. I then polled the group to see where they were. The other three said they definitely wanted to proceed with the consultation. Arnold said it was now clear to him what the others thought. He acknowledged the partnership was in dire straits and he agreed with the others that what we said sounded good. Still he wasn't sure about going ahead with the plan.

Melinda and I were both frustrated when Arnold put up the roadblock as the meeting was ending. It had seemed to us that the owners had agreed to proceed and that we were set to go. I felt a pull to do as the other owners had often done with Arnold in the past – argue with him that he had already made a decision. Instead, I noted that we didn't have to decide in that meeting and that seemed to settle Arnold down, but removing the pressure didn't enable him to act.

I concluded the discussion about whether or not they could work with us by saying that:

1   Arnold was wary of beginning a process solely designed to get him to change.
2   The other three owners were worried that Arnold wouldn't take it seriously.

Reminding Arnold that the others said that he paralyzes decision-making by demanding more and more information obsessively and by saying that he isn't sure everybody is behind a decision, I showed him that this exact dynamic was operative right now. He was actually quiet for a moment, smiled, accepted my observation, and signed the agreement. I said to the group that this type of interaction – using a here-and-now experience to recognize the owners' dynamics – was something that we would be doing with them as we worked together to understand the business.

The interpretation of Arnold's fear that he would be targeted as the sole problem, and the others' fears that he wouldn't take the process seriously, calmed the situation. Frequently, when one man or woman is helped to see that someone else can speak for his or her issue, the distressing feeling of being alone is lessened for that one person and for the group.

In this vignette, we have shown how we experienced the pull of projective identification with the owners' problem dynamics. By resisting the pull, containing the group's anxiety and aggression, and interpreting the process, we made a start on detoxifying the situation in which the struggling business had become a persecutory object to the couples and conversely the couples' dynamics were strangling the business.

Session 2: Individual dynamics and beginning group work

During the morning, we interviewed each partner individually. We were able to understand their conflicts and hopes more clearly. Betty displayed a steady, reasonable, trustworthy presence. Ann came across to us as having the same down-to-earth practicality but she also showed considerable anxiety and an edgy sense of humour. All four owners saw the business as a timely opportunity to make a significant amount of money. Additionally, Betty and Ann had entered the business to work more closely with each other. They felt that they had a good relationship and valued the chance to be even closer. They had also hoped that being owners would allow them to work part-time so as to spend more time with their children but found instead that Com.com placed more than full-time demands on them. This overwork repeated a family pattern that they had wanted to avoid. They described their father as a good man and a creative entrepreneur, but he had been away from the family too much trying to turn around a series of businesses that were barely profitable. Their mother worked in the companies too. As Ann said rather bitterly, 'We've lived family businesses.' In that family, Betty had been the mediator and was closer to their parents. Ann never felt as successful as Betty. We sensed unacknowledged competition between them.

The sisters were overwhelmed by every aspect of their lives. Both were dealing with significant health or behavioural problems with their children and both of their marriages were suffering severe strain during the last few years. The conflict between their husbands was extremely difficult for them. Both women often found themselves acting as messengers between Arnold and Bill – in 'no man's land' as Ann called it – and they felt torn by conflicting loyalties. Throughout it all, however, they felt that their relationship as sisters had not significantly suffered. Although she was functioning effectively at work, Betty was clinically depressed. Moreover, the spectre of cancer hung over both sisters. A year prior to our consultation, Betty had completed a course of chemotherapy for breast cancer. Several years before that, her middle sister had been diagnosed and treated for breast cancer, too. Ann did not have cancer, but she feared with good reason that it would eventually strike her as well. Even Arnold was worried that some fatty lumps he had found under his skin might be cancerous.

We had found Bill to be quite engaging in our first meeting and so were surprised by how unlikeable he seemed when we met with him individually. Of the four partners, he was the most defensive in our individual meeting and we were able to learn the least about him. He deflected questions smoothly and continually returned to complaining about and blaming the problems on Arnold. He had felt humiliated by Arnold regularly and had periodically threatened over the previous six months to quit the partnership. Bill acknowledged that he had failed two years ago to bring in the business that he had promised. By getting additional training and then intensifying his marketing strategies, he had been much more successful in the past year. He was bitter that Arnold and Ann did not appreciate what he had done and did not realize how hard it had been to overcome the difficulties involved.

In contrast, Arnold surprised us by being more appealing than expected. A man with narcissistic vulnerabilities, he nevertheless presented openly in the individual meeting. The appeal to Arnold of starting the company was to be his own boss and to have the opportunity to make a good deal of money. His parents had divorced when Arnold was five and he never really knew his father. He said he was like his mother. As he put it, 'She's controlling but she gets the job done.' His job history was one of quick successes followed by intense interpersonal conflicts that meant that he had to move on to the next job. He presented himself as a heroic martyr who had to work 75 hours per week despite the physical toll on him. 'If I don't do it,' he said, 'it won't get done.' He did acknowledge that he could be too much of a micromanager and that his temper was, at times, abusive and uncontrolled.

That afternoon, we worked with the owners as a group in what proved to be a rather steady, productive session. Bill and Arnold talked directly to each other and the owners agreed upon several ground rules to guide their interactions.

Session 3: The drama intensifies during group work

The third session was quite different. For an hour and a half, it was a difficult, contentious meeting. Finally the owners worked out an agreement for Bill and Arnold to have a weekly meeting. They eventually agreed upon the time, duration, format, and agenda for these meetings. We then took a break and moved on to address a particular business issue: how to determine if a price for software was a good one and how to determine the speed of follow-through on delivery and service for that product.

As the discussion of the group task progressed, the group dynamics actually regressed and overtook the consultants temporarily. I was taking the lead in facilitating this part of the meeting and Arnold was becoming hostile to me. He was yelling, at times, and was frequently cutting me off. Melinda and I tried to deal with this as a group issue but we got nowhere. As the process moved on Ann, Betty, and Melinda became very quiet. Arnold, Bill, and I became increasingly active and intense. For about 30 minutes, I became downright hyperactive and Melinda became extremely quiet. Like a detached spectator I could see what was happening, but as an involved participant I became so captured by the process that I couldn't get out of it. I couldn't stop overfunctioning. Melinda was equally captured by it and she couldn't emerge from her passivity. In situations like this, when the process becomes too intense and spins out of control, we typically call for a brief break for process and review, but both of us were so disabled that we didn't think of doing that. Finally, Betty found her voice and screamed at Arnold to listen to what I was saying. This was very unusual for her and it broke the regressive cycle and lessened the tension somewhat. Melinda and I recovered sufficiently to call for a break and the two of us met briefly to regroup and re-orient ourselves to the consulting task.

For the last 30 minutes we worked on the agenda for the following meeting, our final half day with this business. Arnold said angrily that he sure didn't want another meeting like this one. Melinda and I agreed. I said that the second half of this meeting had been very difficult and that we would work with them to make the next meeting more productive. I asked if what we had all just been through was very much like life at Com.com. They all agreed it was. Betty said, 'I thought we were back at the office.'

During the break and after this difficult meeting, Melinda and I processed our experiences. We had both been caught up in an intense and rather primitive projective identification. As Ogden (1982) has noted, one function of projective identification is as an unconscious, non-verbal form of communication. In this meeting the partners didn't *tell* us about their own experience. Through projective identification, they had us *experience* it.

In the meeting, I had come to feel frustrated, isolated, and alone. Since I was operating predominantly from a paranoid-schizoid mode (Ogden 1989), I was not reflecting on these feelings but rather was bombarded by them and so was unable to think. Asking for help didn't even occur to me at the time. I thought angrily, 'Where's Melinda? Why isn't she helping out here? Do I have to do this whole damn thing on my own?' I was also experiencing wide swings in my narcissistic equilibrium. At times I was feeling absolutely hopeless and woefully inadequate. Alternately I was experiencing myself as incredibly creative and articulate, uniquely capable of turning this meeting around, and even defiant. Especially at some points when Arnold was cutting me off, I was aware of feeling, 'If you're not going to listen to me, fire me. Go ahead, make my day!'

Just like Arnold, I was feeling alone with the burden of responsibility. With too little time for the consultation, I was labouring under a tight deadline. Like him, I felt that I had to be heroic, take charge, and solve the problems myself. No one else could do it, I thought.

Melinda, for her part, was experiencing an equally desperate yet different state of mind. Like me she felt pressured by our time rapidly diminishing, but unlike me she felt unable to speak. She was thinking, 'How do I get in here to help out? I can't find a way in.' She felt guilty that she was letting me down. At times she thought angrily, 'This is ridiculous. What in the hell is Mike doing?' At other times, she thought admiringly, 'Yes, that's just the right comment. That'll work.' She also felt that the emotional intensity was just too high and that, since she wasn't a therapist, she should let me deal with it. Just like Betty and Ann at the office, Melinda in the consultation was seeing a turbulent drama but she felt powerless to do anything about it.

The intense psychological states that the consultants were experiencing had caused a temporary paralysis of our consulting function. These were states of mind that dominated the four partners' experience together. Our own reactions gave us a powerful sample of some of their experience and helped us to understand the business.

Insights about the family business

1   The dynamics at Com.com obviously made it difficult for the owners to think and reflect rather than to react. The dynamics had that effect on us, the consultants, as well. Just as the owners were having a difficult time coping with their tumultuous experiences at Com.com, so the consultants were temporarily unable to contain the family group anxieties. We all needed to find a way to be able to think again.

2   Intense but unconscious attacks on pairing were part of the psychological environment for the partners at Com.com. It became part of the consultants' psychological environment, too. One of the wonderful aspects of co-consulting is that the two consultants can contain and support each other when the going gets tough. Our consultant pair was so disrupted during this point in Session 3 that we were no longer functioning as a couple but rather as individuals under attack. This gave us empathy for the owner pairs. Both marriages were under severe strain. Arnold and Bill, the two top people in the business, were not even talking to each other. The only couple that seemed to be doing well was the sister couple.

3   Although their generally united approach was helpful for the company, the sisters' consciously denied sibling rivalry intensified some of the battles between Arnold and Bill. The husbands were acting out their wives' unrecognized conflicts. Moreover, Arnold seemed to be reliving the pain of his parents' divorce. Bill had not given us enough information so we could not be sure of the contribution of his internal couple except to say that he was fully engaged in the enactment. After the consultation was completed, I realized some other family dynamics were probably persecuting the business. Both married couples were acting out rage against their parents and the sisters were acting together as if to break up their parents who had been wedded to their work.

4   The business was hampered by a dynamic of male hyperactivity and female passivity. One intensified the other, driven by the attacks on pairing and by the sisters' resisting acknowledgement of any significant struggle between them. During a portion of Session 3, all three men were overfunctioning and all three women were silent. Betty finding her own voice and breaking out of her projective identification-

induced role was an important step in bringing about a new ending for old experience (Stadter 1996).

5   All of the owners were struggling with narcissistic issues involved in regulating self-esteem. Fears of doing something wrong, of failing, and of being shamed kept them from being able to make decisions. Mistrust and rivalry made it difficult for them to take responsibility and to give authority to each other.

6   The owners' group dynamics were pushing Arnold into an aggressive executive role. Admittedly, Arnold had a valency for it, and that was why the unconscious group process recruited him for it successfully (Bion 1959). Particularly, Bill's smooth, engaging style and the sisters' avoidance of conflict pressed Arnold into the role of the abrasive boss.

The consultants' strategy

Melinda and I grappled with these points. We regained our thinking capacity and planned our work as a consultant pair for the final meeting. Given that we expected only one more meeting, it was unlikely that we could interpret much. Depending on the participants' psychological mindedness, in a longer consultation we would try to bring more of these dynamics to a conscious level. However, we did resolve to keep aware of the forces that were attacking pairing and promoting male hyperactivity and female passivity. We set as a priority the need to function in a balanced way and, as a team, to contain the process and the affects more adequately. We planned to be a model of co-operation and containment in the final meeting and to talk about the impact of the forces of destruction on us and on the owners. We would watch any distortions in our own self-concepts in the meeting and quickly ask for a break for process and review if either of us felt uncomfortable in role. Also, if Arnold again took on his obstructive, antagonistic role, we would immediately comment on that, suggest that he was performing a group function, and ask the group to think about what might be going on.

Bion (1967, 1970) has written about attacks on the analyst's thinking capacity in analysis and on the difficulty of containing primitive psychic contents. One of the necessary conditions for effective functioning as a business owner, as a consultant, and as a therapist is to be able to think clearly and creatively. Bollas (1987) has written about occasions in psychoanalytic psychotherapy when the therapist becomes 'situationally ill'. This occurs because of the therapist's receptivity to countertransference states that involve reliving disturbed portions of the patient's psyche through projective identification. The therapist's situational illness is a version of the patient's own illness. The same process happens to the organizational consultant. With family businesses, the synergistic power of family and workplace dynamics creates a fertile ground for recruitment by such primitive processes. In Session 3, Melinda and I had become situationally ill. Now our job was to try to think about it, talk about it together, and treat our own 'illness'.

Session 4: Group work and termination

Through phone calls to the business, together with the owners we set the agenda for the final meeting:

1   Give a summary and final recommendations.
2   Work to develop a trial agreement for a decision-making process.
3   Help to set regular partner meetings.

We started the meeting by acknowledging how difficult the last meeting had been and how unbalanced the participation had been, ours and theirs. We said we would do our best to give them contributions from both of us and urged them to do the same. We acknowledged the powerful forces acting on us and on them that can produce such a disruption in the ability to work together. Melinda and I were pleased to learn that Arnold and Bill had kept to their agreement to meet weekly and that the meetings had been productive and were going well. At first we felt surprised, but we later felt pleased that this positive outcome reflected the potentially detoxifying effect of our engagement in the process. Although we had not put into words an interpretation of our countertransference, our painful identification with the owners' struggles had begun to metabolize some of the toxicity.

Impressions and recommendations

At the final meeting, Melinda and I together presented the following summary of our impressions and our recommendations:

1 Given the intense conflicts and dynamics, it was impressive – and a credit to all of them – that the company had been able to turn a profit.

2 The partnership as presently configured could not last. For their partnership to endure, they would need to do much more work on their partnership structure and process.

3 Com.com, a family business, was being conducted like a family and not like a business. The owners needed the following organizational structures: a legal partnership agreement (remarkably, they did not have even a minimal contract), planned performance reviews, clear written definitions of authority for decisions, a decision-making process, and a strategic plan.

4 Neither Bill nor Arnold should report to each other. They needed to report to the ownership as a group of four with each having clear, separate responsibilities.

5 Ann and Betty needed to become more active in their roles as owners rather than as employees of Com.com.

6 The owners had made significant progress by defining a list of guidelines for effective, respectful communication and interactions in the second meeting. They needed to adhere to these guidelines.

7 The owners needed to keep the business in perspective and at the office. Com.com was harming their marriages and their health. We urged them to make their health and relationships their top priorities and not to allow discussion of business to take place at home.

All four owners responded well and were in agreement with our recommendations. The process was calm and collaborative. I had a feeling that their experience of hope for the business as a money-making concern and as a sisterly collaboration had shifted significantly. I thought that they had lost hope of ever being able to make the partnership work in the long run and instead had developed a new and realistic hope that they could find a way in the short run to tolerate working together and to do it effectively.

We then moved to the topic of developing a decision-making process. At the heart of this problem lay their difficulty with taking and giving responsibility and authority. They recognized the urgency of this since they had been unable for months to decide on anything other than the most immediate of operational issues. Yet, the loss of trust among them and the fear of attack for making a wrong decision were paralyzing them. Half of the morning meeting was spent on this.

It was a difficult and conflictual meeting with the owners several times almost giving up on the process. In fact, at one point, they became so discouraged yet so clear about having to break this decision-making paralysis that they seriously entertained the idea of flipping a coin to make a decision. During this work I intermittently felt the pull to become more active as I had in the previous meeting but it was not nearly as compelling. Moreover, Melinda and I were actively keeping an even balance in our participation. Also, we commented repeatedly on the difference in the tone of this meeting and frequently facilitated Ann and Betty to stay active in the process. Eventually, they agreed to a 6-month trial period of a decision-making process that authorized particular partners to have final authority on specific issues.

Finally, we spent a short amount of time helping them to set up monthly partner meetings. At termination, the partners expressed appreciation for the process even though it had been much more painful and difficult than they had expected. They were surprised and impressed with how we were all able to work in such a different manner in this meeting compared to the previous one. Melinda mentioned hopefully that perhaps they could work differently at the office just as they had done in this meeting.

Follow-up seven months later

Arnold and Bill were still meeting weekly and their meetings were going well. Arnold had not yelled at anyone at the office since he had yelled at me in our third meeting. Owners' meetings were occurring, though infrequently. The four owners had been able to make decisions as a team and the new management process was continuing to work. Profits were up and they had even bought out a competitor. They continued to agree with our observation that the partnership could not hold together in its present form. However, they had hope for the future since they were now being wooed by a potential buyer. Although the atmosphere at work had improved it was still tense. Ann and Betty were taking a more active role as owners and working less hard as employees. Betty was in individual psychotherapy, was taking antidepressant medication, and was feeling much better. Both marriages were calmer.

Twelve months later

The Com.com owners had sold their business for what they felt was a good profit. Bill and Arnold had employment contracts to continue with the new company for three years. Each of them would be reporting to a third individual. Arnold was feeling some anxiety and loss, but the other owners were pleased with the outcome.

INTERPRETATION-IN-ACTION

Even though our consultation with this highly dysfunctional organization was brief, we did manage to help the owners break the organizational paralysis, improve their functioning, and decrease their level of interpersonal stress. The detoxification was incomplete, however, and the owners still had not found a way to be a family business for the long run. They had agreed with our observation that the partnership could not hold together as it was constituted, but they did not act to change that fundamental fact. Instead, they looked for and found a successful exit strategy – selling the company. Our practical consultation and mediation techniques did provide help to the owners, but it was our experiencing their inner world and, once there, struggling to think and act effectively as a couple in working with them that began the detoxifying process. In a longer consultation, we could have brought the issues to consciousness through verbal interpretations and then helped the owners work through towards a more benign organization of their inner and outer worlds. In brief interventions like this, many of the dynamics cannot be expressed verbally in interpretation. Instead, we use 'interpretations-in-action' (Ogden 1994). The consultants' non-verbalized activities and their 'way of being' function as the interpretations in action that foster a shift in the transferences (Stadter 1996). Within the limitations of the time frame of this consultation, the ways that we worked together to detoxify the bad objects projected into us functioned as the interpretations in action that facilitated change.

REFERENCES

Ashbach, C. and Schermer, V. L. (1987). *Object Relations, The Self, and the Group.* London and New York: Routledge.

Bion, W. (1959). *Experiences in Groups.* New York: Basic Books, 1961.

—— (1967). *Second Thoughts.* London: Heinemann.

—— (1970). *Attention and Interpretation.* London: Tavistock.

Bollas, C. (1987). *The Shadow of the Object.* New York: Columbia University Press.

Gage, D. (2002). 'Shoulder to Shoulder: How Business Partnerships Can Succeed.' Manuscript in preparation.

Gage, D., Martin, D., and Gromala, J. (1999). What partners often leave unsaid. *Family Business*, 10(2): 21–28.

Greenberg, J. R. and Mitchell, S. A. (1983). *Object Relations in Psychoanalytic Theory.* Cambridge, MA: Harvard University Press.

Higgins, M. (1998). Passing the torch in family owned businesses. *American Bar Association Journal*, 85: 48–53.

Levinson, H. (1971). Conflicts that plague family businesses. *Harvard Business Review*, 49: 90–98.

Menzies-Lyth, I. (1988). *Containing Anxiety in Institutions.* London: Free Association Books.

Obholzer, A. and Roberts, V. Z., eds. (1994). *The Unconscious at Work: Individual and Organizational Stress in the Human Services.* London: Routledge.

Ogden, T. H. (1982). *Projective Identification and Psychotherapeutic Technique.* Northvale, NJ: Jason Aronson.

Ogden, T. H. (1989). *The Primitive Edge of Experience.* Northvale, NJ: Jason Aronson.

Ogden, T. H. (1994). *Subjects of Analysis.* Northvale, NJ: Jason Aronson.

Scharff, D. E. and Scharff, J. S. (1987). *Object Relations Family Therapy.* Northvale, NJ: Jason Aronson.

Scharff, D. E. and Scharff, J. S. (1991). *Object Relations Couple Therapy.* Northvale, NJ: Jason Aronson.

Scharff, J. S. and Scharff, D. E. (1998). *Object Relations Individual Therapy.* Northvale, NJ: Jason Aronson.

Shakespeare, W. *The Unabridged William Shakespeare.* Philadelphia: Running Press, 1989.

Stadter, M. (1996). *Object Relations Brief Therapy: The Therapeutic Relationship in Short-term Work.* Northvale, NJ: Jason Aronson.

Chapter 13

Detoxification possible and impossible

Stanley A. Tsigounis, PhD

We have described various ways of thinking about self-hating persecutory objects and shown how to work with them effectively. knowing from first-hand experience that not all persecutory objects can be detoxified, we must admit that our knowledge and therapeutic techniques in this area have limitations. We will conclude with a discussion from object relations and Kleinian perspectives of various conditions and issues, which interact in unpredictable ways to foil our attempts at detoxification.

LIMITS ON THE PATIENT'S HEALING

The intransigence of the persecutory object

The compelling power of the persecutory object is embedded in years of actual and illusionary experience. The earlier the pathological process begins, the more the trauma is cumulative in nature, the more ingrained is the pathology. The deepest cause of psychopathology is seen as the identification with and flight from the outer world of bad, recalcitrant objects in infancy. The patient's tie to the persecutory object is the only methodology available to the patient to retain a sense of contact with another human being. There is no other way to relate. Patients resist change because they cannot comprehend the existence of more meaningful working models. The anti-libidinal internal object becomes a unifying structure, organizing both the patient's internal object world and the patient's actual, interpersonal relationships (Fairbairn 1943). Unconsciously, they fear the complete loss of contact with the other if they were to abandon the persecutory object. This creates massive resistance to the detoxification of the persecutory object in therapy.

Patients accept the restrictions of the persecutory bad object in preference to facing 'four ultimate psychic dangers' – loss of the ego, disintegration of the ego, absorption of the ego into another's personality, and crushing of the ego under a burden of guilt (Guntrip 1973, p. 438). The anti-libidinal ego, split off from the central ego and developed in relation to the persecutory object, derives from experience with the parents through identification. In proportion to the enormity of the badness of the parental objects, the anti-libidinal ego enlarges and takes over the ego by repression. It attracts bad experience and reduces the opportunity for good experience to enrich the central ego. From the cruel parents, it borrows a sense of power – if only over the self – and fills it with self hatred.

When therapeutic efforts at detoxification reduce the power of the anti-libidinal ego, the patient fears the loss of this familiar object relationship that is such a major part of the personality, and dreads the effects on the self. As therapy proceeds, the patient fears disintegration, total loss of the ego, being taken over by the self of another person who fills the gap, or falling victim to guilt for separating from the identification with the parents and growing beyond their limitations. Since the persecutory object forms a large part of the self and serves a crucial defensive function to hold that self together, work on detoxifying it proceeds slowly and sometimes incompletely.

The death instinct being too strong

If the constitutionally determined death instinct is too strong to be modified by fusion or sublimation, or if the life instinct is too weak in opposing it, the death instinct will have to be deflected by massive defensive projective identification. The self is then surrounded by the persecutory objects of its projection and deals with them by introjection and identification in order to control their powerful threat against it. This is another way of conceptualizing the formation of persecutory objects that resist our therapeutic efforts.

Garma (1971) postulated a source for the death instinct. He wrote that this 'biological field derives from archaic events which were detrimental to human development and the consequences of which are too deeply imprinted biologically on the human psychosomatic unit for the self destructive or death urge to be modified by psychoanalysis beyond a certain limit' (Garma 1971, p. 150).

Whether we hold that the problem lies in the death instinct or the tie to the bad object, we agree that sometimes the internalization of persecutory objects has been so intense, desperate, and fundamental to survival, and the threat to the self of losing that protection so current, that our efforts at detoxification are experienced as an equally great threat that has to be resisted strenuously. At that point, hatred of the self is redirected at the therapist. That is when the therapist's ability to be hated without retaliating, falling apart, or feeling destroyed is the crucial factor that ensures or limits progress in treatment.

Clinical example: criticizing herself and her therapist

Ingrid is a 36-year-old woman who had been in treatment for five years. At times she was introspective and thoughtful. At other times she launched into an attack on the treatment and me. During these assaults she would lose her ability to be thoughtful and link material, and became arrogant and seemed stupid instead.

'You don't understand me at all,' she complained. 'This therapy is a complete waste of time. I don't know who it is that you think you can help. There must be someone that you're good with but I can't figure out who that would be. This therapy is an entire waste. I don't know why I continue to come here. My life is pretty good except for coming here. I'm really disappointed in you. You haven't helped me at all. I am so angry with you. Just f. . . you!'

These attacks on the therapist and treatment were followed by an even more vicious self-attack in which she would criticize herself mercilessly for being a typical, stupid woman without a brain or any degree of dignity and decorum.

Ingrid grew up in a family where her father praised her for actions that mimicked his own male behaviours, told her that women were foolish, and spent many hours complaining to her about his relationship with her mother. She felt both empowered by his attention and by his pairing with her and at the same time frightened, confused, and disappointed. After all, no matter how manly she acted she was still biologically a woman. She felt strong sexual urges towards him that produced both guilt and excitement. She blamed her mother for her parents' poor marital relationship. She did not feel understood or supported by them as a couple and felt attacked by her four sisters who envied her relationship with her father. She became enraged at age 16 when her parents abruptly divorced and her father married 'another stupid woman'. This created a rift between them that continued until his death five years ago, and was echoed in the stand-off between her and her therapist.

This attack on the therapist and then on herself is a pattern that Ingrid repeated numerous times during the treatment. No intervention by her therapist had succeeded as yet in detoxifying this type of persecutory attack on object and self. Similar patients described by Spotnitz directly attack the treatment (cited in Robertiello and Schoenewolf 1989). They arrive at sessions late and sometimes intoxicated, verbally abuse the therapist, and engage in excessive hostile silence. He called this process *treatment-destructive resistance* because it becomes so powerful that it overwhelms both the therapist and the treatment, rendering the treatment ineffectual.

Impaired affect regulation

Traumatized patients have difficulty with ego integration, which further interferes with their abilities to regulate dysphoric affects and metabolize and transform the associated internal persecutory objects. We may not be sure whether this stems from, or causes, a failure of biochemistry in the brain. Whichever is the case, it seems likely that a fault in the ego's ability to regulate responses and use the interpersonal relationship as a container is what leads the patient to experience his affects as intolerable, overwhelming, and unmetabolizable. Severe anxiety propels such patients away from any stimulus perceived as threatening. Their escape routes run the gamut of self hatred from social shyness and schizoid withdrawal to severe forms of acting out such as suicide attempts, alcohol and drug abuse, self-mutilation, sexual acting out, and other self-defeating behaviours.

This self-hating patient often perceives treatment as being the cause of his distress, because the very act of curious introspection is seen as being related to the initial trauma. As Bion observed, 'the very act of analyzing the patient makes the analyst an accessory in precipitating regression and turning the analysis itself into a piece of acting out. From the viewpoint of a successful analysis, this is a development that should be avoided. Yet I have not been able to see how this can be done' (1967, p. 87). Bion goes on to say that at this stage the patient acts as if the only problem he has is the therapist and the therapy, perceived as hurtful, hateful, and discomfiting. Bion described many of his patients as psychotic, but the same phenomenon can be seen in patients who would not warrant such a diagnosis.

The psychological catastrophe

Psychological catastrophe leads to the creation of a primitive superego that prevents the individual from utilizing projective identification in a normal manner (Bion 1967). Patients with psychological catastrophes involving sexual abuse are able to make some progress in treatment but often have great difficulty in bringing the therapeutic relationship to its conclusion. The termination process itself appears to reactivate intolerable affects which force the patient to terminate prematurely and to invoke a sense of trauma in the therapist (Scharff and Scharff 1994). The therapist may think that the treatment is unfinished because part of the trauma remains unmetabolized, but we conclude that a traumatic ending may be the only way for the patient to convey the impact of the catastrophe and the effects of the resulting primitive superego (Scharff and Scharff 1998).

LIMITS ON THE THERAPIST'S EFFECTIVENESS

Limitations of current theory and technique

Concerned and dedicated professional therapists continue advanced training, constantly searching for new theories and techniques. As we develop professionally we begin to recognize the rigidity of the characterological structure of some patients, the depth of their trauma, and how impossible change can appear.

Without understanding projective identification, holding, and containment, we would be lost. While we stay optimistic we nevertheless recognize how difficult our work is and how it stretches our theories and techniques to the limit, and places considerable demands on the therapist's self (Scharff 1992).

Lack of skill in holding and containment

Stolorow and colleagues (1987) point out that some therapists appear better equipped emotionally to relate to more seriously disturbed patients and to tolerate the ambiguities and chaos inherent in these cases. Depending on personal history, personality structure, training and experience, some therapists display greater strength and tolerance in holding and containment than others. Other therapists are prone to identifying with the patient's resistance and are then unable to extricate themselves from this collusive process that prevents therapy from proceeding (Racker 1968). Some of them use personal therapy or psychoanalysis to improve their effectiveness but others remain limited in these areas.

Lack of neutrality

Robertiello and Schoenewolf (1989) describe numerous cases where the therapist's personal bias has entered into the therapeutic relationship. In a case vignette entitled 'The therapist who did not want her patient to be a housewife', they described a stalled treatment where the therapist directly influenced the patient to return to work even though the patient, conflicted and self-persecuting, wanted to remain a housewife.

Poor training

A seldom-discussed factor that limits the possibility of detoxification is the poor training of potentially good therapists. They have not been given a psychodynamic understanding of the difficulties they are experiencing with patients. Overwhelmed by their affective reactions to their own distress and that of their disturbed patients, they lose their ability to contain and think about the projective experience. They enter into re-enactments of the patients' primitive experiences without an understanding of their own roles in the re-enactments. The result is that they fall prey to blaming the patients, often by labelling them pejoratively with diagnostic categories. In these situations, therapists have identified unconsciously with the persecutory object in a complementary countertransference (Racker, 1968). They persecute the patient themselves, unwittingly reinforcing the patient's persecutory world.

Limitations in the therapeutic environment

Finally, the environmental context may not support the therapist to deal with difficult affects. Holding and containment require a safe, consistent environment. Many patients may need multiple sessions per week over many years in order to detoxify the effects of years of persecutory organization and reinforcement. In an age of declining resources for mental health services many patients do not receive adequate treatment and therapists do not receive adequate support and sufficient containment for themselves. Unfortunately institutions for training therapists are promoting short-term methods and pharmacological approaches in keeping with the dictates of managed care. So it is increasingly difficult for therapists who want to do the kind of intensive work that we have been talking about to find adequate training and continuing education, support, and containment in a dedicated learning community (Scharff and Scharff 2000).

SUMMARY

The persecutory object torments both patient and therapist and resists change in the hatred of self and other. We cannot predict prior to treatment which patients will be able to modify their persecutory objects fully or partially, or which will move from self hatred to self-appreciation. When these objects threaten the therapeutic alliance, we hold firmly to the therapeutic frame and the containing stance. We commit ourselves to engaging fully with patients in the therapeutic process and applying our skills and knowledge in the pursuit of resolution. When we sense limitations, speak to our feeling of hopelessness, and accept the possibility of defeat, patients in despair of change feel deeply understood. Together, we may then hope to arrive at detoxification after all.

REFERENCES

Bion, W. R. (1967). *Second Thoughts*. London: Maresfield Library.
Fairbairn, W. R. D. (1944). Endopsychic structure considered in terms of object relationships. In *Psychoanalytic Studies of the Personality*, pp. 82–136. London: Routledge.
Garma, A. (1971). Within the realm of the death instinct. *International Journal of Psycho-Analysis*, 52: 145–154.
Guntrip, H. J. S. (1973). *Personality Structure and Human Interaction*, (third edition of 1961 original). London: Hogarth Press.
Racker, H. (1968). *Transference and Countertransference*. New York: International University Press.
Robertiello, R. C. and Schoenewolf, G. (1989). *101 Common Therapeutic Blunders: Countertransference and Counterresistance in Psychotherapy*. Northvale, NJ: Jason Aronson.
Scharff, J. S. (1992). *Projective and Introjective Identification and the Use of the Therapist's Self*. Northvale, NJ: Jason Aronson.
Scharff, J. S. and Scharff, D. E. (1994). *Object Relations Sexual and Physical Trauma*. Northvale, NJ: Jason Aronson.
Scharff, J. S. and Scharff, D. E. (1998). *Objects Relations Individual Therapy*. Northvale, NJ: Jason Aronson.
Scharff, J. S. and Scharff, D. E. (2000). *Tuning the Therapeutic Instrument: Affective Learning of Psychotherapy*. Northvale, NJ: Jason Aronson.
Stolorow, R. D. Brandchaft, B., and Atwood, G. E. (1987). *Psychoanalytic Treatment: An Intersubjective Approach*. Hillsdale, NJ: Analytic Press.

Index

abandonment 77, 79, 81, 171, 208
abortions 13, 14
Abraham, K. 4
absence 93; unexpected 187
abuse 92, 114, 121; alcohol 71, 228; criminal 111; drug 71; emotional 47, 172; maternal, suspected 116; mutual 65; physical 47, 172; sexual 229; surreptitious 116
acceptance 165, 175, 178; self 85
acting out 218, 229; masochistic 71; severe forms of 228; sexual 228
adaptation 42
addictive behaviours 38, 85, 96
Adler, Alfred 39
admiration 32
adolescence 60, 96; treating persecutory anxiety in 145–64
adoption 107
aesthetics 148
aetiology 146, 159–61
affairs 63
affects 81, 175; aggressive 26; detachment of 166; dysphoric 228; impaired regulation 228–9; intolerable 229; overwhelming 9; psychotic levels of 122; strong 154
affirmation 80
aggression 6, 43, 134, 186, 191; child's 42; ever-present 14; guilt and 81, 82–4; intense 71; life-threatening levels of 26; localized 30; masochism, envy and 81–2; mass 39; oscillation between hate and 15; primitive 208; projected 16, 26; projectively identified 71; recognition of 77; shame-related 82–4; turned against self 29; unbridled 189; unconscious 74; underlying 190
agony 64
Akira (Japanese film) 145, 146, 148, 149, 150, 159, 160, 161
alcohol abuse 71, 228
Alexander, F. 25, 30, 32, 39
alienation 123
allegiances 115
aloneness 165
alpha elements 28, 197
ambivalence: defence against the pain of 182; divorce 176–7; introspection of self-objects experienced with 4; maternal 114, 117; profound 114
anal phase 6
anger 7, 8, 61, 140, 187; notable lack of 113
animals 28–9, 40
annihilation 43, 84, 123, 159, 175; fears of 23, 65, 74–5, 186; imminent 111; of object 31; self 26, 32, 42; threat of 6
antidepressants 150, 223
anti-libidinal trends 41
anti-Semitism 24

Index compiled by Frank Pert